To our wives,
JANICE, JANE, *and* ANNE

TAX
RESEARCH
TECHNIQUES

Eighth Edition

AMERICAN INSTITUTE OF CERTIFIED PUBLIC ACCOUNTANTS

Robert L. Gardner, Ph.D.
Robert J. Smith Professor
Brigham Young University

Dave N. Stewart, CPA, Ph.D.
Rachel Martin Professor
Brigham Young University

Ronald G. Worsham, Jr., CPA, Ph.D.
Associate Professor
Brigham Young University

1770-356

Preface

Tax Research Techniques is designed to aid tax advisers in the development of their research skills. The book employs a systematic approach to tax problems based on five steps, namely: the critical role of facts, the elusive nature of tax questions, locating and assessing appropriate authority, applying the authority to the fact pattern, and communicating the findings. Included are specific examples explaining in detail the five steps employed by successful tax advisers.

For more than thirty years, the book has aided practicing tax advisers, researchers, and students in the development and implementation of effective research skills. The eighth edition updates the examples and illustrations to reflect the changes that have taken place in the tax law over the past several years. Also, new and updated sections reflect the continuously evolving advances in the technology of Web based research.

The authors express appreciation to Ray M. Sommerfeld and G. Fred Streuling, who were coauthors of the earlier editions of this book.

Acknowledgments

The authors wish to acknowledge the assistance of the following AICPA staff personnel who contributed to the development, editorial, production, and design of this publication:

Linda Cohen, Director of Publishing/Publisher, Professional Publications
Amy Stainken, Senior Manager, Specialized Publications
Erin Valentine, Acquisitions Editor
Laura LeBlanc, Copy Editor
Annmarie Piacentino, Copy Editor
Robert DiCorcia, Senior Manager, Production Services
Michael Laches, Production Manager, Production Services
Amy Sykes, Production Administrator, Production Services
Nancy Karmadi, Graphic Designer, Creative Services

Contents

1

Tax Research in Perspective

This book is designed to provide a working knowledge of tax research methodology for the individual who is not already a tax specialist. After a careful reading of this book—and many hours of experience in implementing the procedures suggested here—the reader should be capable of finding and using relevant information dealing with tax questions encountered in tax practice today.

This book is not intended to increase an individual's knowledge of specific technical tax provisions per se. However, as a secondary benefit, readers may learn more than they previously knew about some tax provisions as they study the examples offered as problem-solving illustrations. When solving similar problems of their own, however, readers should not rely on the conclusions reached in these examples without updating them. Although this book is periodically revised, it is not intended as a substitute for a current tax reference service. Furthermore, it is not intended or written to be used, and cannot be used, for the purpose of avoiding penalties imposed under the Internal Revenue Code (IRC) and applicable state or local tax law provisions.[1]

Meaning of Research in General

Ideally, a book devoted to tax research would begin with an unambiguous definition of the word *research*. Unfortunately, no such definition has come to the authors' attention; therefore, we will have to be satisfied with a general, rather than a precise, definition. This general description should adequately reveal the nature of the process envisioned within the phrase *tax research* as it is used here. However, the word *research* is used to describe a wide variety of diverse activities. For example, at one extreme it can include the search for anything not presently known by the person making the search. In this context, looking up an unknown telephone number in a directory would constitute research. At the other extreme, a scientist might restrict his or her use of the word *research* to exhaustive experimentation under tightly controlled conditions solely for the purpose of revising previously accepted conclusions in light of recently determined facts. Between these two extremes lie infinite alternative definitions.

Thus, this book does not purport to deal with all types of tax research. Except for a few introductory comments in this chapter, this book is restricted to a description of the procedures commonly used by a diverse group of professionals—including CPAs—to determine a defensibly "correct" (and in some instances, an optimal) conclusion to a tax question. Totally different kinds of work undertaken by these professionals or by other individuals might be properly included within the meaning of the phrase *tax research*. Our objective is neither to define nor to reconcile conflicting definitions. We desire only to place the general characteristics of the different types of tax research in perspective. Very few persons become expert in each of the research methodologies noted. Nevertheless, anyone engaged in any facet of tax work should at least be generally aware of what other individuals working in the same general field are doing. Often, experts in one area of taxation are

---

[1] See Appendix B for Treasury Department Circular 230 considerations.

asked to express an informed opinion on a wholly different aspect of taxation. In these circumstances, it is especially desirable that the expert be aware of what others have done, and thereby move with appropriate caution in dealing with tax matters with which he or she is not intimately familiar.

Perhaps the easiest and most desirable way to place the different types of tax research in meaningful perspective is to create a general classification system based on the purpose of the inquiry. Although other possible classification systems might be used, one based upon the purpose behind the research effort is probably the most useful for this statement of perspective. At least three distinct purposes for tax research come immediately to mind: implementation of rules, policy determination, and advancement of knowledge.

Research for Implementation of Rules

Tax professionals spend a great deal of time researching the applicability of general tax laws to specific fact situations. After a tax law is enacted, implementation of the law is the responsibility of the taxpayer. Although we have what purports to be a self-assessment tax system in this country, both tax rules and business practices have become so complex that many taxpayers seek the assistance of specially trained individuals to ensure not only their compliance with the tax rules, but also their achievement of that compliance at minimal tax cost.

In this context, five elementary steps constitute a total research effort: (1) establishing the facts; (2) from the facts, determining the question; (3) searching for an authoritative solution to that question or issue to be resolved; (4) determining a proper application of the frequently incomplete and sometimes conflicting tax authorities; and (5) communicating the conclusion to the interested party. Although a thorough examination of what each of these five steps involves is deferred to later chapters, a summary of each step is included here.

Establishing the Facts. Many tax statutes and their related administrative regulations are necessarily written in general terms. Effective rules must be stated in terms that adequately describe the vast majority of factual circumstances envisioned by those who determine the rules. Rules stated too broadly invite conflicting interpretation; those stated too narrowly often fail to achieve their intended objective. However, no matter how carefully the words of a statute are selected, general rules cannot possibly describe every conceivable factual variation that might be subject to the intended rules. Consequently, the first step in implementation-oriented research necessarily involves the process of obtaining all of the facts so that the researcher can determine which tax rule or rules might apply to those particular events.

Determining the Question. Questions arise when specific fact situations are examined in light of general rules or laws. Complex tax questions frequently evolve through several stages of development. Based on prior knowledge of tax rules, a researcher usually can state the pertinent questions in terms of very general rules. For example, the tax researcher may ask whether the facts necessitate the recognition of gross income by the taxpayer, or whether the facts permit the taxpayer to claim a deduction in the determination of taxable income. After making an initial search of the authorities to answer the general question, the researcher often discovers that one or more specific technical questions of interpretation must be answered before the general question can be resolved. These secondary questions frequently involve the need to determine the exact meaning of certain words or phrases as they are used in particular tax rules. For example, the tax researcher may have to determine if a particular payment made in the fact situation under consideration is *ordinary, necessary,* or *reasonable* as those words are used in various sections of the IRC. Alternatively, he or she may have to determine the meaning of the word *primarily* or, perhaps, the meaning of the phrase *trade or business.* Once the general question is restated in this more specific way, the researcher often must return briefly to the process of collecting more facts. From a study of the authorities, the researcher might learn that facts initially not considered important may actually be critical to the resolution of the revised question. After obtaining all necessary facts and resolving the more technical questions, the tax researcher may discover that the general question is also resolved. Often an answer to a related question must be resolved before the researcher can proceed to a conclusion. For example, even if a tax researcher determines that a particular expenditure is not tax deductible, he or she may have to determine whether or not the expenditure can be capitalized (that is, added to the tax basis of an asset) or whether it must simply be ignored in the tax determination procedure.[2] In effect, raising collateral questions often requires the researcher to move back and forth between fact discovery and issue identification. This procedure continues until all pertinent questions have been satisfactorily answered.

Searching for Authority. Authority in tax matters is voluminous. It nearly always begins with the IRC, as amended, but it quickly expands to include Treasury regulations, judicial decisions, administrative pronouncements, and sometimes congressional committee reports. Judicial decisions in federal tax disputes are issued by U.S. district courts, the Tax Court, the U.S. Court of Federal Claims, the circuit courts of appeals, and the Supreme Court. Administrative pronouncements are issued in various forms, including revenue rulings, revenue procedures, IRS notices and announcements, and technical information releases. Reports of the House Ways and Means Committee, the Senate Finance Committee, and the Joint Committee may be pertinent to the resolution of a tax question. Obviously, the task of locating all of the potential authority before reaching a conclusion can be a very demanding and time-consuming task. Furthermore, the search for authority often raises additional questions that can be answered only after the determination of additional facts. Thus, the research process often moves back from step three to step one before it proceeds to a resolution of the general question.

Resolving the Question. After locating, reading, and interpreting all of the pertinent authority, a tax adviser must be prepared to resolve the questions that have been raised. The taxpayer must make the final decision about what course of action to take. However, in many circumstances, the taxpayer's decision is guided by the conclusions

---

[2] In a tax planning situation, of course, the tax adviser may recommend an alternative way of structuring the transaction to achieve the most desirable tax result.

reached by the adviser. Thus, a tax adviser really must resolve the question to his or her own satisfaction before recommending action to anyone else.

Communicating the Conclusion. Having thoroughly researched the tax issue and having reached a conclusion, a tax adviser must communicate the information to the interested parties. Drafting tax communications is unusually difficult. Often, highly technical questions must be phrased in layman's language. Positions sometimes must be carefully hedged without omitting or misstating any critical fact or any applicable rule. At the same time, tax advisers must protect their own rights and professional integrity. Therefore, great care must be exercised in this final step of the implementation-oriented research procedure. This is especially critical in today's world because of the penalties that may be imposed on the tax adviser if certain standards are not met. Currently, under IRC Section 6694, these standards imposed on the tax adviser are actually higher than the standards imposed on the taxpayer.

The arrangement of the material in this book follows the sequence of steps suggested above. That is, chapter 2 deals with the search for facts; chapter 3 is a discussion of the process by which a tax researcher prepares a statement of the pertinent question. Chapter 4 discusses the type of authority that tax practitioners may rely on in resolving tax issues; chapter 5 explains how relevant authority may be found. Chapter 6 suggests what to do if the authority is incomplete or conflicting. Chapter 7 describes the many factors that must be considered in drafting the communication that will convey the results of the research effort to the concerned persons. Chapters 8 and 9 give detailed examples of this tax research process under two different circumstances; chapter 8 illustrates the research process in a compliance setting, and chapter 9, in a planning situation.

Research for Policy Determination

Our tax laws are enacted by Congress to produce federal revenues and to achieve designated economic and social objectives. For example, the objective of the Child and Dependent Care Credit and the

Earned Income Credit is to help ease the tax burden of persons who work and also have the responsibility for the care of dependent children. The purpose of the bonus depreciation deduction and the increased IRC Section 179 immediate deduction for certain business assets is to stimulate the economy. The purpose of the domestic manufacturing deduction is to help the economy in creating jobs. These and many other tax provisions should be investigated thoroughly to determine whether they are efficiently achieving the intended objectives. The research methodology common to such investigations draws heavily from the discipline of economics. Often econometric models are constructed and much aggregate data obtained to formulate tax policy.

As they attempt to achieve these economic goals, our government representatives should also have factual information about voter preferences. They should know, for example, whether a majority of the voters prefers to deal with problems of pollution through fines and penalty taxes, through incentive provisions in the tax laws, or through nontax legislation. Those who enact laws should know how the voters feel about funding public medical care, employee retirement programs, mass transit systems, interstate highways, and a host of other government projects. Policy makers should also understand the economic impact of shifting the relative tax burden between various economic groups in the general population. The research methodology common to determining voter preferences draws heavily on survey techniques developed by sociologists, demographers, and other social scientists.

Every change in tax law has a direct impact on the federal budget and on monetary policies, the magnitude and direction of which should be determined as accurately as possible before the law is finalized. Operations research techniques and computer technology are useful in making such determinations. Some of the research techniques used to make these predictions are similar to those used by the econometrician in building models that tell us whether a law can achieve its intended objectives. In other ways, the techniques used are quite different. The point is simply that, even within the confines of the work that must be undertaken to provide tax policy prescriptions, the procedures that must be used to make those determinations vary substantially. Yet all of these diverse procedures are commonly referred to as *tax research.*

Research for Advancement of Knowledge

Another purpose for undertaking tax research is the advancement of knowledge in general. Research undertaken to determine a preferable tax policy, as well as that undertaken to implement tax rules, has a pragmatic objective. The researcher in each instance has a very practical reason for wanting to know the answer. Some research, on the other hand, is undertaken solely for the purpose of disseminating general knowledge. There is, however, no single, common methodology for such research. Rather, the methodology selected depends entirely upon the nature of the investigation being undertaken. If it involves economic predictions, economic modeling is necessary. If it involves taxpayer attitudes, preferences, or both, surveys based on carefully selected statistical samples are equally mandatory. And if it involves compliance considerations, a studied opinion of pertinent authority is just as essential.

Tax practitioners, as well as academicians, government employees, and foundation personnel, often engage in tax research work intended solely for the advancement of knowledge. The results are published in journals and presented in proceedings that appeal to two fundamentally different audiences. Policy-oriented journals and proceedings primarily attract persons who are economists by education and training. Implementation-oriented journals and proceedings primarily attract those who are either accountants or lawyers by education and training. Academicians are found in both camps.

Examples of Tax Research

Chapter 8 is an example of implementation-oriented, or compliance, tax research. The objective of chapter 8 is simply to illustrate how a tax researcher might determine the "correct" tax treatment of incorporating a sole proprietorship under certain stated facts. Chapter 9 demonstrates how tax planning can be used to minimize the tax dangers and maximize the tax opportunities implicit in a different fact setting.

Before we turn our attention to the details of implementation-oriented research in subsequent chapters, however, we note some examples of policy-oriented tax research and documents. Among some of the most significant are the AICPA's Statements on Standards for Tax Services. These statements contain the AICPA's standards of tax practice which delineate members' responsibilities to taxpayers, the public, the government, and the profession. To date, the AICPA has issued eight Statements on Standards for Tax Services dealing with various issues that a CPA might encounter in providing tax services. The AICPA has also issued certain interpretations of these statements. These statements replace the Statements on Responsibilities in Tax Practice, which the AICPA had issued to provide a body of advisory opinions on good tax practice, and which had come to be relied on as the appropriate articulation of professional conduct in a CPA's tax practice.

In addition to these standards, the AICPA has published various studies that address policy issues dealing with revenue collection and the tax law itself. The AICPA issued its first Statement of Tax Policy in 1974.[3] Eight additional statements were issued in the next seven years. In 1993, the AICPA issued an exposure draft of Statement of Tax Policy 10, *Integration of the Corporate and Shareholder Tax Systems*. More recent examples include the AICPA's *Understanding Tax Reform: A Guide to 21st Century Alternatives* issued in 2005, and *Understanding Social Security Reform: The Issues and Alternatives*, March 2005, 2nd edition.

Tax-policy-oriented research has also been done at institutions such as the National Bureau of Economic Research and the Brookings Institute. An example is Brookings' Studies on Governmental Finance, which is devoted to examining issues in taxation and public expenditure policy. One book in this series is *Federal Tax Policy* by Joseph A. Pechman.[4] This book discusses individual and corporate income taxes, consumption taxes, payroll taxes, estate and gift taxes, and state and local taxes. The emphasis of the book, however, is on other issues such as the effects of taxation on economic incentives and changes in fiscal relations between the federal and the state and local governments.

---

[3] *Taxation of Capital Gains* (New York: American Institute of Certified Public Accountants, 1974), 28 pages.

[4] This book, published in 1987 (5th ed.), by the Brookings Institution, 1775 Massachusetts Avenue, Washington, D.C. 20036, is still available through vendors, such as Amazon.com.

In recent years, the AICPA and individual CPA firms have become more active in their efforts to influence tax policy and procedure by committing significant resources to support policy-oriented research. These efforts include funding tax research symposia for academicians and practitioners, research grants for established academicians, and dissertation awards for aspiring researchers. In addition, the AICPA regularly responds to tax policy issues considered by Congress. For example, in 2002, Congress passed the Sarbanes-Oxley Act in response to perceived audit failures. Although this act does not address specific tax provisions found in the IRC, the act does specify certain rules and procedures that must be followed by CPA firms that provide auditing and other services, including tax. As Congress deliberated the passage of this act the AICPA provided input to the debate. Additionally, after the act was passed, the AICPA again provided input as regulations associated with the act were created. Other more recent examples include the AICPA's input to Congress opposing any codification of an "economic substance standard" in the IRC and its comments on IRC Section 6694, which imposes a "more likely than not" standard that must be met by tax advisers in order to avoid preparer penalties. This standard is much higher than the standard imposed on taxpayers themselves.

In summary, the phrase *tax research* is commonly used to refer to widely divergent processes. All are legitimate, socially productive endeavors that may be included in a definition of tax research. A broad outline of the different processes is mentioned in this perspectives chapter for two reasons: first, to give the reader some idea of what is and what is not to be described in the study, and second, to suggest to accountants and others, who, by their own inclination are implementation-oriented, the kinds of efforts that should be included in policy-oriented projects they might undertake.

In closing this chapter, the authors join many others who have called for a broader participation and cooperation in the determination of tax policy. In the past, the tax research efforts of theoreticians have all too often wholly ignored all practical consequences, including the behavioral adaptation of those most directly affected by their recommendations. On the other hand, the policy prescriptions rendered by the implementation-oriented groups have often over-looked important empirical evidence accumulated in the more theoretical studies. An important first step in this hoped-for cooperation is the acquaintance of each with the aims and the methodologies of the other. This volume should help to describe the tax research methodology commonly used by the more implementation-oriented group.

2

The Critical Role of Facts

A tax result is dependent upon three variables: the pertinent facts, applicable law, and an administrative (and occasionally judicial) process. In arriving at a conclusion about the tax consequences of a particular transaction (either completed or proposed), a tax adviser must completely and fully examine and analyze all three variables. Frequently, an adviser not trained in the practice of law is apt to underestimate the significance of facts to the resolution of a tax question. At times, the study of law tends to concentrate on general rules, often overlooking the impact the pertinent facts have on the application of the general rules. For the tax adviser, however, general rules will not suffice. It is essential that every tax adviser understand why a thorough knowledge of *all* the facts is critical to the resolution of any tax question.

The Importance of Facts to Tax Questions

As used here, the word *fact* means an actual occurrence or an event or thing; facts are the who, what, when, why, where, and how of daily existence. Questions and conclusions arise from facts. A tax adviser must be able to distinguish a conclusion from a fact. This distinction may be illustrated by a simple example. A statement that an individual is married really is a conclusion rather than a fact. The facts that support such a conclusion may include such real world events as these:

- On February 6, 2008, that person appeared with a member of the opposite sex before a third person duly authorized to perform marriages.
- That person exchanged certain oral vows with the specified member of the opposite sex.
- The person authorized to perform marriages made certain declaratory statements to those present.
- The exchange of vows and the declaratory statements were made in the presence of a designated number of witnesses.
- Certain documents were signed by designated parties to this ceremony, and those documents were filed in a specified repository.
- No events that might change this relationship have subsequently transpired.

Change any one of these facts, and the conclusion—that is, that a person is married—may no longer be valid. Furthermore, depending upon the context of the question or issue being addressed, the presence of additional facts may also change the conclusion. A statement of pertinent facts is almost always much longer and clumsier than is a simple statement of the conclusion drawn from them. Consequently, much of the time our conversations and thoughts are based on conclusions rather than on elementary facts.

In tax work it often is necessary to pursue facts at length to be certain of the validity of a particular tax conclusion. To continue the foregoing illustration, a person cannot file a "joint income tax return" unless he or she is married. Obviously, most people know if they are married or not, and most tax advisers accept their client's word on this important conclusion. If, in the course of a conversation or in an investigation related to the preparation of a tax return, it becomes apparent that there is reason to doubt the validity of the client's conclusion, a full-scale investigation of all the facts is necessary. For example, a client may state that she has recently been widowed. This simple statement should be sufficient to cause an alert tax adviser to make further investigation because a person may be deemed to be married for tax purposes even after that person believes that he or she once again is single. In this case, the widow may still file a joint return (that is, she is still treated as married for tax purposes) for the year in which her husband died, even though she is no longer married at the end of the year. Furthermore, individuals who are married (that is, all the facts listed above have transpired) may be treated as single for tax purposes because of the existence of additional facts. For example, certain married individuals who are living apart from their spouses may be treated as single so that they may file as a head of household. Likewise, persons married to nonresident aliens may not be eligible to file joint income tax returns, even though they are obviously married.

On the other hand, a tax adviser must also know that persons who have never exchanged marriage vows may be considered as married for tax and other purposes by virtue of their actions (that is, by virtue of "the facts") and the law of the state in which they reside. In all these cases, facts other than the ones listed above play a critical role in the determination of whether the individual is treated as married or single for purposes of the particular tax question being resolved. Here again, additional facts that may seem insignificant or irrelevant (for example, how many days has the taxpayer's spouse been physically present in the United States) play a critical role in arriving at the proper conclusion.

Tax work is often made difficult and risky precisely because the taxpayer may not understand the significance of the pertinent facts, and a tax adviser often cannot spend the time to verify every alleged fact (or absence of fact) without charging an exorbitant fee. When a tax adviser is (or reasonably should be) alerted to the possibility that a further investigation of the facts may lead to a significantly different conclusion in a tax determination, however, it is the tax adviser's professional obligation to investigate those facts in sufficient depth to permit a correct conclusion. In situations involving aspects of the law beyond the confines of taxation—as in the marriage example—the accountant may very well find it necessary to advise a client to engage legal counsel before proceeding with the client's tax problem.

Facts—Established and Anticipated

Taxpayer compliance and tax planning constitute two major portions of any successful tax adviser's work. The initial and critical difference between these two phases of tax practice is simply a difference in the state of the facts. In compliance work, all the facts have already transpired, and the tax adviser's task is to establish what those facts are in order to determine the tax result implicit in those facts. As discussed later in this chapter, this process may at times be more difficult than it appears. In planning work, the tax adviser researches alternative ways of achieving established goals and recommends to a client those actions that will—considering all operational constraints, personal and financial objectives, and personal and business history—minimize the resulting tax liability. In other words, the tax planner must determine and help the taxpayer achieve the desired economic or business goals while at the same time establishing an optimal set of facts from the standpoint of desired tax results, given certain objectives and constraints. The operational procedures applied in these two phases of tax practice are quite different.

Compliance

The first step in taxpayer compliance work is a determination of the facts that have already taken place. This is an especially critical step because an inadequate job of determining all the facts may cause the tax adviser to arrive at an incorrect conclusion. Furthermore, the tax adviser must always keep in mind that the client generally does not even know which facts are important to the tax issue at hand. The procedures used to determine facts differ significantly depending upon the relationship existing between the tax adviser and the taxpayer. The less personal the relationship, the greater the amount of time that must be devoted to a discovery of facts. In most instances, the fact-discovery process can be divided into at least four distinct steps: initial inquiry, independent investigation, additional inquiry, and substantiation.

Initial Inquiry. At one extreme, the tax adviser will not have known the taxpayer before the request for services. In that event, if the initial request is for tax return preparation services, it is common for the tax adviser to complete a predetermined checklist of facts during (or immediately following) an initial interview. Many firms have devised their own forms to facilitate this information-gathering process; others use standard forms prepared by tax return computer services or other agencies. If the initial request is for assistance in an administrative proceeding, a less structured interview is typically used. In every instance the objective of the inquiry is the same: to establish all the facts essential to an accurate determination of the tax liability.

Tax advisers who are intimately familiar with their clients' affairs often are able to extract sufficient facts from existing files and personal knowledge without extended personal contact with the taxpayer. For example, the CPA who regularly maintains a client's financial records may require only minimal additional contact with the client to establish the information necessary to resolve the tax question.

Independent Investigation. Regardless of the extent of personal contact involved in the initial inquiry, all but the simplest taxpayer compliance engagements require some independent investigation on the part of the tax adviser. The specific reasons for undertaking an independent investigation vary from one situation to another, but all stem from the need for additional facts to determine a tax result. Sometimes the impetus for obtaining more facts comes from something the client said; at other times, from what he or she did not say. At still other times, the need for further facts becomes apparent when the tax adviser begins to examine the client's financial records. For example, a canceled check made payable to an unknown Dr. Fred Jones may or may not be tax deductible. The tax adviser must determine what kind of doctor Jones is and what service he rendered to the taxpayer before deciding whether the payment can be deducted.

Whatever the cause, the tax adviser frequently does detective work to determine necessary facts. An independent investigation may involve a detailed review of financial records, old files, correspondence, corporate minutes, sales agreements, bank statements, and so forth. It may involve interviews with friends, family, employees, business associates, or others. In some cases, that search may extend to reviews of general business conditions and practices. Because of the relatively high cost of some investigations, taxpayers and their advisers often delay incurring these costs until absolutely necessary. Often this means deferring the costs from the time of the initial act of taxpayer compliance to the time of a dispute, that is, from the time of filing the tax return to the time when the IRS challenges a tax conclusion previously reported by the taxpayer. Because the IRS challenges only a very small percentage of all tax returns filed in an average year, the reason for delaying a costly in-depth investigation of all the facts is obvious. Nevertheless, the competent tax adviser should always be alert for situations that are apt to require further investigation later. Often it is easier and cheaper to obtain facts and to assemble related evidence at the time events transpire than it is to reconstruct them at a later date. Furthermore, occasionally facts may become impossible to determine if too much time has elapsed between the events and the inquiry. A tax adviser's services are often more efficient and less costly if the client collects much of the necessary evidence to support the facts. Again, the probability of the client's obtaining this evidence successfully is much greater if the facts relate to recent events. Deferring an investigation of pertinent facts nearly always increases the costs. The tradeoff is clear: incur a smaller cost now at the risk that the cost was incurred unnecessarily, or incur greater cost later in the unlikely event that the documented evidence is needed.

Additional Inquiry.   Even in situations in which an in-depth investigation of the facts has been completed, the tax adviser frequently will need to make further factual inquiries after beginning a search of the law. A search for the tax law applicable to a given set of facts often uncovers the need for information not originally deemed relevant by the taxpayer or the tax adviser. By reading revenue rulings and judicial decisions in situations similar to that of the client, an adviser may become aware of the importance of facts not originally considered. Being alerted to their possible importance, the tax adviser must return to the fact determination process once again. In highly complex situations, this process of moving between finding facts and determining the law may repeat itself several times before the tax question is finally resolved.

Substantiation of Facts. Determining what the facts are and proving or substantiating those facts can be two entirely different things. In certain situations, the law requires proper substantiation of the facts to even be able to take a particular position on a tax return. For example, in order to take a deduction for certain charitable contributions, the taxpayer must properly document the fact that the contribution has been made. This current documentation is also required in order to deduct certain automobile business expenses. In other situations where the tax law does not require substantiation in order to take a particular position, the nature and quality of the proof that is required varies significantly, depending on who is receiving the proof. In tax matters, the person who must be convinced of the authenticity of the facts can be anyone from an IRS agent to a Supreme Court justice. The methods used to substantiate facts vary tremendously. Generally, fact substantiation procedures are much less formal in dealings with an administrative agency such as the IRS than in dealings with a court. Even with the judicial system, the rules of evidence vary from one court to another. Obviously, the closer one moves to formal litigation the greater the need for the opinion and the assistance of a qualified trial attorney. Only such a professional can adequately assess the hazards of the litigation procedure, including the rules of evidence and the burden-of-proof problems.

The CPA engaged in tax practice should not lose sight of the fact that the vast majority of all tax disputes are settled at the administrative level. Therefore, it is necessary for the tax adviser to be fully prepared to determine, present, and substantiate all of the facts critical to the resolution of a tax dispute in any administrative proceeding. In doing this, the adviser must exercise caution to avoid stipulation of any fact that might be detrimental to the client in the unlikely event that a dispute should move beyond administrative hearings and into the courts. Because of this ever present

danger, the CPA should consult with a trial attorney at the first
sign of significant litigation potential.

Planning

If events have not yet occurred and the facts have not yet been
established, a taxpayer has an opportunity to plan the anticipated
facts carefully. As noted earlier, tax planning is nothing more than
achieving the desired business or economic goal while at the same
time determining and establishing an optimal set of facts to achieve
the desired tax results. The procedures followed in making such
a determination differ significantly from the procedures used in
taxpayer compliance work.

Determination of the Preferred Alternative. The first step in the determination of the tax preferred alternative involves a client interview.
In this instance, however, the purpose of the interview is not to
determine exactly what has happened in the past but, rather, to
determine (1) the future economic objectives of the client and (2)
any operative constraints in achieving those objectives. If the tax
planner is to perform successfully, *all* of the client's history, present
circumstances, and future ambitions must be fully understood. For
example, the optimal tax solution in organizing a new business
for a client may best be determined by understanding the client's
future desires and goals and helping the client establish a proper
exit strategy from the business. That kind of information can seldom
be obtained in a single interview. Ideally, it is derived through a
long, open, and trusting relationship between the client and tax
adviser. When tax planning is based on such an ongoing relationship, any particular client interview may be brief and directly to
the point. Even relatively major plans can sometimes be developed,
at least initially, with no more than a simple telephone conversation.
Additionally, throughout this process, the tax adviser should
always keep in mind that the goal of proper tax planning is to
achieve economic or business objectives in the most tax effective
way rather than merely to reduce or eliminate taxes with no real
economic or business purpose.

When the tax adviser fully understands a client's objectives and
constraints, he or she should spend a sufficient amount of time

simply thinking about alternative ways of achieving the objectives specified by the client before beginning the research. Generally, there are diverse ways to achieve a single goal; failure to spend enough time and effort in creative thinking about that goal usually results in taking the most obvious route to the solution. In many instances, the most obvious route may not be the preferred alternative. A vivid imagination and creative ability have their greatest payoff in this "thinking step."

Although in all probability no one can do much to increase his or her native imagination or creative ability, many people simply do not take advantage of that which they already possess. By far the most common cause of unimaginative tax planning is the failure of the adviser to spend sufficient time *thinking about* alternative ways to achieve a client's economic or business objectives. A common tendency is to rush far too quickly from the initial inquiry to a search of the law for an answer. By rushing to a solution, we often completely overlook the preferred alternative.

An example of creative imagination appears in *John J. Sexton,* 42 T. C. 1094 (1964), where a taxpayer successfully defended the right to depreciate a hole in the ground. The facts of the case are both interesting and instructive. The taxpayer was an operator of refuse dumps. He acquired land with major excavations primarily to use in his dumping business, and he allocated a substantial portion of the purchase price of the land to the holes in the ground. As the holes were filled, he depreciated the value so allocated. Because the taxpayer carefully documented all the pertinent facts in this case, including the business purpose for purchasing the ground, the court allowed the deduction. Many less imaginative persons might have totally overlooked this major tax advantage simply because it is unusual and because they did not spend enough time just thinking about the facts of the case.

After a tax adviser has determined a client's economic or business objectives and after thinking about alternative ways of achieving those objectives, the tax adviser should systematically go about researching the tax law and calculating the tax result of each viable alternative. The preparation of a "decision tree" or diagram is often very helpful in determining which of several alternatives is the tax preferred one (see chapter 9). This process forces the adviser to think through each alternative carefully, and it demonstrates vividly the dollar significance of the tax savings in the preferred set of facts. Throughout this thinking process, the tax adviser should also carefully ensure that the critical facts can be established in order for the alternative to be viable. For example, taxpayers may elect to treat certain types of organizations or entities as either a partnership or a corporation. This process is known as *checking the box*. However, taxpayers may not "check the box" for other types of entities, called *per se entities*. A great deal of thinking and tax planning can be wasted if the tax adviser doesn't first establish whether the check the box option is available for the particular entity involved in the planning scheme. Ultimately, it is up to the client to implement the plan successfully.

Substantiation of Subsequent Events. The client and the tax adviser, working together, must take every precaution to accumulate and preserve sufficient documentation of the facts to support the tax plan selected. In relatively extreme circumstances, a court will not hesitate to apply any one of several judicial doctrines—most notably the doctrine of substance-over-form—to find that an overly ambitious tax plan is not a valid interpretation of the law. If, however, the tax adviser exercises reasonable caution against plans that lack substance, and if he or she takes sufficient care to document each step of the plans, the chance of succeeding is considerably improved. Of course, the process of substantiating carefully selected facts is primarily the responsibility of the taxpayer. The tax adviser, however, will often supervise the process of implementation to make certain that the intended event actually transpires in the sequence intended and that the proof of these events will be available when and if it is needed.

Some Common Fact Questions

Many tax disputes involve questions of fact, not questions of law. In working with fact questions, a tax adviser's job is to assemble, clarify, and present the facts in such a way that any reasonable person would conclude that they conform to the requirements outlined in the tax law. Demonstrating the facts so clearly is often very difficult. Some fact questions are necessarily much more involved and difficult to prove than others. Following are brief examples of common but difficult questions of fact.

Fair Market Value

The determination of the fair market value of a property is a frequently encountered fact question. It arises in connection with income, estate, and gift taxes. The applicable law common to many of these situations is relatively simple if the fair market value of the properties can be established. For example, section 61 of the Internal Revenue Code (IRC) provides that "gross income means all income from whatever source derived," and Treas. Reg. Sec. 1.61-2(d)(1) goes on to state, "if services are paid for in property, the fair market value of the property taken in payment must be included in income as compensation." Generally, the application of this law is simple enough once the valuation question is settled.

A legal definition of *fair market value,* stated concisely in Estate Tax Reg. Sec. 20.2031-1(b), is

> The fair market value is the price at which the property would change hands between a willing buyer and a willing seller, neither being under any compulsion to buy or to sell and both having reasonable knowledge of relevant facts.[1]

Fact problems are involved in making that brief definition operational. What is a willing buyer? A willing seller? A compulsion to buy? A compulsion to sell? Reasonable knowledge? A relevant fact? Only in the case of comparatively small blocks of listed securities, and in the case of selected commodities, do we have access to an organized market that will supply us with ready answers to those questions. In all other instances we must look to all of the surrounding facts and circumstances to find an answer.

Many articles and books have been written to delineate the circumstances that must be considered in determining fair market

---

[1] **Fair market value** (FMV) is the price that property would sell for on the open market. It is the price that would be agreed on between a willing buyer and a willing seller, with neither being required to act, and both having reasonable knowledge of the relevant facts [IRS Publication 561].

value. Even a cursory review of those books is outside the scope of this tax study. Suffice it to observe here that valuation is a fact question and that, ordinarily, the party to any tax valuation dispute who does the best job of determining, clarifying, and presenting all of the pertinent facts is the party who wins that dispute.

Reasonable Salaries

The determination of what constitutes a reasonable salary has long been a troublesome tax problem. As usual, the applicable law is relatively simple if we could only determine what is reasonable within a particular fact setting.

In determining reasonableness, both IRS agents and judges often look, for comparison, to such obvious facts as salaries paid to other employees performing similar tasks for other employers, any unique attributes of a particular employee, the employee's education, the availability of other persons with similar skills, and prior compensation paid to the employee. In addition, tax authorities trying to determine the reasonableness of salaries also look to the dividend history of the employer corporation, the relationship between salaries and equity ownership, the time and method of making the compensation decision, the state of the economy, and many other facts. Again, we cannot examine here all of the detailed facts that have been important to reasonable salary decisions in the past. We need only observe that the question of reasonableness is a fact question. The taxpayer who marshals all of the pertinent facts and presents them in a favorable light stands a better chance of winning an IRS challenge of unreasonable salaries than does the taxpayer who ignores any critical facts. The best reason for carefully studying regulations, rulings, and cases in such a circumstance is to make certain not to overlook the opportunity to determine and prove a fact that could be important to the desired conclusion.

Casualty and Theft Losses

Taxpayers may lose their right to claim a casualty or theft loss deduction for income tax purposes because they did not take sufficient care to establish the facts surrounding that loss. The law authorizes a tax deduction for losses sustained on property held for personal use only if the property is damaged or destroyed by a casualty or theft. Thus, the loss sustained because of the disappearance of a diamond ring will not give rise to a tax deduction unless the taxpayer can prove that the disappearance is attributable to a casualty or theft, rather than to carelessness on the part of the owner. If the taxpayer has photographs, newspaper accounts, police reports, testimony of impartial persons, or other evidence that a casualty or theft has occurred, he or she will have relatively little trouble convincing a skeptical IRS agent or a judge of the right to claim that deduction.

Gifts

Section 102 provides that receipt of a gift does not constitute taxable income. In many situations, however, it is difficult to determine whether a particular property transfer really is a gift or compensation for either a past or a contemplated future service. Once again the facts surrounding the transfer are what will control that determination. Facts that demonstrate the intent of the transferor to make a gratuitous transfer—that is, one without any expectation of something in return—are necessary to the determination that the transfer was a gift. Relationships existing between the transferor and the transferee may be important; for example, it generally will be easier to establish the fact that a gift was made if the two persons involved are closely related individuals (for example, mother and daughter). On the other hand, if the two are related in an employer-employee relationship, it will be especially difficult to establish the presence of a gift. Although the broad outline of many other abstract but common fact questions could be noted here, let us consider in somewhat greater detail a few examples of some real world tax disputes that were based on fact questions.

Illustrative Fact Cases

To better illustrate the critical role of facts in the resolution of tax questions, an examination of four previously litigated tax cases follows. The four cases can be divided into two sets of two cases each. One set deals with the question of distinguishing between the receipt of a gift (not taxable income to the recipient) and the receipt of income for services rendered; the other set deals with the deductibility of payments made by a taxpayer to his or her parent. None of the four cases is particularly important in its own right, but together, they serve to illustrate several important conclusions common to tax research and fact questions. The court decisions in these cases are relatively brief, and the facts involved are easy to comprehend.

Gifts or Income?

Under the IRC, gifts do not constitute an element of taxable income. The present rule is stated in section 102 as follows: "(a) General Rule—Gross income does not include the value of property acquired by gift, bequest, devise, or inheritance." The first two cases to be examined consist largely of a judicial review of the facts necessary to determine whether particular transfers of property constitute gifts or taxable income for services rendered.

The first case involves a taxpayer named Margaret D. Brizendine and her husband, Everett. In this case, the taxpayers are referred to as the *petitioners* and the IRS is referred to as the *respondent*. The case was heard by the Tax Court in 1957, and the decision, rendered by Judge Rice, reads in part as follows:

Case 1. Everett W. Brizendine, *T.C.M. 1957-32*

Findings of Fact

Petitioners were married in 1945 and throughout the years in issue were husband and wife and residents of Roanoke, Virginia. They filed no returns for the years 1945 through 1949, inclusive, but did file returns for 1950 and 1951 with the former collector of internal revenue in Richmond.

Prior to the years in issue, petitioner, Margaret D. Brizendine, was convicted and fined on five separate occasions for operating a house of prostitution, or for working in such a house. Petitioner, Everett W. Brizendine, prior to the years in issue, had served a term in the penitentiary. During the years in issue, he was convicted and fined seven times for violation of the Roanoke City Gambling Code, for operating a gambling house, and for disorderly conduct.

Prior to the years in issue, petitioner, Margaret D. Brizendine, met an individual in a Roanoke, Virginia, restaurant with whom she became friendly. The individual promised her that if she would discontinue her activities as a prostitute he would buy her a home and provide for her support. In 1945, the individual paid Margaret $2,000 with which sum she made the down payment on a house; he also arranged for her to secure a loan to pay the balance of the purchase price. From 1945 and until the time of his death in March 1950, the individual provided money with which Margaret made payments on such loan. In addition, he paid her approximately $25 per week in cash and also paid her money to provide for utilities, insurance, furniture, and clothing. In 1946, he paid her $500 which she used to buy a fur coat.

In determining the deficiencies herein, the respondent arrived at petitioners' adjusted gross income by adding annual estimated living expenses in the amount of $2,000 to the known expenditures made by them. The amounts of adjusted gross income so determined were as follows:

1945	$4,784.80
1946	3,300.70
1947	2,645.00
1948	2,978.62
1949	2,763.37
1950	4,812.82
1951	3,641.57

Petitioners' living expenses did not exceed $1,200 in addition to the known personal expenditures made by them during each of the years in issue.

Petitioners' failure to file returns for the years 1945 through 1949 inclusive, was not due to reasonable cause. The deficiencies in issue were due to petitioners' negligence or intentional disregard of rules and regulations. The petitioners' failure to file declarations of estimated tax was not due to reasonable cause and resulted in an underestimate of estimated tax.

Opinion

Petitioners contended that the amount received by Margaret from the individual, with which she made a down payment on a house, as well as all other amounts received from him until the time of his death in 1950, were gifts to her and, therefore, did not constitute taxable income. The respondent, while accepting petitioner's testimony as to the source of the sums, argues that she has not established that the amounts received from the individual were really gifts. He further points out that Margaret testified that the payments received from the individual were in consideration of her forbearance to refrain from engaging in prostitution, and to grant him her companionship, and argues that her promise constituted valid consideration for the payments which causes them to be taxable as ordinary income.

Both petitioners testified at the hearing in this case. Their demeanor on the stand, coupled with their long criminal records, leaves considerable doubt in our mind that the payments from the individual to Margaret were the only source of petitioner's income during the years in question, or that such amounts as the individual paid to Margaret were gifts. Since petitioners thus failed to establish that those amounts were in fact gifts, we conclude that such amounts were correctly determined by respondent to be taxable income which petitioners received during the years in issue. We further think that there is considerable merit to the respondent's argument that Margaret's promise to the individual to forbear from engaging in prostitution, and to grant him her companionship, constituted sufficient consideration for the money received from him to make it taxable to her.

The second case involves a taxpayer named Greta Starks. Here again, the taxpayer is referred to as the *petitioner*. The case was heard by the Tax Court in 1966, and the decision, rendered by Judge Mulroney, reads in parts as follows:

Case 2. Greta Starks, *T.C.M. 1966-134*

Findings of Fact

Petitioner, who was unmarried during the years in question, lives at 16900 Parkside, Detroit, Michigan. She filed no federal income tax returns for the years 1954 through 1958. She was 24 years old in 1954 and during that year and throughout the years 1955, 1956, 1957, and 1958 she received from one certain man, amounts of money for living expenses, and a house (he gave her the cash to buy it in her name), furniture, an automobile, jewelry, fur coats, and other clothing. This man was married and about 55 years old in 1954.

Respondent in his notice of deficiency stated that he determined that the property and money petitioner received each year constituted income received by petitioner "for services rendered" and in his computation he held her subject to self-employment tax. He explained his computation of the deficiency for each year by reference to Exhibit A which was attached to the notice of deficiency. Page 13 of this Exhibit A is as follows:

Analysis of Living Expenses and Assets Received
for Services Rendered

Year 1954	
1955 Oldsmobile automobile	$ 3,000.00
Weekly allowance ($150.00 × 20 weeks)	3,000.00
Total	$ 6,000.00

Year 1955	
16900 Parkside	$22,211.08
Roberts Furs	5,038.00
Saks Fifth Avenue	828.18
Piano and furniture	6,000.00
Weekly allowance ($150.00 × 52 weeks)	7,800.00
Total	$41,877.26

Year 1956	
Roberts Furs	$ 1,570.00
Saks Fifth Avenue	3,543.17
Miscellaneous household expenses	1,500.00
Total	$ 6,613.17

Year 1957	
Furs by Roberts	$ 121.00
Saks Fifth Avenue	1,353.19
Living expenses	4,000.00
Total	$ 5,474.19

Year 1958	
Furs by Roberts	$ 35.00
Saks Fifth Avenue	978.79
Living expenses	4,000.00
Total	$ 5,013.79

The money and property received by petitioner during the years in question were all gifts from the above described man with whom she had a very close personal relationship during all of the years here involved.

Opinion

The question in this case is whether the advancements made by respondent's witness were gifts under section 102, Internal Revenue Code of 1954, or in some manner payments that would constitute taxable income. The question is one of fact.

There were two witnesses in this case. Petitioner took the stand and testified she was not gainfully employed during the years here involved except for an occasional modeling job in 1954 for which her total receipts did not exceed $600. She said she had no occupation and was not engaged in any business or practicing any profession and had no investments that yielded her income during the years in question. She in effect admitted the receipt of the items of money and property recited in respondent's notice of deficiency but said they were all gifts made to her by the man she identified as sitting in the front row in the courtroom. She testified that this man gave her money to defray her living expenses, and about $20,000 cash to buy the house at 16900 Parkside in 1955. She testified that she mortgaged this house for about $9,000 and she and this man lived for a time off of the proceeds of this loan. She said that this man gave her the furniture, jewelry, and clothing but she never considered the money and property turned over to her by this man as earnings. She said she had during the years in question, love and affection for this man and a very personal relationship.

The only other witness in the case was the alleged donor who sat in the courtroom during all of petitioner's testimony. He was called to the stand by respondent. He admitted on direct examination (there was no cross-examination) that he had advanced petitioner funds for the purchase of a house, clothes, fur coat, and furniture for the house. He was asked the purpose of the payments and he replied: "To insure the companionship of Greta Starks, more or less of a personal investment in the future on my part." The only other portion of his testimony that might be said to have any bearing on whether the advancements were gifts or not is the following:

Q. In advancing Greta Starks monies to purchase the properties I previously mentioned, what factors did you take into consideration pertaining to your wish or desire of securing the permanent companionship of Greta Starks?

A. The monies were advanced as I considered necessary. The purchase of a house was considered a permanent basis to last ten, twenty years not for a short while.

Respondent, of course, asks us to believe the testimony of his witness for respondent's counsel stated he was not to be considered a hostile witness. The witness was only asked a few questions. He had heard all of petitioner's testimony to the effect that the money, home, car, furniture, clothing, etc. were gifts by him to her. It is somewhat significant that he was not asked the direct question as to whether the advancement of money and property, which he admits he made, were gifts by him to her. We have quoted the only two statements he made that throw any light at all on the issue of whether the advancements were gifts or earnings. Such passages in his answers to the effect that he was making a "personal investment in the future" or the house purchase was "considered a permanent basis" are incomprehensive and rather absurd as statements of purpose. His testimony, in so far as it can be understood at all, tends to corroborate petitioner. He gives as his purpose for making the advancements "to insure the companionship" of petitioner. This can well be his purpose for making the gifts. It certainly serves no basis for the argument advanced by respondent on brief to the effect that her "companionship" was a service she rendered in return for the money and property she received. Evidently respondent would argue the man paid her over $41,000 for her companionship in 1955 and $5,000 or $6,000 for her companionship in the other years.

We are not called upon to determine the propriety of the relations that existed between petitioner and her admirer during the five years in question. He testified he had not seen her for five or six years. Petitioner was married in 1961 and is now living with her husband and mother. It is enough to say that all of the circumstances and the testimony of petitioner and even of respondent's witness support her statement that she received gifts of money and property during the five years in question and no taxable income.

A Comparison of Facts. Even a cursory examination of these two Tax Court memorandum decisions reveals that the two cases have many facts in common. In both instances, a female taxpayer received substantial sums of money and other valuable property each year for several years, from a specific man, in exchange for her companionship.

On the other hand, the two decisions also suggest several fact differences between the two cases. For example, consider the following:

1. The names, dates, and places of residence of the principal parties differ in the two instances.
2. The woman involved in the one case was, throughout the years in question, married; the other woman was single.
3. One of the male companion/transferors had died before the legal action; the other was alive and testified at the trial.
4. One of the taxpayer/transferees had a criminal record as a prostitute before the years in question; the other had no such record.

Because the pertinent tax issue is the same in both cases, the question is whether the facts common to the two cases are sufficiently alike to warrant a common result or whether the facts are sufficiently dissimilar to justify different results. Brizendine had to report taxable income; Starks was found to have received only gifts and, therefore, had no taxable income to report. The law was the same in both instances; therefore, the different results must be explained either by the differences in the facts or by differences in the judicial process. Theoretically, the judicial process should work equally well in every case; if so, the different results can be explained only by different facts.

An Analysis of the Divergent Results. The published decision rendered by any court is, quite obviously, much less than a complete transcript of the judicial proceeding. It is, at best, a brief synopsis of those elements of the case deemed to be most important to the judge who has the responsibility of explaining why and how the court reached its decision. A review of the two judicial decisions under consideration here suggests at least two hypotheses that might explain the different results reached in these two cases.

On the one hand, the fact that Margaret Brizendine was found to have received taxable income rather than gifts may be attributable primarily to the fact that she had a record of prior prostitution. The fact that during the years 1945 through 1951 she elected to "discontinue her activities as a prostitute" may suggest that the taxable status of her receipts really had not changed all that significantly. Before 1945, her receipts apparently were derived from numerous persons; thereafter, from one individual. If the same explanation for the receipts is common to both time periods, the tax results should not differ simply because of the number of transferors involved. If, however, the pertinent facts surrounding those transfers differed materially during the two time periods, a history of prostitution should have no material impact on the present decision.

An alternative hypothesis that might also adequately explain the divergent results in these two cases would emphasize the differences in the judicial process rather than the differences in the facts. Perhaps Brizendine and her attorney simply failed to convince the judge that the facts warranted treating the transfers as gifts.

Two adjacent statements in *Brizendine* support each of the above hypotheses. Judge Rice first says, "Since petitioners thus failed to establish that those amounts were in fact gifts, we conclude that such amounts were correctly determined by respondent to be taxable income which petitioners received during the years in issue." This sentence clearly suggests that Brizendine's primary problem was one of inadequate substantiation. In the next sentence, however, the judge suggests the alternative hypothesis in the following words: "We further think that there is considerable merit to the respondent's argument that Margaret's promise to the individual to forebear from engaging in prostitution, and to grant him her companionship, constituted sufficient consideration for the money received from him to make it taxable to her."

The ultimate basis for a judicial decision often is not known with much certainty. Any impartial reading of *Brizendine* could not pass lightly over the judge's observation that the taxpayers' "demeanor on the stand, coupled with their long criminal records, leaves considerable doubt in our mind that the payments from the individual to Margaret ... were gifts." Although initially it may be difficult to understand how courtroom behavior or criminal records relate to the presence or absence of a gift, those facts may help to establish the credibility of any statements made by a witness. The process of taxation is, after all, not a laboratory procedure but a very human process from beginning to end. Any attempt to minimize the significance of the human element at any level of the taxing process runs the risk of missing a critical ingredient.

Starks may be viewed as further evidence of the importance of the human element in the taxing process. This time, however, the record suggests that human sympathies were running with the taxpayer and against the IRS. Judge Mulroney seems to have been less than pleased with the performance of the government's attorney. The judge, commenting on the government's interrogation of the male transferor, observes, "He was not asked the direct question as to whether the advancements of money and property, which he admits he made, were gifts by him to her. We have quoted the only two statements he made that throw any light at all on the issue of whether the advancements were gifts or earnings. Such passages in his answers to the effect that he was making a 'personal investment in the future' or the house purchase was 'considered a permanent basis' are incomprehensible and rather absurd as statements of purpose. His testimony, in so far as it can be understood at all, tends to corroborate petitioner." In summary, the failure of the government's attorney to ask the obvious question and to pursue related questions when a witness gave "incomprehensive" answers seems to have influenced the judge in this instance. In any event, the court did conclude that "all of the circumstances and the testimony of petitioner and even of respondent's witness support her statement that she received gifts of money and property during the five years in question and no taxable income."

Lessons for Tax Research. Even though the specific technical tax content of these two cases is trivial, a tax adviser can learn several things from these two cases. History—that is, facts that took place well before the events deemed to be critical in a given tax dispute— may significantly influence the outcome of the decision. Therefore, in gathering the facts in a tax problem, the tax adviser can never be too thorough in getting all of the facts of a case.

A study of these two cases also reveals the intricate balance between facts and conclusions. If the trier of facts—IRS agent, conferee, or judge—can be convinced of the authenticity or even the reasonableness of the facts presented for consideration, he or she has ample opportunity to reach the conclusion desired by the taxpayer. If those facts are not presented or are presented inadequately, the decision maker cannot be blamed for failing to give them full consideration. Disputes are often lost by the party who fails to capitalize on the opportunity to know and present all pertinent facts in the best light.

Finally, some further reflections on these two cases are instructive for tax planning generally. If the parties to this litigation had correctly anticipated their subsequent tax problems, what might they have done to reduce the probabilities of an unfavorable result? For example, would the results have differed if neither party had included a "weekly allowance" in their financial arrangements? What if all transfers had been made on such special occasions as a birthday, an anniversary, Christmas, Chanukah, or some other holiday? What if gift cards had accompanied each transfer and those cards had been saved and "treasured" in a scrapbook? Would the filing of gift tax returns by the transferor have helped the income tax conclusion? Obviously, each of the additional facts suggested here would lend credence to the conclusion that the transfers were indeed gifts. At some point, the evidence—perhaps the filing of the gift tax return—would be so overwhelming that no one would question the conclusion in anything but the most unusual circumstances.

The important point of this review is, of course, that the tax adviser often plays a critical role in settings very remote from the courtroom. If the tax adviser correctly anticipates potential problems, it may be easy to recommend the accumulation of supporting proof that will almost insure the conclusion a client is interested in reaching, without going to court. Even when the tax adviser has been consulted only after all of the facts are "carved in stone," the thoroughness with which those facts are presented is often critical to the resolution of the tax question. No one can make a good presentation of the facts until all of the facts are known, down to the very last detail. A study of two more cases can yield additional insight into the critical role that facts play in tax questions.

Deductible or Not?

In general, we know that income earned for services rendered must be reported by the person who rendered the services, and that income from property must be reported by the person who owns the property. If a taxpayer arranges for someone else to pay to one of his or her parents a part of the compensation that was originally owed to him or her for services rendered, generally, that payment is still taxed to the individual rendering the service, and the payment made to the parent ordinarily is not deductible by him or her. Payments made to parents, like payments made to anyone else, are deductible for income tax purposes only if the parent renders a business-related service to the child, and the payment made for such a service is reasonable in amount. What exactly, however, do those words mean?

The third case to be reviewed here involves a professional baseball player named Cecil Randolph (Randy) Hundley, Jr. The Tax Court heard the case in 1967, and the decision, rendered by Judge Hoyt, reads in part as follows:

Case 3. Cecil Randolph Hundley, Jr., *48 T.C. 339 (1967)*

Findings of Fact

The stipulated facts are found accordingly and adopted as our findings.

Cecil Randolph Hundley, Jr. (hereinafter referred to as petitioner), filed his 1960 income tax return with the district director of internal revenue, Richmond, Va.; Martinsville, Va., was his legal residence at the time petitioner filed the petition herein. Petitioner is a professional baseball player and at the time of trial was a catcher for the Chicago Cubs of the National League.

Petitioner's father, Cecil Randolph Hundley, Sr. (hereinafter referred to as Cecil), is a former semiprofessional baseball player, and he has also been a baseball coach. Cecil played as a catcher throughout his baseball career, and received numerous injuries to his throwing hand while using the traditional two-handed method of catching. This is a common problem of catchers. A few years before Cecil retired from active participation in baseball as a player, he developed a one-handed method of catching which was unique and unorthodox. This technique was beneficial because injuries to the catcher's throwing hand were avoided. Cecil became actively engaged in the construction and excavation business in 1947 and was still engaged in that business at the time of trial.

Petitioner attended Basset High School near Martinsville, Va., from which he graduated in June of 1960. During 1958 petitioner was a member of his high school baseball team and the local American Legion team. He played catcher for both teams and was an outstanding player. In the spring of 1958, while a sophomore in high school, petitioner decided that he wanted to become a good major league professional ball player. Petitioner believed that Cecil was best qualified to coach and train him for the attainment of this goal. After discussing his ambition with Cecil, an oral agreement was reached between petitioner and Cecil. Cecil agreed to devote his efforts to a program of intensive training of petitioner in the skills of baseball, to act as petitioner's coach, business agent, manager, publicity director, and sales agent in negotiating with professional baseball teams for a contract. His role may best be described in petitioner's own words when he first asked Cecil to handle things for him in 1958: "Daddy, do the business part and let me play the ball."

As compensation for Cecil's services, it was agreed that Cecil would receive 50 percent of any bonus that might be received under the terms of a professional baseball contract if one should later be signed. This contingent payment agreement was thought to be fair and reasonable by the parties since it was unknown at that time whether petitioner would ever develop into a player with major league potential or sign a professional baseball contract or receive a bonus for signing. Moreover, petitioner could not sign a baseball contract while still a minor without his parent's consent or until he graduated from high school. The size of baseball bonuses obtainable at some unknown time, years in the future, was extremely conjectural. A rule limiting bonuses to $4,000 for signing baseball contracts had been suspended in 1958 and its reinstatement was a definite possibility before 1960. It was not expected by petitioner or Cecil at that time that an exceptionally large bonus would ever be received. Later on they estimated that at most $25,000 might be paid to petitioner as a bonus.

Between the spring of 1958 and petitioner's graduation from high school in 1960, Cecil devoted a great deal of time to petitioner's development into the best baseball player possible. Cecil became petitioner's coach and taught petitioner the skill of being a one-handed catcher. While this method is advantageous, it is difficult to master because it is contrary to natural instincts. The perfection of this unorthodox technique therefore required an inordinate amount of time and effort by the teacher and the pupil. Cecil also taught petitioner to be a power hitter in order to enhance petitioner's appeal to professional baseball teams. Petitioner weighed only 155 pounds during his high school days which was a decided handicap for him both as a hitter and a catcher hoping to break into the big leagues.

Cecil attended every baseball practice session and every home and away game in which petitioner participated between 1958 and 1960. On many of these occasions he met with scouts for big league teams. By mutual agreement, Cecil relieved petitioner's high school and American Legion coach from any duties with respect to petitioner. It was agreed between the coach and Cecil that it would be in the petitioner's interest for Cecil to be in complete charge of the training program. Cecil supplied petitioner with baseball equipment at his own expense during this period.

In order to obtain the best possible professional baseball contract for petitioner, Cecil had many meetings with members of the press during the 2-year period from the spring of 1958 to June 16, 1960, to publicize petitioner's skill as a baseball player. Cecil handled all the negotiations with representatives of the many professional baseball teams that became interested in petitioner. This undertaking involved numerous meetings at home and out of town. Cecil left Sundays open for such negotiations for the entire 2-year period but negotiations often occurred on other days of the week. Cecil was never paid anything for the considerable expenses he incurred over the 2-year period.

The amount of compensation to be received by Cecil was contingent on the obtainment and size of a bonus to be paid petitioner for signing a professional baseball contract. In determining the percentage of the possible bonus to be received by Cecil, the parties also gave consideration to Cecil's increased expenses and the anticipated loss of time and income from his construction business. Cecil had to neglect his business and he lost several substantial contracts during the period of petitioner's intensive training. The amount of time he devoted to his grading and excavating business was substantially reduced during 1958, 1959, and 1960 with corresponding loss of business income.

Petitioner developed into an outstanding high school baseball player under Cecil's tutorage and by 1960 many major league clubs had become interested in signing him. Due to the rule requiring high school graduation before signing a baseball contract, extensive final negotiation sessions with representatives of the various major league baseball teams did not begin until after petitioner's graduation in 1960.

The final negotiation sessions were held at Cecil's home and after 2 weeks resulted in a professional baseball contract signed by petitioner on June 16, 1960. All of the negotiations with the many major league clubs bidding for petitioner's contract were handled by Cecil in such a way that the bidding for petitioner's signature was extremely competitive. Representatives of the various baseball teams were allowed to make as many offers as they wanted during the 2-week period, but the terms of any offer were not revealed to representatives of other teams. Cecil's expert and shrewd handling of the negotiations was instrumental in obtaining a most favorable contract and an extraordinarily large bonus for the petitioner.

The baseball contract finally signed by petitioner was with a minor league affiliate of the San Francisco Giants of the National League. The contract provided for a bonus of $110,000 to petitioner and $11,000 to Cecil, and a guaranteed salary to petitioner of not less than $1,000 per month during the baseball playing season for a period of 5 years. Cecil bargained for and insisted upon the minimum salary provision in addition to the large bonus because of his expectation that petitioner would be playing in the relatively low paying minor leagues for at least 5 years. Cecil also signed the contract because under the rules of professional baseball the signature of a minor was not accepted without the signature of his parent.

The baseball contract contained the following pertinent provisions:

> 1. The Club hereby employs the Player to render and the Player agrees to render, skilled services as a baseball player in connection with all games of the Club during the year 1960, including the Club's training season, the Club's exhibition games, the Club's playing season, any official series in which the Club may participate, and in any game or games in the receipts of which the Player may be entitled to share. The Player covenants that at the time he signs this contract he is not under contract or contractual obligation to any baseball club other than the one party to this contract and that he is capable of and will perform with expertness, diligence and fidelity the service stated and such other duties as may be required of him in such employment.
>
> 2. For the service aforesaid subsequent to the training season the Club will pay the Player at the rate of one thousand dollars ($1,000) per month ... after the commencement of the playing season ... and end with the termination of the Club's scheduled playing season and any official league playoff series in which the Club participates.

> • • • •

> 14. Player is to receive cash bonus of one hundred and ten thousand dollars ($110,000) payable as follows:

Eleven thousand dollars ($11,000) upon approval of this contract by the National Association of Professional Baseball Leagues. Also eleven thousand dollars ($11,000) on Sept. 15, 1961; Sept. 15, 1962; Sept. 15, 1963; Sept. 15, 1964.

The father, Cecil R. Hundley, is to receive eleven thousand dollars ($11,000) upon approval of contract by the National Association of Professional Baseball Leagues. Also eleven thousand dollars ($11,000) on Sept. 15, 1961; Sept. 15, 1962; Sept. 15, 1963; Sept. 15, 1964.

• • • •

The designation of $11,000 to be paid annually to Cecil for 5 years was a consequence of the agreement between Cecil and petitioner to divide equally any bonus received by petitioner for signing a professional baseball contract. The scout for the San Francisco Giants who negotiated the contract was aware of the aforementioned agreement before the contract was written, and the terms of the contract reflected the prior understanding of the contracting parties with respect to the division of the bonus payments. Petitioner's high school coach also knew of the 50-50 bonus agreement between petitioner and Cecil and had been aware of it since its inception in 1958.

During the 1960 taxable year which is in issue, petitioner and Cecil each received $11,000 of the bonus from the National Exhibition Co. pursuant to the terms of the contract. Petitioner did not include the $11,000 payment received by Cecil in his gross income reported in his income tax return for 1960. Cecil duly reported it in his income tax return for that year.

The notice of deficiency received by petitioner stated that income reported as received from the National Exhibition Co. was understated by the amount of $11,000. The parties are apparently in agreement that petitioner understated his income for 1960 in the determined amount, but petitioner contends that an offsetting expense deduction of $11,000 should have been allowed for the payment received by Cecil as partial compensation for services rendered under the 1958 agreement between petitioner and Cecil. Respondent's position on brief is that only a $2,200 expense deduction, 10 percent of the total bonus payment in 1960, is allowable to petitioner in 1960 as the reasonable value of services performed by Cecil.

The contract between Cecil and petitioner was made in 1958; it was bona fide and at arm's length, reasonable in light of the circumstances existing when made in the taxable year before us. The payment of 50 percent of petitioner's bonus thereunder to Cecil in 1960 was compensation to him for services actually rendered to petitioner. He received and kept the $11,000 of the bonus paid directly to him by the ball club.

Opinion

Respondent's determination that an additional $11,000 should have been included in petitioner's income for 1960 is based upon section 61(a) which provides that gross income includes compensation for services and section 73(a) which provides that amounts received in respect of the services of a child shall be included in the child's gross income even though such amounts are not received by the child.

It is beyond question and on brief the parties agree that the $11,000 received by Cecil actually represented an amount paid in consideration of obtaining petitioner's services as a professional baseball player. Petitioner, while agreeing with the foregoing conclusion, argues that a deduction in the amount of $11,000 should be allowed for 1960 under section 162 or 212. Respondent has conceded that such a deduction should be allowed but only in the amount of $2,200.

Section 162 provides that a deduction shall be allowed for an ordinary and necessary expense paid during the taxable year in carrying on any trade or business including a reasonable allowance for compensation for personal services actually rendered. Section 212 provides that an individual may deduct all ordinary and necessary expenses paid or incurred during the taxable year for the production or collection of income.

Respondent argues there is insufficient evidence to establish an agreement in 1958 to share any bonus equally and that even if there were such an agreement no portion paid for Cecil's services to petitioner prior to 1960 is deductible because prior to his graduation petitioner was not in the trade or business of being a baseball player. He contends that the only service performed by Cecil for which petitioner is entitled to a deduction was the actual negotiation of the June 16, 1960, contract. He concedes on brief that a reasonable value for the services rendered by Cecil during the 2-week period from graduation to signing the contract is $2,200, 10 percent of the total bonus paid in 1960.

Petitioner has introduced persuasive and convincing evidence that the agreement was in fact reached in the spring of 1958, and we have so found. This finding is essential to petitioner's position that a deduction for an ordinary and necessary business expense deduction in the amount of $11,000 should be allowed in 1960. He argues that a contingent right to 50 percent of any bonus obtained was a reasonable value for services rendered by Cecil between the spring of 1958 and the signing of the contract in 1960, and that payment for such services was therefore an ordinary and necessary expense associated with his business of professional baseball.

We agree that the 50 percent contingent compensation agreement was reasonable in amount. Section 1.162-7(b)(2) of the regulations sets forth a test for the deductibility of contingent compensation which we have accepted as correct in *Roy Marilyn Stone Trust,* 44 T. C. 349 (1965). We apply the test here.

The primary elements considered by petitioner and Cecil in determining Cecil's contingent compensation were the amount of time that would be spent in coaching, training, and representing petitioner during the uncertain period between 1958 and an eventual contract. Cecil's exclusive handling of all publicity and contract negotiations and the income that would probably be lost due to less time spent on Cecil's construction business were also important factors. In addition to the foregoing considerations, emphasis should be placed on the fact that the ultimate receipt of a bonus of any kind was uncertain and indefinite. The amount was indeterminable and in 1958 neither petitioner, Cecil, nor the high school coach who was aware of the agreement had any notion that an exceptionally large bonus would be paid 2 years hence. Petitioner might well never have become a professional ballplayer, nor was it at all certain that he would be paid a bonus in the future. Viewing the circumstances at the time the agreement was made in the light of all of the evidence before us we conclude and hold that the test of reasonableness has been met even though the contingent compensation may be greater than the amount which might be ordinarily paid.

• • • •

While it is true that an agreement of this sort between a father and his minor son cannot possess the arm's-length character of transactions between independent, knowledgeable businessmen and must be most carefully scrutinized, the agreement here stands every searching test. Independent and trustworthy witnesses verified its existence since 1958. It was in our judgment and in the opinion of both petitioner and Cecil, then and at trial, fair to both parties. See *Olivia de Havilland Goodrich,* 20 T.C. 323 (1953).

• • • •

Respondent contends further, however, that even if the bonus splitting agreement arose in 1958 and was intended to ultimately result in a reasonable amount of compensation for services rendered throughout the 2-year period, the full amount received by Cecil is still not deductible because petitioner was not engaged in a trade or business or any other income-producing activity until graduation from high school when he became eligible to sign a professional baseball contract. In order for an expenditure to qualify for deductibility under section 162 or 212, it must have been paid or incurred in carrying on any trade or business or for any other income producing or collecting activity.

The contingent compensation agreement was so closely bound up with the existence of the petitioner's business activity of professional baseball that payments made thereunder must be considered as paid in carrying on a trade or business. If petitioner had never entered the business of professional baseball or had not been paid a bonus therefore, no payments would have been made to or received by Cecil. The whole basis of the agreement was the ultimate existence and establishment of the contemplated business activity and the collection of a bonus. We therefore conclude that payments made under the terms of the agreement were paid for services actually rendered in carrying on a business. The obligation to make the payments to Cecil was an obligation of the business since there would be no obligation without the business. If the business were entered without payment of a bonus there also would be no obligation to share it with Cecil. The unique relationship of Cecil's compensation to the professional baseball contract and petitioner's income derived therefrom in 1960 is most persuasive of the deductible nature of the compensation payment made that year.

Respondent's final argument, raised herein for the first time on brief, is based on the premise that the services rendered prior to high school graduation were basically educational in nature, and that educational expenditures are personal and nondeductible if undertaken primarily for the purpose of obtaining a new position or substantial advancement in position. See sec. 1.162-5(b), Income Tax Regs. We have previously held that claimed deductions for educational expenditures of the foregoing type are not allowable. *Mary O. Furner*, 47 T.C. 165 (1966); *Joseph T. Booth* III, 35 T.C. 1144 (1961); and *Arnold Namrow*, 33 T.C. 419 (1959), aff'd. 288 F. 2d 648 (C.A. 4, 1961).

However, petitioner is not claiming a deduction in the amount of $11,000 for educational expenditures, and indeed he could not. It is clear that a significant portion of Cecil's compensation was not for coaching and training petitioner in the skills of baseball, if that be deemed education, but for other services rendered throughout the 2-year period.

• • • •

We hold, therefore, that whereas respondent acted correctly in including the entire $22,000 bonus in petitioner's taxable income, petitioner should be nevertheless allowed a deduction in the amount of $11,000 in 1960 as a business expense for the portion of the bonus paid directly to Cecil for his personal services actually rendered with such rewarding financial results for both petitioner and his father.

The last case to be reviewed in this chapter involves another professional baseball player named Richard A. Allen. His case was heard by the Tax Court in 1968, and the decision, rendered by Judge Raum, reads in part as follows:

Case 4. Richard A. Allen, *50 T.C. 466 (1968)*

Findings of Fact

Some of the facts have been stipulated and, as stipulated, are incorporated herein by this reference along with accompanying exhibits.

Petitioners Richard A. and Barbara Allen are husband and wife, who at the time of the filing of the petitions and amended petitions herein resided in Philadelphia, Pa. Richard A. Allen filed his individual returns for the calendar years 1960, 1961, and 1962, and a joint return with his wife Barbara Allen for 1963, on the cash receipts and disbursements method of accounting, with the district director of internal revenue, Pittsburgh, Pa. Barbara Allen is a party to this proceeding solely by virtue of the joint return filed for 1963, and the term 'petitioner' will hereinafter refer solely to Richard A. Allen.

Petitioner was born on March 8, 1942. In the spring of 1960 petitioner, then age 18, was living with his mother, Mrs. Era Allen, in Wampum, Pa., and was a senior at a local high school. Mrs. Allen had been separated from her husband since 1957. She had eight children, of whom three, including petitioner, were dependent upon her for support during 1960. She received no funds from her husband, and supported her family by doing housework, sewing, or laundry work.

In the course of his high school years, petitioner acquired a reputation as an outstanding baseball and basketball player. He was anxious to play professional baseball, and had even expressed a desire to leave high school for that purpose before graduation, but was not permitted to do so by his mother. During the petitioner's junior year in high school, word of his athletic talents reached John Ogden (hereinafter "Ogden"), a baseball "scout" for the Philadelphia National League Club, commonly known and hereinafter referred to as the Phillies. Ogden's attention was drawn to petitioner through a newspaper article about petitioner which, while primarily describing him as a great basketball player, also mentioned that he had hit 22 "home runs" playing with a men's semiprofessional baseball team the summer before his junior year in high school, and that the player who had come closest to his total on the team, which otherwise comprised only grown men, had hit only 15 home runs. Ogden's function as a scout for the Phillies was to select baseball talent capable of playing in the major leagues, i.e., with the Phillies, and after reading this article he made up his mind to see petitioner.

Ogden had himself played baseball for around 16 to 18 years, was general manager of one baseball club and owner of another for 7 or 8 years, and at the time of the trial herein had been a baseball scout for the preceding 28 years—a total of about 52 years in professional baseball. After interviewing petitioner and watching him play basketball and baseball, Ogden determined that petitioner was the greatest prospect he had ever seen. He conveyed this impression to John Joseph Quinn (hereinafter "Quinn"), vice president and general manager of the Phillies, and told Quinn that petitioner was worth "whatever it takes to get him." Quinn thereupon gave Ogden authority to "go and get" petitioner, i.e., to sign him to a contract to play baseball for the Phillies.

From this point on, Ogden became very friendly with petitioner's family. He hired Coy Allen, petitioner's older brother of about 36 or 37 who had played some semiprofessional baseball in the past, as a scout for the Phillies. He also signed Harold Allen, another brother of petitioner, to a contract to play baseball in the Phillies organization. He visited the Allen home often, and talked to petitioner about playing baseball. He did not, however, attempt immediately to sign petitioner to a contract because of a rule adhered to by the Phillies and other baseball teams prohibiting the signing of any boy attending high school to a baseball contract until after his graduation.

Ogden, as well as representatives of a dozen or more other baseball teams that also desired petitioner's services, discussed petitioner's prospects with his mother, Era Allen. She was the head of the family, and she made all the family decisions. Although petitioner discussed baseball with the various scouts, he referred them to his mother in connection with any proposed financial arrangements, and he felt "bound" to play for whichever club his mother might select.

Era Allen conducted all negotiations with Ogden in respect of the financial arrangements that might be made for petitioner if it should be determined that he would play for the Phillies. However, she knew nothing about baseball, particularly the financial aspects of baseball, and she relied almost entirely upon advice from her son Coy Allen. After petitioner had entered into a contract to play for the Phillies organization, as hereinafter more fully set forth, Era Allen paid Coy $2,000 in 1960 for his services out of the funds which she received under that contract, and she deducted that amount from her gross income on her 1960 individual income tax return.

One of the principal items of negotiation with Ogden was the amount of "bonus" to be paid for petitioner's agreement to play for the Phillies organization. Such bonus was in addition to the monthly or periodic compensation to be paid petitioner for services actually rendered as a ballplayer. The purpose of the bonus was to assure the Phillies of the right to the player's services, if he were to play at all, and to prevent him from playing for any other club except with permission of the Phillies. Scouts for other teams had made offers of a bonus of at least $20,000 or $25,000. During the course of the negotiations Ogden made successive offers of a bonus in the amounts of $35,000, $50,000, and finally $70,000. The $70,000 offer was satisfactory to petitioner's mother, but she wanted $40,000 of that amount paid to her and $30,000 to petitioner. She thought that she was entitled to a portion of the bonus because she was responsible for his coming into baseball by her hard work, perseverance, taking care of petitioner, and seeing that he "did the right thing." Although it had been informally agreed prior to petitioner's graduation that he would go with the Phillies, the contract was presented to and signed by petitioner some 30 or 40 minutes after he had received his high school diploma on June 2, 1960.

The contract was formally between petitioner and the Williamsport Baseball Club, one of six or seven minor league teams affiliated with the Phillies through a contractual arrangement known as a "working agreement" whereby, in general, the Phillies were entitled, in exchange for a stated consideration, to "select" the contracts of any of the players on the Williamsport Club for their own purposes and under which the Phillies further agreed, among other things, to reimburse the Williamsport Club for any bonus paid to a player for signing a contract with that club. The Williamsport Club was under the substantial control of the Phillies, and the contract between petitioner and the Williamsport Club was signed on behalf of the latter by an official of the Phillies, who was in charge of all the Phillies' minor league clubs, or what was called their "farm system," and who was authorized to sign on behalf of the Williamsport Club. The contract was on the standard form prescribed by the National Association of Professional Baseball Leagues. Since petitioner was a minor, his mother gave her consent to his execution of the contract by signing her name under a printed paragraph at the end of the form contract entitled "Consent of Parent or Guardian." Such consent was given explicity [sic] "to the execution of this contract by the minor player party hereto," and was stated to be effective as to any assignment or renewal of the contract as therein specified. She was not a party to the contract. The Phillies, in accordance with their usual practice, would not have entered into any such contract, through the Williamsport Club or otherwise, without having obtained the consent of a parent or guardian of the minor player.

In addition to providing for a salary of $850 per month for petitioner's services as a ballplayer, the contract provided for the $70,000 bonus payable over a 5-year period, of which $40,000 was to be paid directly to petitioner's mother and $30,000 to petitioner. The contract provided in part as follows:

1. The Club hereby employs the Player to render, and the Player agrees to render, skilled services as a baseball player in connection with all games of the Club during the year 1960 . . . The Player covenants that at the time he signs this contract he is not under contract or contractual obligation to any baseball club other than the one party to this contract and that he is capable of and will perform with expertness, diligence and fidelity the service stated and such other duties as may be required of him in such employment.

2. For the service aforesaid subsequent to the training season the Club will pay the Player at the rate of eight hundred fifty dollars per month.

• • • •

5. (a) The Player agrees that, while under contract and prior to expiration of the Club's right to renew the contract, and until he reports to his club for spring training, if this contract is renewed, for the purpose of avoiding injuries he will not play baseball otherwise than for the Club except that he may participate in postseason games as prescribed in the National Association Agreement.

(b) The Player and the Club recognize and agree that the Player's participation in other sports may impair or destroy his ability and skill as a baseball player. Accordingly, the Player agrees he will not engage in professional boxing or wrestling and that, except with the written consent of the Club, he will not play professional football, basketball, hockey or other contact sport.

• • • •

Player is to receive bonus of $6,000 payable June 2, 1960
$8,000 ... on ... June 1, 1961
$8,000 ... on ... June 1, 1962
$4,000 ... on ... June 1, 1963
$4,000 ... on ... June 1, 1964

Mother, Mrs. Era Allen is to receive bonus of $16,000 payable June 2, 1960

Mother, Mrs. Era Allen is to receive bonus of $10,000 payable June 1, 1961

Mother, Mrs. Era Allen is to receive bonus of $6,000 payable June 2, 1962

Mother, Mrs. Era Allen is to receive bonus of $4,000 payable June 2, 1963

Mother, Mrs. Era Allen is to receive bonus of $4,000 payable June 2, 1964

Total bonus seventy thousand dollars guaranteed.

• • • •

It was generally the practice in baseball to have the signature of a parent or guardian when signing a player under the age of 21 to a contract, and a contract lacking such signature would probably not have been approved by the president of the National Association of Professional Baseball Leagues.

The installments of the $70,000 bonus agreed to by the Williamsport Baseball Club in its contract with petitioner were actually paid by the Phillies under their "working agreement" with the Williamsport Club. The Phillies viewed such bonus arrangements as consideration to induce a player to sign a contract which thus tied him to the Phillies and prevented his playing baseball for any other club without the consent of the Phillies. These bonus arrangements represented a gamble on the part of the Phillies, for a player might not actually have the ability to play in the major leagues, or might decide on his own that he no longer wanted to play baseball. The Phillies could not recover bonus money already paid, and as a matter of baseball practice felt obligated to pay a bonus, once agreed to, in all events, even if some part of the bonus still remained unpaid when the player left or was given his unconditional release by the club. Nevertheless, in light of petitioner's future potential and ability, Ogden, who negotiated petitioner's bonus, and Quinn, who had the final say in these matters, felt that $70,000 was a fair price to pay to "get" the right to petitioner's services as a professional baseball player. It was a matter of indifference to them as to whom the bonus was paid or what division was made of the money. The previous year, in 1959, the Phillies had paid a bonus of approximately $100,000 to one Ted Kazanski and in 1960, at about the same time they signed petitioner, the Phillies paid a bonus of approximately $40,000 to one Bruce Gruber.

Following the execution of the foregoing contract in June 1960 with the Williamsport Club, petitioner performed services as a professional baseball player under annual contracts for various minor league teams affiliated with the Phillies until sometime in 1963. From that time, he has performed his services directly for the Phillies, and in 1967 his annual salary as a baseball player was approximately $65,000.

Petitioner (and his wife Barbara Allen in the taxable year 1963) reported as taxable ordinary income in his (their) Federal income tax returns for the taxable years 1960, 1961, 1962, and 1963 the bonus payments received by petitioner in each of said years, as follows:

1960	$ 6,000
1961	8,000
1962	8,000
1963	4,000

Petitioner's mother, Era Allen, reported as taxable ordinary income in her Federal income tax returns for the taxable years 1960, 1961, 1962, and 1963 the payments received by her in each of said years, as follows:

1960	$16,000
1961	10,000
1962	6,000
1963	4,000

In his notice of deficiency to petitioner in respect of the taxable years 1961 and 1962, and his notice of deficiency to petitioner Richard and his wife Barbara Allen in respect of the taxable year 1963, the Commissioner determined that the bonus payments received by petitioner's mother in 1961, 1962, and 1963 represented amounts received in respect of a minor child and were taxable to petitioner under sections 61 and 73 of the Internal Revenue Code of 1954; he increased petitioner's taxable income in each of those years accordingly.

Opinion

1. *Inclusion of Bonus in Petitioner's Gross Income.* (a) Petitioner was only 18 years old when the event giving rise to the bonus payments in controversy took place. Accordingly, if the payments made during the years in issue (1961-63) by the Phillies to Era Allen, petitioner's mother, constitute "amounts received in respect of the services" of petitioner within the meaning of section 73(a), I.R.C. 1954, then plainly they must be included in petitioner's gross income rather than in that of his mother. Although petitioner contends that the statute does not cover the present situation, we hold that the payments made to his mother during the years in issue were received solely in respect of petitioner's services, and that all such amounts were therefore includable in his income.

Petitioner argues that the payments received by his mother, totaling $40,000 over a 5-year period, were not part of his bonus for signing a contract to play baseball for the Phillies organization, but rather represented compensation for services performed by her, paid by the Phillies in return for her influencing petitioner to sign the contract and giving her written consent thereto. But there was no evidence of any written or oral agreement between the Phillies and Era Allen in which she agreed to further the Phillies' interests in this manner, and we shall not lightly infer the existence of an agreement by a mother dealing on behalf of her minor child which would or could have the effect of consigning her child's interests to a secondary position so that she might act for her own profit. Moreover, we think the evidence in the record consistently points to the conclusion that the payments received from the Phillies by Era Allen were considered and treated by the parties as part of petitioner's total bonus of $70,000. This sum was paid by the Phillies solely to obtain the exclusive right to petitioner's services as a professional baseball player; no portion thereof was in fact paid for his mother's consent.

We note, first of all, that there was no separate written agreement between the Phillies and Era Allen concerning the payment of $40,000 to her, and that in fact the sole provision of which we are aware for the payment of this sum appears in the contract between petitioner and the Williamsport Baseball Club, a minor league baseball club affiliated with the Phillies under a "working agreement" which entitled the Phillies to claim the contract and the services of any player on the club at any time. Petitioner's contract, a uniform player's contract standard in professional baseball, contained a paragraph requiring the parties to set forth any "additional compensation" (aside from the regular payment of salary) received or to be received from the club "in connection with this contract" and it is in the space provided for such "additional compensation" that all the annual installments of petitioner's bonus, both those payable to petitioner and those payable to his mother, are set forth. After a description of all such installments, identifying the payee (petitioner or his mother), the amount and the date due, appear the words: "Total bonus seventy thousand dollars guaranteed." Moreover, if further proof be needed that the Phillies did not consider any part of the $70,000 bonus as compensation for Era Allen's services it is provided by the testimony of John Ogden, the baseball scout responsible for petitioner's signing a contract with the Phillies' organization. Although Ogden resisted being pinned down, the clear import of his testimony was that the total bonus paid was determined solely by petitioner's ability to play baseball and his future prospects as a player, that the Phillies considered $70,000 a fair price to pay for the right to petitioner's services, and that it made little difference to them whether petitioner's mother received any part of the bonus so determined.

Era Allen herself did not claim to be entitled to $40,000 by virtue of any services performed for or on behalf of the Phillies, and in fact made clear in her testimony that she bargained, as one would expect, "for whatever was best for my son." Rather, she insisted upon a large portion of petitioner's bonus because she felt that petitioner would never have reached the point at which he was able to sign a lucrative contract with a professional baseball team had it not been for her hard work and perseverance in supporting him. And indeed, as the mother of a minor child, one who by the fruits of her own labor had contributed to the support of her minor child without the help of the child's father, she appears to have been entitled to *all* petitioner's earnings under Pennsylvania law. Pa. Stat. tit. 48, sec. 91 (1965).

Prior to 1944, the Commissioner's rulings and regulations "required a parent to report in his (or her) return the earnings of a minor child, if under the laws of the state where they resided the parent had a right to such earnings," even if none or only part of the child's earnings were actually appropriated by the parent. Because parents were not entitled to the earnings of their minor children in all States, and because even in those States following this common-law doctrine the parents' right to the earnings of a minor child could be lost if it was found that the child had been emancipated, the result of the Commissioner's policy was that:

> for Federal income tax purposes, opposite results obtain(ed) under the same set of facts depending upon the applicable State law. In addition, such variations in the facts as make applicable the exceptions to the general rule in each jurisdiction tend(ed) to produce additional uncertainty with respect to the tax treatment of the earnings of minor children.

H. Rept. No. 1365, 78th Cong., 2d Sess., p. 21 (1944); S. Rept. No. 885, 78th Cong., 2d Sess., p. 22. To remedy these defects, Congress in 1944 enacted the substantially identical predecessor of section 73 of the Internal Revenue Code of 1954, providing the easily determinable and uniform rule that all amounts received "in respect of the services of a child" shall be included in his income. Thus, even though the contract of employment is made directly by the parent and the parent receives the compensation for the services, for the purpose of the Federal income tax the amounts would be considered to be taxable to the child because earned by him. H. Rept. No. 885, 78th Cong., 2d Sess., p. 22, 23. We think section 73 reverses what would have been the likely result in this case under pre-1944 law wholly apart from the contract, and that the $70,000 bonus is taxable in full to petitioner.

Petitioner stresses the fact that the $70,000 bonus paid by the Phillies did not constitute a direct payment for his "services" as a professional baseball player, which were to be compensated at an agreed salary of $850 per month, for the $70,000 was to be paid in all events, whether or not petitioner ever performed any services for the Phillies organization. Therefore, it is argued, the bonus payments could not have constituted compensation for *services* which alone are taxed to a minor child under section 73. Cf. Rev. Rul. 58-145, 1958-1 C.B. 360. This argument misreads the statute, which speaks in terms of "amounts received *in respect of* the services of a child," and not merely of compensation for services performed. True, petitioner performed no services in the usual sense for his $70,000 bonus, unless his act of signing the contract be considered such, but the bonus payments here were paid by the Phillies as an inducement to obtain his services as a professional baseball player and to preclude him from rendering those services to other professional baseball teams; they thus certainly constituted amounts received "in respect of" his services.

(b) Even if amounts in issue were not received "in respect of the services" of a child under section 73, we think that the bonus installments paid to petitioner's mother during the tax years 1961–63 are nevertheless chargeable to him under the general provisions of section 61. It has long been established that one who becomes entitled to receive income may not avoid tax thereon by causing it to be paid to another through "anticipatory arrangements however skillfully devised." *Lucas v. Earl*, 281 U.S. 111, 114-115; *Helvering v. Horst*, 311 U.S. 112; *Helvering v. Eubank*, 311 U.S. 122; *Harrison v. Schaffner*, 312 U.S. 579.

As indicated above, the entire $70,000 bonus was paid as consideration for petitioner's agreement to play baseball for the Phillies or any team designated by the Phillies. We reject as contrary to fact the argument that part of that amount was paid to his mother for her consent to the contract. It was petitioner, and petitioner alone who was the source of the income and it is a matter of no consequence that his mother thought that she was entitled to some of that income because of her conscientious upbringing of petitioner. . . .

2. *Petitioner's Alternative Contention—Deduction of Bonus Payments From His Gross Income.* Finally petitioner argues alternatively that if his entire $70,000 bonus is includable in his income, he should be allowed to deduct the bonus payments received by his mother as an "ordinary and necessary" expense incurred in carrying on his trade or business as a professional baseball player. He places great reliance in this argument upon *Cecil Randolph Hundley, Jr.,* 48 T.C. 339, acq. 1967-2 C.B. 2, a case recently decided by this Court in which a professional baseball player was allowed to deduct that portion of his bonus for signing a baseball contract which was paid directly to his father, the result of an agreement entered into some 2 years before the contract was signed as a means of compensating the father for his services as a baseball coach and business agent. However, the special facts in *Hundley,* which supported a finding of reasonableness for the amount of the deduction claimed and warranted the conclusion that the amounts paid there in fact represented a bona fide expense incurred in carrying on the taxpayer's trade or business of being a professional baseball player, are almost entirely absent here.

It is unnecessary to determine the exact sum which would have constituted a reasonable payment to Era Allen for her services, though we note that only $2,000 was paid to her son Coy Allen for the advice she so greatly relied on, for we are certain that in any case it could not have exceeded the $16,000 received by her in 1960. Although the year 1960 is not before us in these proceedings, we can and do take into account the payment made to her in that year in determining whether the deductions now claimed by petitioner for payments made to her in the years 1961, 1962, and 1963 are reasonable in amount and deductible as "ordinary and necessary" business expenses. We think they clearly are not, and hold that petitioner is not entitled to deductions in any amount for payments made to his mother in those years.

A Comparison of the Facts. Once again, even a cursory examination of these two Tax Court decisions reveals that the cases have several facts in common. In both instances

1. A professional baseball player arranged to have a portion of what, at that time was a sizable bonus paid to one of his parents.
2. Both the parent and the ball playing minor child signed the professional contract.
3. The bonus payments actually were made by the ball club to the parent over several years.
4. The parent reported the amount received as ordinary taxable income and paid the tax liability thereon.

The two cases also differ in several factual respects.

1. The names, dates, amounts, and places of residence of the principal parties differ in the two cases.
2. The parent involved in one case was the baseball player's father; the other case involved the baseball player's mother.
3. One parent was knowledgeable about, and deeply involved in, training the child in the skill of ball playing; the other parent knew relatively little about baseball.
4. One parent-child pair had a prior oral agreement about how they would divide any bonus that might eventually be received; the other parent-child pair had no such prior agreement.

Once again, it is pertinent to inquire whether the common facts are sufficient to require a common result or whether the different facts justify different results. The decisions of the court again were very different. Cecil Hundley, Jr., was allowed to deduct the portion of the bonus paid to his father; Richard Allen was denied the right to deduct the portion of the bonus paid to his mother. Because the law was the same in both cases, and because there is little basis in the reported decisions to conclude that differences in the judicial process had much influence on these results, we must conclude that the different facts adequately explain the divergent results.

An Analysis of the Divergent Results. Judge Hoyt makes it clear that the decision in *Hundley* is critically dependent on the existence of the oral agreement between the father and the son. He states, "Petitioner has introduced persuasive and convincing evidence that the agreement was in fact reached in the spring of 1958, and we have so found. This finding is essential to petitioner's position. . . ." Judge Raum makes it equally clear in *Allen* that he could find no contractual agreement in that case. He states, "Petitioner argues that the payments received by his mother . . . were not part of his bonus for signing a contract to play baseball for the Phillies organization, but rather represented compensation for services performed by her, paid by the Phillies in return for her influencing petitioner to sign the contract and giving her written consent thereto. But there was no evidence of any written or oral agreement between the Phillies and Era Allen in which she agreed to further the Phillies' interests in this manner, and we shall not lightly infer the existence of an agreement by a mother dealing on behalf of her minor child. . . ."

One cannot help but wonder exactly how it is possible for a person to present convincing evidence of an oral agreement made between a father and his tenth-grade son some nine years before the litigation. Two brief statements in the reported decision provide the only clues. One statement notes that the high school coach knew of the oral agreement since its inception; the other statement suggests that the scout for the San Francisco Giants, who negotiated the Hundley contract, also knew of the oral agreement since its inception. We can only conclude, therefore, that these statements are either based on an oral examination of witnesses at the trial or that written depositions were obtained from these persons and submitted as evidence at the trial to substantiate the existence of the oral contract.

Lessons for Tax Research. For the student of tax research, perhaps the most instructive aspect of the last two cases is their demonstration of the importance of favorable testimony by impartial witnesses.

Proper preparation of a tax file sometimes may include the need to provide supporting evidence available only from disinterested third parties. The longer one waits to locate such a party, the greater the difficulty in finding one capable of giving the testimony needed. To the maximum extent possible, considering economic and other constraints, the tax adviser should anticipate the importance of all supporting documents, including sworn statements from third parties. If strong evidence of one or two critical facts can be provided to an IRS agent or to a conferee, the probability of litigation may be significantly reduced.

A careful reading of these two decisions also reveals that very similar facts or situations may sometimes be argued on radically different grounds. In other words, even though the facts are similar, the questions raised may be different. Although this observation really is more pertinent to the next chapter of this book than it is to the present chapter, and even though the more unusual argument did not prove to be fruitful in this instance, we observe in passing that *Allen* argues for a favorable result in the alternative. First, the taxpayer contends that the payments made to his mother were not for his services as a ballplayer. Only later, should the first argument fail does he argue that the payments to his mother are deductible business expenses. In *Hundley,* on the other hand, the taxpayer never raised the former issue. The fact that both questions deserve consideration stems directly from a careful review of the facts and the law.

In *Allen,* the argument is made that a bonus payment really is not a payment for *services rendered.* At least in part, that payment really is to compensate the ballplayer for *not* rendering services (to a competitor club).

The pertinent statutory provisions refer to "amounts received *in respect of the services of a child"* [*emphasis added*]. The question raised, then, deals with whether a ballplayer's bonus properly falls within the meaning of the "in respect of" clause. After reviewing the congressional intent behind those words, the court determined that it did and, thus, rejected the taxpayer's first line of argument.

Nevertheless, this observation should remind the tax adviser to consider the facts of a case in every possible way before selecting a single line of argument. The next chapter examines in greater detail the subtle relationship between the facts and a statement of the pertinent questions.

In summary, for the tax adviser, knowledge of the statutes alone is insufficient. An adviser must carefully delineate facts important to the tax question and recognize the need to document significant facts in the event that they must be retrieved and substantiated during a later audit. The next chapter addresses the task of extracting or anticipating tax questions from the fact situation.

3

The Elusive Nature
of Tax Questions

Tax questions arise when a unique set of facts is examined in light
of general rules of tax law. Learning to identify and phrase the
critical tax questions implicit in any set of facts is no small accom-
plishment, for in many instances, the most important questions are
by no means obvious. The more experienced the tax adviser, the
easier it is to identify and ask the right questions. For the beginner,
asking the right question is often the most difficult part of tax
research. However, even the most seasoned tax veteran can easily
overlook a very important question. For this reason, successful tax
practitioners make it a general practice to require an internal review
of all tax research before stating an opinion to anyone outside
the firm. This precaution often is extended to even include the
preparation of a written record of all oral responses made to infor-
mal inquiries. The probability of overlooking either an important
tax question or a part of the law is simply too great to permit any
less thorough procedure.

The difficulty experienced in properly identifying and stating
the pertinent tax questions is largely attributable to the high degree

of interdependence that exists between the facts, questions, and law. If the tax adviser fails to determine all of the pertinent facts, the chance of overlooking a critical question is greatly increased. Similarly, even if the tax adviser has determined all of the critical facts, the failure to consider a critical part of the law may also lead to the overlooking of a critical question. Finally, even if the tax adviser knows all of the facts and all of the law pertinent to a case, he or she still may overlook an obvious question simply because of human error.

Errors in stating questions are often related to either (1) failure to think originally or creatively about tax problems or (2) failure to pay sufficient attention to detail. A veteran tax adviser will seldom fail to heed detail. On the other hand, precisely because of long years of experience, a tax adviser may be prone to overlook new and different ways of viewing recurring problems.[1] In some instances, therefore, it is desirable to have the most complex tax situations reviewed by inexperienced as well as experienced personnel. The former individuals might ask the obvious question that otherwise would be overlooked, but only the latter individuals can fully appreciate the significance of even the obvious question once it has been asked. Frequently, one good tax question raises two or more related questions, and before long, the tax result depends on a network of closely related but separate questions.

Initial Statement of the Question

The resolution of a tax problem often evolves through several stages of development. In many instances, the initial statement of the question may be only remotely related to the questions that turn out to be critical to its solution. The greater the technical competence of the researcher, the fewer steps in the evolution of identifying the correct questions and answers.

---

[1] For example, in *Allen* (see chapter 2) it would have been very easy to overlook the first of the two alternative arguments considered, that is, what exactly was Allen being paid for in the bonus? If it was for not rendering a service, a different result might apply. Admittedly, the argument was not successful in that particular case, but it was pertinent and could have been important.

The technical competence of tax researchers is, in all likelihood, normally distributed on a continuum ranging from little or no competence to very great expertise. Any attempt to separate these individuals into discrete groups is obviously unrealistic. Nevertheless, for purposes of discussing the difficulties encountered in identifying tax questions, tax advisers could be categorized into one of three groups: those with "minimal" technical competence, those with "intermediate" technical competence, and those with "extensive" technical competence relative to the subject at hand. Technical competence in one area of taxation does not guarantee equal competence in other areas. Individuals who have an extensive technical knowledge in one aspect of taxation must move with a beginner's caution when approaching another area of the law. Although the problems are often similar, the applicable rules are sometimes quite different. As was stated earlier, a final tax result depends upon three variables: facts, law, and an administrative (and judicial, if necessary) process. Just as the facts of one case may differ from another, so also may the law.

Minimal Technical Competence

A tax adviser with minimal technical competence usually can state tax questions in only the broadest of terms. After reviewing the facts, the beginner typically is prepared to ask such general questions as the following:

1. Is gross income recognized "in these circumstances"?
   a. If so, how much income must be recognized?
   b. If so, is that income ordinary or capital?
2. Can a deduction be claimed "in these circumstances"?
   a. If so, how much can be deducted?
   b. If so, in which year can the deduction be claimed?
   c. If not, can the tax basis of an asset be increased?
3. What is the tax basis of a specific asset?

In any real situation, of course, the actual facts of the case must be substituted for the phrase "in these circumstances" in the hypothetical questions posed in this list. For example, the facts underlying the first question might justify a question such as "Can an individual shareholder of a corporation whose stock is completely redeemed by a cash distribution from that corporation recognize a capital gain on the sale of his or her stock?" Observe that even the initial statement of a tax question should be very carefully phrased to include what appears to be all of the important facts of the situation.

Because beginning staff members typically enter the tax departments of accounting firms with minimal technical competence, usually they are prepared to ask only broad, general questions. If properly phrased, however, the broad questions posed by the new staff person are ultimately the same questions that the more knowledgeable tax adviser seeks to answer. The more senior adviser tends, however, to phrase initial questions in somewhat different terms.

Intermediate Technical Competence

The tax adviser with an intermediate level of technical competence often can review a situation and state the pertinent questions in terms of specific statutory authority. For example, the question already considered for the beginning adviser might be verbalized by a person with more experience in words such as, "Can an individual shareholder whose stock is completely redeemed by a cash distribution from a corporation waive the family constructive ownership rules of section 318 to recognize a capital gain on the sale of his or her stock under section 302, even though the remaining outstanding stock is owned by his or her children and the individual continues to do consulting work for the corporation?"

A comparison of the same two hypothetical questions, as phrased by the person with minimal competence versus that phrased by the person with an intermediate level of competence, reveals several interesting differences.

First, the more experienced person generally understands the statutory basis of authority applicable to the tax questions. Or, to put this same difference in another way, the more experienced person (1) knows that most tax questions have a statutory base and (2) knows which Internal Revenue Code sections apply to the facts under consideration.

Second, the tax adviser with intermediate technical competence often phrases questions in such a way that they imply the answer to a more general question, subject only to the determination of the applicability of one or more special provisions to the facts under consideration. For example, the phrasing of the question suggested earlier for the person with intermediate-level skills may really imply something like this: "The distribution of cash by a corporation to a shareholder in his or her capacity as a shareholder will result in dividend income under the general rule of section 301 unless the distribution qualifies for sale or exchange treatment under either section 302 or 303."[2] Note that questions phrased by persons with greater technical competence frequently suggest where at least the foundation for an answer can be located. If a researcher knows which Code sections are applicable to a given fact situation, the task of locating pertinent authority is greatly simplified.

Third, the more competent tax adviser is more apt than the beginning adviser to include more facts in any statement of the question. Thus, for example, the adviser recognizes the importance of determining the ownership of the remaining outstanding stock by adding the phrase, "even though the remaining outstanding stock is owned by his or her children." Furthermore, the adviser recognizes that continuing to work for the corporation even as an independent contractor may also be critical. This tendency to add more facts to the statement of the question is the result of experience. The inclusion of additional information to the statement of the question indicates that the more experienced person recognizes some of the apparently innocent facts that can so critically modify a tax result.

In daily tax practice, a person with minimal technical tax competence acquires a great deal of knowledge by seeking answers to

---

[2] This statement assumes that the corporation has sufficient earnings and profits to cover the distribution. If the transaction is treated as a dividend, an individual shareholder reports the entire distribution as ordinary income. A corporate shareholder may be eligible for a dividend received deduction. If the transaction is treated as a sale, the amount of the distribution is reduced by the basis of the stock redeemed to arrive at the amount of capital gain or loss. Furthermore, capital gains may be offset by capital losses and, if realized by an individual, may be subject to preferential tax rates. Thus, the purpose of section 302 is to distinguish between distributions that are to be taxed as dividends and distributions that are to be taxed as capital gains realized on the sale of stock.

the specific questions posed by more competent colleagues. This saves valuable and expensive time by directing the beginner to look in the right places. Without this assistance, the beginner must spend many hours just locating the general authority that is pertinent to a question.[3] We might note, however, that the beginner typically prepares working papers detailing the research steps undertaken to answer the questions posed by supervisors. These working papers allow the supervisor to review the adequacy of the staff person's conclusions as well as leave a permanent record of the facts and the authorities that were considered in solving any given tax problem. These records may prove to be invaluable should the IRS later question the way the tax adviser handled a particular tax problem.

Extensive Technical Competence

The tax adviser with an extensive level of technical competence in a given area can often review a situation and state the pertinent question in a still more refined manner. For example, the tax expert may ask questions such as, "Does the reasoning used in *Estate of Lennard* allow the section 302(c)(2) waiver of family attribution in this case, thus allowing sale or exchange treatment? Or does *Lynch* apply in this case to prevent the waiver of family attribution under section 302(c)(2), thus causing dividend treatment?" By stating a question in this way, the expert implies not only the general statutory authority for an answer, but also specific interpretative authority that would, in all likelihood, apply to the facts under consideration. The expert often needs only to determine the most recent events to resolve a tax question. Unless something new has happened, this phrasing of the question suggests that a very specific answer can be found to the general, but unstated, question.

Thus, the expert's question—"Does the reasoning used in *Estate of Lennard* allow the section 302(c)(2) waiver of family attribution in this case, thus allowing sale or exchange treatment?"—may in reality be the same question that the beginner phrased this way:

---

[3] A discussion of the various types of tax authority is found in chapter 4. The tools used in locating this authority are discussed in chapter 5.

"Can an individual shareholder of a corporation whose stock is completely redeemed by a cash distribution from that corporation recognize a capital gain on the sale of his or her stock?" The former question implies that the answer to the latter question may be found in judicial or administrative interpretations of the statute. The phrasing of the expert's question recognizes, however, that there may be ample reason why specific interpretative authority would not apply. For example, the facts of the two cases may differ in some material way—perhaps the taxpayer lives in a different judicial circuit from the *Lynch* or *Estate of Lennard* decisions—or perhaps these decisions have otherwise been modified by a regulation, ruling, or subsequent judicial decision. If one knows his or her way around a tax library, it obviously will require even less time to answer the question posed by the expert than it will to answer the question posed by the adviser with intermediate competency. Unfortunately, however, not all tax questions are so easily stated or resolved, even by the expert.

Restatement of the Initial Question After Some Research

In some circumstances, even an expert must move cautiously from facts to questions to authority and then back to more facts, more questions, and more authority before resolving a tax problem. The search for authority to resolve an initial question sometimes leads to the realization that facts previously deemed unimportant are critical to the resolution of the problem. In that event, the tax adviser returns to the fact determination procedure before looking any further for answers. At other times, the initial search suggests considering other tax law rather than isolating more facts. Sometimes it suggests the need to consider both additional facts as well as additional law. Before reaching the administrative or judicial process, the tax adviser has only two raw materials with which to work: facts and law. Therefore, the tax adviser must learn how to identify and phrase pertinent questions by examining facts in light of the applicable law. That microscopic examination is what reveals the need for further discovery and analysis of facts, law, or both. The tax research process is not complete until all of the facts have been fully examined in light of all of the applicable law, and all pertinent questions have been resolved to the extent possible.

This "research procedure" is illustrated conceptually in figure 3.1.

The spiral line shows how the researcher proceeds from an initial statement of the facts (F_1), to an initial statement of the questions (Q_1), to an initial search for authority (A_1). If the initial authority suggests new and different questions (Q_2), as it often does, the researcher continues by making additional fact determinations (F_2), by considering additional authority (A_2), or both. The procedure continues over and over until all the facts are known, all the relevant authority is considered, and all the questions are answered, at least tentatively. At this juncture, the tax adviser evaluates the facts and authority just identified and reaches a conclusion.

Dangers Inherent in Statements of Questions

The danger of overlooking pertinent alternatives is greatly increased if tax questions are stated too narrowly. This danger is particularly acute for the more experienced tax adviser because, as noted earlier, he or she generally knows where to begin looking. Once the search for pertinent authority is restricted to a particular segment of the IRC, for all practical purposes, all other alternatives may be eliminated.

This danger has been vividly demonstrated to the authors on several occasions. While teaching a university course in tax research methodology, it is necessary to design sample cases that lead stu-

Figure 3.1

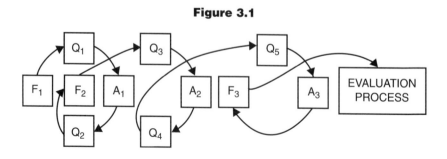

dents to make important discoveries of their own. A large number of the sample cases are drawn from live problems suggested by various tax practitioners. In some cases, possibly the best solutions have been those never considered by either the authors or by those who initially suggested the problems to us. Beginning students, unhampered by predilection and blessed by natural curiosity and intelligence, have managed on more than one occasion to view the problem in an entirely different light. This is mentioned to stress the importance of imagination and creativity in tax research and planning. As was noted in chapter 2, the "thinking step," the point at which the practitioner spends time considering facts, alternatives, and options, is an indispensable and critical segment of the research process.

A second danger inherent in the statement of the question is the tendency to phrase the question using conclusions rather than elementary facts. The important distinction between conclusions and facts was noted in chapter 2. The use of conclusions in stating questions is hazardous because conclusions tend to prejudice the result by subtly influencing the way one searches for pertinent authority. If, for example, one begins to search for authority on the proper way to handle a particular expenditure for tax purposes, the question posed might be, "Should the expenditure of funds for 'this-and-that' be capitalized?" The answer possibly will be affirmative. On the other hand, the answer will possibly be affirmative if the same question is rephrased in terms such as, "Can the expenditure of funds for 'this-and-that' be deducted?" Obviously, if the facts are the same (that is, if the "this-and-that" in the two questions are identical), both answers cannot be correct. The explanation for the conflicting results probably can be traced to the place where the researcher looks for authority. The first question tends to lead the researcher to decisions in which section 263 is held to be of primary importance, whereas the latter question leads to decisions in which section 162 is of greater importance.[4] Conse-

---

[4] Section 263 reads in part as follows: "No deduction shall be allowed for—(1) Any amount paid out for new buildings or for permanent improvements or betterments made to increase the value of any property or estate." Section 162 reads in part as follows: "There shall be allowed as a deduction all the ordinary and necessary expenses paid or incurred during the taxable year in carrying on any trade or business. . . ." Obviously, reasonable persons can and do differ in their application of these rules to specific fact situations.

quently, the statement of the question may assume unusual importance because it may influence or lead a researcher down a particular line of thought that is too narrow. To the maximum extent possible, tax questions should be phrased neutrally and without conclusions to permit the researcher greater freedom in finding the best possible authority for resolving the question.

A Comprehensive Example

The remainder of this chapter is a detailed review of a comprehensive example that demonstrates the elusive nature of tax questions. In the process of developing this example, we shall attempt to illustrate the way in which facts, law, and questions are inextricably interrelated in tax issues. In following this example, the reader should not be concerned with the problem of locating pertinent authority. The next two chapters will explain how the reader might find that same authority if he or she is working alone on this problem. To begin, let us assume the following statement of facts.

> On February 10 of the current year, Ima Hitchcock, a long-time client of your CPA firm, sold one-half of her equity interest in General Paper Corporation (hereafter, GPC) for $325,000 cash. Ms. Hitchcock has owned 60,000 shares (or 20 percent) of the outstanding common stock of GPC since its incorporation in 1988. During the past 20 years, she has been active in GPC management. Following this sale of stock, however, she plans to retire from active business life. Her records clearly reveal that her tax basis in the 30,000 shares sold is only $25,000 (one-half of her original purchase price).

Given no additional facts, both the beginner and the seasoned tax adviser would be likely to conclude that Ms. Hitchcock should report a $300,000 long-term capital gain in the current year because of her sale of the GPC stock. The case appears to be wholly straightforward and without complication as long as no one asks any questions or volunteers any additional information. Although few persons would ask for the statutory authority in this case, sections 1001, 1012, 1221, 1222, and 1223 are the basis for the suggested conclusion. Section 1221 establishes the fact that the stock is a capital asset; sections 1222 and 1223 determine the long-term status of the capital gain realized; section 1012 specifies the cost basis of the shares sold; section 1001 defines the gain realized as the difference between the $325,000 received and the $25,000 cost basis surrendered and requires the entire $300,000 realized gain be recognized. If, however, someone happened to ask who purchased Ms. Hitchcock's shares, problems could quickly arise.

Diagramming the Facts

Before this example is considered in more detail, a simple stick-figure diagram of the transaction possibly should be made (see figure 3.2). In the authors' opinion, every tax adviser should become

Figure 3.2

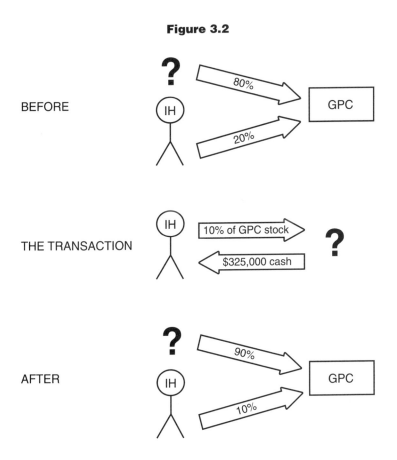

accustomed to preparing such simple diagrams of the essential facts of any case before asking any questions or searching for any authority. In addition to diagramming the transaction itself, the practitioner should diagram a simple portrayal of the fact situation as it existed both before and after the transaction under examination. Each person can create his or her own set of symbols for any problem. This illustration, however, uses only a stick figure to represent an individual taxpayer (Ima Hitchcock) and a square to represent a corporate taxpayer (General Paper Corporation).

First Questions Call for Additional Facts

As is evident in figure 3.2, the first two critical questions appear to be: (1) Who owns the other 80 percent of GPC stock? and (2) Who purchased the shares from Ms. Hitchcock? The answers to these two questions obviously call for the determination of more facts, not for additional authority.

Suppose the tax adviser knows from prior work with this client that GPC is a closely owned corporation; that is, it has been equally owned by five local residents (including Ms. Hitchcock) since its incorporation. However, the CPA needs to know who purchased the stock. Under these circumstances, we can easily imagine a conversation between Ms. Hitchcock and her CPA as follows:

CPA: Who purchased your stock in GPC, Ms. Hitchcock?

Ms. H: Ghost Publishing, Incorporated.

CPA: That's a name I haven't heard before. Is it a local firm?

Ms. H: Yes, it's my grandson's corporation.

From there, this conversation would proceed to establish the facts that Ghost Publishing, Incorporated (hereafter, GPI) is indeed a small but very profitable corporation whose stock is entirely owned by Ms. Hitchcock's favorite grandson, Alvred Hitchcock. GPI decided to purchase the GPC stock both to guarantee its own supply of paper, and because Alvred was convinced that GPC was a sound financial investment.

Before we proceed to examine additional authority, we should emphasize these two apparently innocent facts that have vital importance to the resolution of this tax problem: (1) The GPC shares were purchased from Ms. Hitchcock by GPI, and (2) GPI is owned by Ms. Hitchcock's grandson. Unless these two facts are discovered and their importance fully appreciated, this problem could not continue any further. Furthermore, we might arrive at the incorrect conclusion. We might also pause briefly to rediagram both our transaction and the after-the-transaction situation to accommodate the new facts that we have just discovered (see figure 3.3). Once again, this diagram serves to highlight the potential problems that lie ahead of us.

The discovery of these additional facts may begin to separate the beginner from the more experienced tax adviser. The beginner quite possibly would not modify the conclusion concerning Ms. Hitchcock's need to report a $300,000 long-term capital gain. An experienced researcher, however, would realize the danger implicit in sales between related parties and would want to determine whether this transaction should be treated in some other way because of the potential relationships involved. The tax adviser with extensive technical competence in the taxation of corporations and corporate shareholder relations might realize this is a potential section 304 transaction and would turn directly to that section to

Figure 3.3

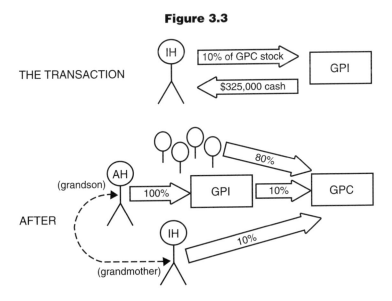

determine the next appropriate question: "Does section 304 apply to Ms. Hitchcock's sale of 30,000 shares of GPC stock to GPI?"

The Authority

Understanding section 304 may be difficult. However, a basic understanding of at least some of this provision is critical in determining which facts and issues in this transaction must be examined. The purpose of section 304 is to ensure that certain sales of stock of one corporation to a related corporation do not avoid the section 302 tests. As mentioned previously, the section 302 tests are used to make the distinction between distributions that are to be taxed as dividends and distributions that are to be taxed as capital gains.[5] Section 304 reads, in part, as follows:[6]

SEC. 304. REDEMPTION THROUGH USE OF RELATED CORPORATIONS.

(a) TREATMENT OF CERTAIN STOCK PURCHASES.—

(1) ACQUISITION BY RELATED CORPORATION (OTHER THAN SUBSIDIARY).—For purposes of sections 302 and 303, if—
(A) one or more persons are in control of each of two corporations, and
(B) in return for property, one of the corporations acquires stock in the other corporation from the person (or persons) so in control, then (unless paragraph (2) applies) such property shall be treated as a distribution in redemption of the stock of the corporation acquiring such stock. . .

(2) ACQUISITION BY SUBSIDIARY.—For purposes of sections 302 and 303, if—
(A) in return for property, one corporation acquires from a shareholder of another corporation stock in such other corporation, and
(B) the issuing corporation controls the acquiring corporation, then such property shall be treated as a distribution in redemption of the stock of the issuing corporation.

---

[5] See note 2, supra.
[6] Because section 304 is a difficult provision, only those parts that are important for our illustrations are reproduced here.

(b) SPECIAL RULES FOR APPLICATION OF SUBSECTION (a).

(1) RULE FOR DETERMINATIONS UNDER SECTION 302(b).— In the case of any acquisition of stock to which subsection (a) of this section applies, determinations as to whether the acquisition is, by reason of section 302(b), to be treated as a distribution in part or full payment in exchange for the stock shall be made by reference to the stock of the issuing corporation. . .

(c) CONTROL.—

(1) IN GENERAL—For purposes of this section, control means the ownership of stock possessing at least 50 percent of the total combined voting power of all classes of stock entitled to vote, or at least 50 percent of the total value of shares of all classes of stock. . . .

(3) CONSTRUCTIVE OWNERSHIP.—(A) IN GENERAL.—Section 318(a) (relating to constructive ownership of stock) shall apply for purposes of determining control under this section.

Although the beginner might require assistance in interpreting and applying this IRC section to the facts of Ms. Hitchcock's sale, every beginner must learn how to read and understand the language of the IRC if he or she is ever to succeed as a tax adviser.[7]

Learning how to understand the IRC is most certainly a time consuming process. After a careful reading of section 304, however, even a beginner will realize that certain words and phrases deserve special attention. For example, understanding whether section 304 applies to this transaction necessarily requires (1) an understanding of sections 302 and 303, (2) the ability to identify an acquisition of stock in a controlled corporation by another controlled corporation (for example, an acquisition by a related corporation that is not a

---

[7] Certainly the beginner might take comfort in knowing that even tax experts can find this to be a formidable assignment. For example, Learned Hand, a distinguished judge, once said, "In my own case the words of such an act as the Income Tax, for example, merely dance before my eyes in a meaningless procession: cross-reference to cross-reference, exception upon exception— couched in abstract terms that offer no handles to seize hold of—leave in my mind only a confused sense of some vitally important, but successfully concealed, purport, which it is my duty to extract, but which is within my power, if at all, only after the most inordinate expenditure of time." (Learned Hand, "Thomas Walter Swan," *Yale Law Journal* 57 [December 1947]: 169.)

subsidiary) and an acquisition of stock of a corporation that controls the corporation acquiring the stock (such as, an acquisition of a parent corporation's stock by a subsidiary corporation), and (3) an understanding of the way in which the constructive ownership rules of section 318 are applied in determining control. For both the beginner and the experienced tax adviser, these issues constitute the next pertinent set of questions.

Additional Questions

Stated in the order in which they must be answered, these questions are as follows:

1. Both before and after the sale of 30,000 shares of GPC common stock to GPI, how many shares of GPC common stock does Ms. Hitchcock own, directly and indirectly, for purposes of section 304, giving full consideration to the constructive ownership rules of section 318?

2. Does section 304 apply to this sale of stock? That is, can the sale of 30,000 shares of GPC stock to GPI by Ms. Hitchcock be considered, for purposes of section 304, as either (a) an acquisition by a related (but not subsidiary) corporation or (b) an acquisition by a subsidiary corporation?

3. If the answer to either question in (2) above is affirmative, what is the tax effect of section 302, 303, or both on this disposition of stock?

To solve these three questions we must turn to the constructive ownership rules found in section 318.

More Authority

Fortunately, section 318 does not, at least at the outset, appear to be as confusing as section 304. Section 318 reads in part as follows:[8]

---

[8] Here, again, only the pertinent parts of section 318 are reproduced.

SEC. 318. CONSTRUCTIVE OWNERSHIP OF STOCK.

(a) GENERAL RULE.—For purposes of those provisions of this subchapter to which the rules contained in this section are expressly made applicable—

(1) MEMBERS OF FAMILY.—
(A) IN GENERAL.—An individual shall be considered as owning the stock owned, directly or indirectly, by or for—
(i) his spouse (other than a spouse who is legally separated from the individual under a decree of divorce or separate maintenance), and
(ii) his children, grandchildren, and parents.

(2) ATTRIBUTION FROM PARTNERSHIPS, ESTATES, TRUSTS, AND CORPORATIONS.—

• • • •

(C) FROM CORPORATIONS.—If 50 percent or more in value of the stock in a corporation is owned, directly or indirectly, by or for any person, such person shall be considered as owning the stock owned, directly or indirectly, by or for such corporation, in that proportion which the value of the stock which such person so owns bears to the value of all the stock in such corporation.

(3) ATTRIBUTION TO PARTNERSHIPS, ESTATES, TRUSTS, AND CORPORATIONS.—

• • • •

(C) TO CORPORATIONS.—If 50 percent or more in value of the stock in a corporation is owned, directly or indirectly, by or for any person, such corporation shall be considered as owning the stock owned, directly or indirectly, by or for such person.

• • • •

(5) OPERATING RULES.—
(A) IN GENERAL.—Except as provided in subparagraphs (B) and (C), stock constructively owned by a person by reason of the application of paragraph (1), (2), (3), or (4), shall, for purposes of applying paragraphs (1), (2), (3), and (4), be considered as actually owned by such person.

More Questions and More Facts

A careful reading of section 318 suggests the need to determine some additional facts before proceeding toward a solution. More specifically, we must know exactly who it is that owns the other 80 percent of GPC. Earlier it was stated that GPC was "equally owned by five local residents." After reading the quoted portion of section 318, it should be obvious that we must ask if any of the other four GPC owners are related to Ms. Hitchcock within any of the family relationships described in section 318(a)(1). At the same time, we probably should make certain that none of the other four original owners has sold any of the original stock in GPC. If they have, we also must determine the relationship, if any, between those purchasers and Ms. Hitchcock. Let us assume that two of the other four owners of GPC are Ms. Hitchcock's sons, and that all of the other four original owners continue to own all of their shares in GPC. Having determined this, we can now reach our first tentative conclusions.

First Tentative Conclusions

Specifically, we are now prepared to answer the first of the three questions. "Both before and after the sale of 30,000 shares of GPC common stock to GPI, how many shares of GPC stock does Ms. Hitchcock own, directly and indirectly, for purposes of section 304, giving full consideration to the constructive ownership rules of section 318?" Before the sale, Ms. Hitchcock is deemed to own 60 percent of GPC (20 percent actually and 40 percent constructively), because pursuant to section 318(a)(1)(A)(ii), she is deemed to own the stock of GPC that her two sons own. Furthermore, Ms. Hitchcock is deemed to own 100 percent of GPI (all constructively) because under the same authority, she is deemed to own the stock in GPI that her grandson owns. After the sale of GPC stock, Ms. Hitchcock is still deemed to own 100 percent of GPI because of her grandson's ownership in that corporation. For the beginner, Ms. Hitchcock's ownership in GPC after the sale may be unexpected. First, pursuant to section 318(a)(2)(C), Alvred is deemed to own the 30,000 shares of GPC that GPI purchased. Furthermore, as mentioned previously, Ms. Hitchcock is treated as owning the stock owned by her grandson. Pursuant to section 318(a)(5)(A), this includes the GPC stock that Alvred is deemed to own.[9] This means, of course, that Ms. Hitchcock is, for purposes of section 304, deemed to own the stock that she just sold. Thus, after the sale she owns 60 percent of GPC (10 percent actually, 40 percent constructively through her two sons, and 10 percent constructively through GPI and her grandson). In summary, Ms. Hitchcock is treated as owning 60 percent of GPC and 100 percent of GPI both before and after the sale of her stock.[10]

Having made this determination, we can now also answer the second of the three questions posed earlier: "Does section 304 apply to this sale of stock?" In other words, is the purchase of the 30,000 shares by GPI either an acquisition by a related, but nonsubsidiary corporation (that is, does Ms. Hitchcock control both GPC and GPI), or an acquisition by a subsidiary corporation (that is, is GPI controlled by GPC)? The answer to this question depends upon the term *control.*

Pursuant to section 304(c)(1), control is defined as the ownership of at least 50 percent of the stock of a corporation, taking into account the constructive ownership rules of section 318. Because under section 318, Ms. Hitchcock is deemed to own 60 percent of GPC and 100 percent of GPI, she is in control of both corporations. Thus, the purchase of stock by GPI is the acquisition of stock in a controlled corporation by another controlled corporation, and section 304(a)(1) applies to the transaction.[11]

---

[9] The only possible exception to this reattribution of stock ownership rule is stated in section 318(a)(5)(B), which reads as follows: "Stock constructively owned by an individual by reason of the application of paragraph (1) [*that is, by family attribution*] shall not be considered as owned by him for purposes of again applying paragraph (1) in order to make another the constructive owner of such stock." Because Alvred's indirect ownership of GPC shares comes about by application of paragraph (2)(C) of section 318 and not by application of paragraph (1), section 318(a)(1)(A)(ii) requires that Ms. Hitchcock also include in her indirect ownership any shares that GPI owns.

[10] Incidentally, the revised diagram of the facts pictured in Figure 3.3 actually suggests this conclusion with much less confusion than do all of the words of the Internal Revenue Code. Perhaps one picture can be worth a thousand words. Note that simply following the dotted lines of that diagram back from Alvred to Ms. Hitchcock shows that the conclusion just reached is not really so farfetched.

[11] Taken literally, this transaction is also the acquisition of parent stock by a subsidiary corporation because using the constructive ownership rules, GPC controls GPI. However, for reasons that go well beyond this illustration, a section 304 parent-subsidiary transaction occurs only if the stock of the subsidiary is

The careful reader will have observed that, even at this point, we have not yet determined the correct tax treatment of Ms. Hitchcock's stock disposition. Before we can make that determination, we must ask still more questions.

More Questions, More Authority

IRC section 304(a)(1) simply provides that Ms. Hitchcock's sale should be treated as a distribution in redemption of stock, and it directs us to examine two additional IRC sections to see what that means. Our next question, then, must be: "If Ms. Hitchcock's disposition of GPC stock is to be treated as a stock redemption under section 302, 303, or both, what, if anything, do those sections say about the tax treatment of the transaction?"

Searching further, we could quickly discover that section 303 deals only with distributions in redemption of stock to pay death taxes. Clearly, the facts of our problem do not suggest anything about Ms. Hitchcock's making this disposition to pay death taxes. Thus, we may safely conclude that section 303 is not applicable to our situation. We turn, therefore, to section 302, which reads, in pertinent part, as follows:

SEC. 302. DISTRIBUTIONS IN REDEMPTION OF STOCK.

(a) GENERAL RULE.—If a corporation redeems its stock (within the meaning of section 317(b)), and if paragraph (1), (2), (3), or (4) of subsection (b) applies, such redemption shall be treated as a distribution in part or full payment in exchange for the stock.

(b) REDEMPTIONS TREATED AS EXCHANGES.—

(1) REDEMPTIONS NOT EQUIVALENT TO DIVIDENDS.—Subsection (a) shall apply if the redemption is not essentially equivalent to a dividend.

(2) SUBSTANTIALLY DISPROPORTIONATE REDEMPTION OF STOCK.—

---

owned by the parent, either actually or constructively, in a direct chain of ownership. For a discussion of this issue, see Bittker and Eustice, *Federal Taxation of Corporations and Shareholders* (RIA, now in its seventh edition).

(A) IN GENERAL.—Subsection (a) shall apply if the distribution is substantially disproportionate with respect to the shareholder.

(B) LIMITATION.—This paragraph shall not apply unless immediately after the redemption the shareholder owns less than 50 percent of the total combined voting power of all classes of stock entitled to vote.

(C) DEFINITIONS.—For purposes of this paragraph, the distribution is substantially disproportionate if—

　　(i) the ratio which the voting stock of the corporation owned by the shareholder immediately after the redemption bears to all the voting stock of the corporation at such time,

is less than 80 percent of—

　　(ii) the ratio which the voting stock of the corporation owned by the shareholder immediately before the redemption bears to all of the voting stock of the corporation at such time.

For purposes of this paragraph, no distribution shall be treated as substantially disproportionate unless the shareholder's ownership of the common stock of the corporation (whether voting or nonvoting) after and before redemption also meets the 80 percent requirement of the preceding sentence.

(3) TERMINATION OF SHAREHOLDER'S INTEREST.—Subsection (a) shall apply if the redemption is in complete redemption of all of the stock of the corporation owned by the shareholder.

(4) REDEMPTION FROM A NONCORPORATE SHARE-HOLDER IN PARTIAL LIQUIDATION.—Subsection (a) shall apply to a distribution if such distribution is—(A) in redemption of stock held by a shareholder who is not a corporation, and (B) in partial liquidation of the distributing corporation.

· · · ·

(c) CONSTRUCTIVE OWNERSHIP OF STOCK.—

(1) IN GENERAL.—Except as provided in paragraph (2) of this subsection, section 318(a) shall apply in determining the ownership of stock for purposes of this section.

· · · ·

(d) REDEMPTIONS TREATED AS DISTRIBUTIONS OF PROPERTY.—Except as otherwise provided in this subchapter, if a corporation redeems its stock (within the meaning of section

317(b)), and if subsection (a) of this section does not apply, such redemption shall be treated as a distribution of property to which section 301 applies.

Obviously, this relatively lengthy IRC section simply brings more questions to mind. The careful reader should observe that section 302(a) provides a general rule that a redemption will be treated as *"a distribution in part or full payment in exchange for the stock"* if the conditions of any one of four paragraphs are satisfied [*emphasis added*]. This means that if the conditions of any one of the four subsections can be satisfied, a taxpayer from whom stock is redeemed can treat the disposition as a sale. In most instances, this would result in a capital gain computed by subtracting the basis of the stock redeemed from the amount received. The general rules of subsection (a) say nothing, however, about the proper tax treatment of the redemption proceeds if those conditions cannot be satisfied. That possibility is treated in subsection (d), which says, "such redemption shall be treated as *a distribution of property to which section 301 applies"* [*emphasis added*]. On further investigation, we discover that section 301 generally provides dividend treatment for property distributed by a corporation to its shareholder. This means, of course, that the redeemed shareholder would have to report the entire amount of the distribution as ordinary income rather than computing a capital gain on the sale of stock.

If we continued to examine the facts of our illustrative problem in detail against all of the rules of section 302, we would have to proceed through another relatively complex set of IRC provisions not unlike those we have just examined in some detail. Because this procedure is no longer new, and because we really are interested only in demonstrating the complex relationship that exists between facts, authorities, and tax questions, we shall discontinue our detailed step-by-step approach and state the remainder of this analysis in more general terms. We can begin such a summary treatment of our problem as follows:

1. *Question:* Is Ms. Hitchcock's disposition of stock a redemption within the meaning of section 317(b), as required by section 302(a)?

   Authority: Section 317(b) reads as follows:

REDEMPTION OF STOCK.—For purposes of this part, stock shall be treated as redeemed by a corporation if the corporation acquires its stock from a shareholder in exchange for property, whether or not the stock so acquired is cancelled, retired, or held as treasury stock.

Conclusion: The intended meaning of this section is not obvious. It seems to suggest that what the acquiring corporation does with shares it acquires from its shareholders will in no way affect the classification of the stock acquisition as a stock redemption. Furthermore, the section seems initially not to apply to our case because it refers to a corporation acquiring *its* stock from a shareholder. A more general reflection on how this section is made applicable to related corporations through section 304 suggests, however, that these words must be stretched to include the stock of a related corporation if the purpose of section 304 is not to be circumvented. Hence, we would likely conclude that Ms. Hitchcock's disposition probably is a redemption within the meaning of section 317(b).

2. *Question:* Is Ms. Hitchcock's sale (redemption) of 30,000 shares of GPC stock to GPI a redemption that falls within the meaning of any one of the exceptions of section 302(b)(1) through (b)(4)?

Authority: Read again section 302(b)(1) through (b)(4) as quoted previously.

Conclusions (in reverse order):
a. Upon further investigation of the facts, it is found that GPC is not involved in a partial liquidation. Thus, section 302(b)(4) is not applicable.
b. Clearly, the exception of section 302(b)(3) is not applicable. Ms. Hitchcock continues to own directly 30,000 shares of GPC stock even after her sale of 30,000 shares to GPI.
c. Clearly, the exception of section 302(b)(2) is not applicable. Considering her indirect ownership as well as her direct ownership, Ms. Hitchcock owns after the sale exactly what she owned before the sale. (Note that section 302(c) requires that the attribution rules of section 318 be applied to stock redemptions.)

The Final Question

Without having carefully examined each of the intermediate questions and authorities suggested above, the reader might have some trouble in stating the final question. If you took the time to do so, however, it would seem that the final question might be stated thus: "Is Ms. Hitchcock's sale of 30,000 shares of GPC to GPI properly treated as a 'redemption not essentially equivalent to a dividend' as that phrase is used in section 302(b)(1)?" The implied conclusion stems importantly from (1) the requirement in section 304 (with assistance from section 318) that Ms. Hitchcock's apparent sale be treated not as a sale at all but as a redemption of a corporation's stock, and (2) the requirement in section 302 that a stock redemption be treated as a dividend unless one of the four exceptions in section 302(b) is satisfied.

Any detailed assessment of the authority that is pertinent to an interpretation of section 302(b)(1) would lead us well into the objective of chapter 6 of this book. Consequently, we shall not undertake that assessment here. We shall note, in passing, some general observations that would become pertinent to a resolution of the problem, were we actually to undertake a detailed assessment. First, the Treasury regulations indicate that the application of section 302(b)(1) depends upon the facts and circumstances in each case.[12] Second, in the Treasury regulations, the only example of a stock redemption qualifying for exchange treatment under section 302(b)(1) is as follows: "For example, if a shareholder owns only nonvoting stock of a corporation which is not section 306 stock and which is limited and preferred as to dividends and in liquidation, and one-half of such stock is redeemed, the distribution will ordinarily meet the requirements of paragraph (1) of section 302(b) but will not meet the requirements of paragraphs (2), (3), or (4) of such section."[13] This example obviously lends no support to the case at hand because the facts of Ms. Hitchcock's ownership are radically different from those described in this regulation. Third, in *Davis*,[14] the Supreme Court held that the business purpose of a

---

[12] Treas. Reg. Sec. 1.302-2(b).
[13] Treas. Reg. Sec. 1.302-2(a).
[14] *U.S. v. Davis*, 397 U.S. 301, 70-1 USTC paragraph 9289 (1970).

transaction is irrelevant in determining dividend equivalence. In summary, the authority for granting Ms. Hitchcock sale (that is, capital gain) treatment by operation of the exception stated in section 302(b)(1) appears to be relatively weak. In addition, if the exception of section 302(b)(1) does not apply, Ms. Hitchcock must report $325,000 dividend income by operation of section 302(d).[15]

Summary

The foregoing example demonstrates the critical role of facts, the interdependency of facts and law, and the elusive nature of pertinent tax questions. If all the facts are discovered and all the applicable law is known and understood, apparently simple transactions have a way of creating relatively complex tax problems in all too many situations. The tax adviser must ask the right questions, not because he or she desires to convert a simple situation into a complex problem and a larger fee, but because the correct reporting of a tax result depends so directly upon asking those questions. Questions often evolve from fact determination to law application. For example, in our illustration, the first critical questions were (1) Who purchased the shares? and (2) Who owned the purchaser? Certainly those are fact questions. Nevertheless, unless a person has some appreciation of the applicable law, it would be highly unlikely for that person to continue to ask the right questions. After the facts are determined, the critical questions concerned the application of law to known facts; for example, (1) Does section 304 apply to Ms. Hitchcock's sale of 30,000 shares of GPC to GPI? (2) Does section 318 apply to make this transaction a section 304 brother-sister transaction? and (3) Does the exception of section 302(b)(1) apply to this same disposition? Each question appears to be more esoteric than the preceding one. Yet, to an important degree, every question depends upon the tax adviser's knowledge of the authority that is applicable to the given fact situation.

---

[15] Our conclusion assumes a sufficiency of earnings and profits as required by section 316, which defines the word *dividend*. In actual practice, of course, this would constitute another critical fact determination.

4

Identifying Appropriate Authority

In chapters 2 and 3 we discussed the importance of facts and the methodology employed to delineate questions that must be answered to solve tax problems successfully. Once the facts are correctly understood and the issues are identified, the tax adviser must then attempt to answer or resolve the issue. To determine a technically correct answer to a tax question, the tax adviser may need to find and analyze various types of authority. This process consists of two distinct phases: (1) The tax adviser must locate the appropriate authority and (2) he or she must assess the importance of that authority, augment it if incomplete and, on occasion, choose between conflicting authorities. To find the tax authority and assess its relevance and importance, however, a tax adviser must first be familiar with and understand the various types of tax authority that exist. Thus, chapter 4 identifies and discusses the major types of tax law. Chapter 5 focuses on locating that authority, and chapter 6 concentrates on the analysis and assessment of these authorities.

The three basic categories or types of tax authority include statutory, administrative, and judicial law. In addition, editorial interpretation, although not authoritative tax law per se, serves a valuable role in locating and assessing the law. In general, statutory law has been enacted by the appropriate legislative body and signed into law by the chief government executive. Examples of statutory law that a tax adviser may need to consult include the Internal Revenue Code (IRC), tax treaties, state tax law, and occasionally other law, such as the Federal Bankruptcy Code. The IRC, of course, is the primary source of tax law for the United States. At times, to understand the IRC, a tax adviser must understand its origin and the process by which it is amended.

Statutory Law

The Tax-Legislation Process

The United States' authority to tax income originates with the 16th Amendment to the U.S. Constitution, ratified in 1913. Since that time, numerous revenue acts have been enacted into law. At first, each of these revenue acts contained the entire tax law of the United States and was passed every year or two. However, due to their number and increasing complexity, existing revenue acts were codified in 1939 into a single document called the Internal Revenue Code of 1939. Revenue acts enacted after this codification merely amended the Internal Revenue Code of 1939. However, in 1954 Congress revised, reorganized, and re-enacted the IRC. Because the reorganization and revision was so extensive, Congress named it the Internal Revenue Code of 1954. Then in 1986, Congress again substantially revised the Internal Revenue Code, calling it the Internal Revenue Code of 1986. Thus, since 1939, revenue acts enacted into law simply amend the 1939, the 1954, and the 1986 Internal Revenue Codes, depending on the date the act was passed. Furthermore, since 1954, the organization of the Internal Revenue Code has remained the same even though it has been amended many times.

Although suggestions or proposals to amend the IRC may come from various sources, by virtue of article I, section 7, of the U.S. Constitution, all revenue bills must originate in the House of Representatives. Most of the actual work the House of Representatives does on a revenue bill takes place in the House Ways and Means Committee. In many cases, the House Ways and Means Committee schedules public hearings. Upon conclusion of the hearings, the committee, with the help of the staff of the Joint Committee, develops a proposed bill and the House Ways and Means Committee report.[1] This report includes the proposed bill drafted in legislative language, an assessment of its effect on revenue, and a general explanation of the provisions in the bill. The report details the reasons for the committee's actions and, therefore, constitutes an important reference source for the courts, the IRS, and practitioners in determining legislative intent in connection with each section of the bill. Upon completion of the committee report, the bill is reported to the floor of the House for action.

Any debates or hearings on the floor of the House are generally included in the *Congressional Record*. After approval by the House, a tax bill is sent to the Senate, where it is immediately referred to the Senate Finance Committee. Often the Senate Finance Committee schedules its own hearings and prepares its own committee report. This report also constitutes part of the legislative history of a tax act. Any debates or hearings on the Senate floor also become part of the *Congressional Record*, which must be consulted if it becomes necessary to understand the reason for an amendment that was introduced on the Senate floor.

If the House and Senate pass different versions of the same bill, a Conference Committee, which consists of members of both the Senate Finance Committee and the House Ways and Means Committee, attempts to iron out the differences. Like the House Ways and Means Committee and the Senate Finance Committee, the Conference Committee may prepare its own committee report, concentrating on the areas of disagreement. This report also becomes part of the legislative history. Statements made on the floor of either chamber before the final vote on the conference report are entered in the *Congressional Record*. At times, these statements can shed light on congressional intent. In addition to these committee reports, the staff of the Joint Committee on Taxation

---

[1] The Joint Committee on Taxation is another congressional committee (not the same as a conference committee, discussed later) that consists of members of both the Senate Finance Committee and the House Ways and Means Committee. In general, its responsibilities include collecting data, investigating the administration of the U.S. tax system, and proposing ways to simplify the tax system.

often prepares its own explanation of major tax statutes. This explanation is typically written after the new bill has been enacted into law and is often called the *Blue Book*. Many tax advisers find these explanations very useful. Technically, the *Blue Book* is not part of the legislative history of a tax act. However, it does constitute substantial authority for purposes of avoiding the penalty imposed by section 6662 for the substantial understatement of income tax.[2]

After approval of the conference bill by both the House and the Senate, the bill is sent to the President to be signed. Once signed, the new law receives a two-part Public Law (P.L.) number. The first part of the number refers to the Congress that passed the law. Each Congress sits for two years, based on the two-year term of the House of Representatives. The 110th Congress, for example, sat for 2007 and 2008. The second number is that particular P.L.'s number.

An understanding of this legislative process is important to a tax adviser for a number of reasons. First, to fully understand the application of the law itself, often the adviser must understand Congress' intent in enacting the law. This is especially important when a law is new and the Treasury, the IRS, or the courts have not issued regulations, other administrative pronouncements, or judicial decisions that interpret the new statute. In such a case, the committee reports, the *Congressional Record*, and the *Blue Book* may provide some help in applying and understanding the law. Second, although generally all of a particular tax act is codified into the IRC, at times certain provisions are not. Typically provisions that are not included in the IRC contain transitional rules (sometimes called *grandfather clauses*) under which the old law is phased out or the new law is phased in. Although not incorporated into the IRC, these transitional rules, nevertheless, are law. Thus, at times a tax adviser must refer to the public law itself to find these rules. Chapter 5 contains a discussion of how and where a tax adviser can find these public laws with their associated committee reports, applicable portions of the *Congressional Record*, and the *Blue Book*.

The Internal Revenue Code

All federal statutes, including all tax acts passed by Congress, are compiled and published in the *United States Code* (USC). The USC

---

[2] Treas. Reg. Sec. 1.6662-4(d)(3)(iii).

contains many different areas of statutory law (for example, federal statutes dealing with criminal law, interstate commerce, and bankruptcy) and is organized or subdivided by area of law into "Titles." The Internal Revenue Code—often referred to by its acronym, IRC, or simply "the Code"—is Title 26 of the USC.[3]

As mentioned previously, the basic organization of the IRC (Title 26 of the USC) has remained the same since 1954. Any amendment to the IRC is merely incorporated into the IRC in its appropriate location. Furthermore, the IRC is somewhat logically organized by topic. For example, the tax law dealing with partnerships generally is organized together into a particular subdivision of the IRC that is commonly referred to as *subchapter K* (as explained later, this is subchapter K of chapter 1 of the IRC). Thus, an understanding of the organization of the IRC can be very helpful to a tax adviser in understanding and researching the statute. As you study the following discussion about the IRC's organization, keep in mind that it is constantly changing. Thus, there may have been changes since the publication of this book. The important thing to understand is the overall structure.

The Internal Revenue Code of 1986 (Title 26 of the USC) is divided into subtitles and is then further subdivided into the following chapters:

Subtitles	*Chapters*
A. Income Taxes	1–6
B. Estate and Gift Taxes	11–14
C. Employment Taxes	21–25
D. Miscellaneous Excise Taxes	31–47
E. Alcohol, Tobacco, and Certain Other Excise Taxes	51–54
F. Procedure and Administration	61–80
G. The Joint Committee on Taxation	91–92
H. Financing of Presidential Election Campaigns	95–96
I. Trust Fund Code	98
J. Coal Industry Health Benefits	99
K. Group Health Plan Requirements	100

---

[3] The IRC, as well as Treasury Regulations and additional IRS guidance, is available on the IRS Web site at www.irs.gov/taxpros/article/0,,id=98137,00.html. These documents may not be updated for the latest amendments and changes.

Each chapter within the IRC is further subdivided into its own subchapters, which are designated by a capital letter. For example, chapter 1 (Normal Taxes and Surtaxes) consists of 25 subchapters, designated as subchapters A–Y. These subchapter designations are often used by tax practitioners as part of their everyday vocabulary in identifying general areas of income taxation. Some of the most frequently used subchapter designations of chapter 1 are as follows:

Subchapter

B	Computation of Taxable Income
C	Corporate Distributions and Adjustments
E	Accounting Periods and Methods of Accounting
J	Estates, Trusts, Beneficiaries, and Decedents
K	Partners and Partnerships
N	Tax Based on Income from Sources Within or Without The United States
O	Gain or Loss on Disposition of Property
P	Capital Gains and Losses
S	Tax Treatment of S Corporations and Their Shareholders

Each subchapter is further subdivided into parts, which may themselves be subdivided into subparts. Parts are designated by large Roman numerals, whereas subparts are designated by capital letters. For example, subchapter C of chapter 1 is divided into seven parts (two have been repealed), each containing provisions that deal with different aspects of corporate distributions and adjustments, such as liquidations or corporate reorganizations. Continuing this example, Part I of subchapter C, titled Distributions by Corporations, contains three subparts: Subpart A—Effects on Recipients, Subpart B—Effects on Corporation, and Subpart C—Definitions; Constructive Ownership of Stock.

    Sections are a basic subdivision of the IRC and are designated by Arabic numerals. IRC section numbers run consecutively through the entire IRC and are assigned to a specific subchapter of a particular chapter of the IRC. For example, subchapter A of chapter 1, which deals with the determination of an entity's income tax liability, includes section numbers 1–59A. On the other hand, subchapter A of chapter 11, which deals with the estate tax and comes sequentially much later in the IRC, includes section numbers 2001–2058. To the extent that section numbers are unassigned, the arrangement is suitable for future expansion of the IRC. For example, even though subchapter A of chapter 11 ends with section 2058, subchapter B of chapter 11 starts with section 2101, leaving some room for future expansion. On the other hand, at times a new provision is enacted that, because of the topic it deals with, should be included properly in a particular location of the IRC where additional numbers may not be available. In this case, the new IRC section is inserted in the proper place by adding a capital letter to its numerical designation, such as section 59A. Thus, for example, subchapter B of chapter 1, in addition to many other sections, contains eight different sections numbered from section 280A through section 280H. Because IRC section numbers run consecutively through the entire IRC, the numbers are helpful in indicating to tax advisers the general tax topic contained in the section. For example, IRC section numbers in the 300 series deal with the income tax topic of corporate distributions and adjustments (subchapter C of chapter 1).

Each section is further broken down into smaller and smaller subdivisions. In descending order of size, these include the following:

- Subsections, designated by small letters in parentheses
- Paragraphs, designated by Arabic numerals in parentheses
- Subparagraphs, designated by capital letters in parentheses
- Clauses, designated by small Roman numerals in parentheses
- Subclauses, designated by large Roman numerals in parentheses

An example of the use of these designations is found in exhibit 4.1. Thus, for example, clause ii of section 318, subsection a, paragraph 3, subparagraph B, which is cited as §318(a)(2)(B)(ii), states that "Stock owned, directly or indirectly, by or for a person who is considered the owner of any portion of a trust under subpart E of part I of subchapter J (relating to grantors and others treated as

Exhibit 4.1

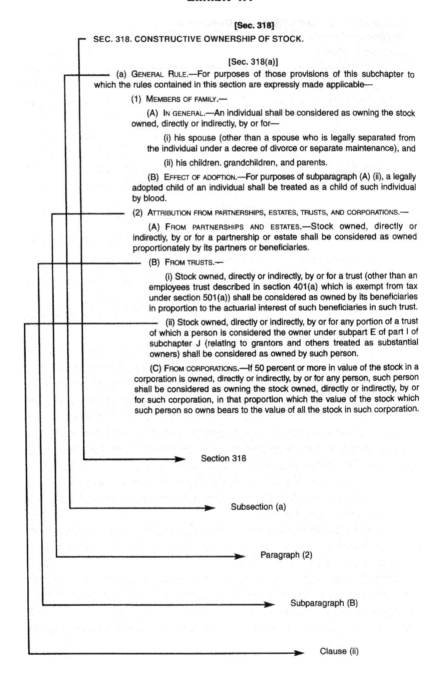

[Sec. 318]

SEC. 318. CONSTRUCTIVE OWNERSHIP OF STOCK.

[Sec. 318(a)]

(a) GENERAL RULE.—For purposes of those provisions of this subchapter to which the rules contained in this section are expressly made applicable—

(1) MEMBERS OF FAMILY.—

(A) IN GENERAL.—An individual shall be considered as owning the stock owned, directly or indirectly, by or for—

(i) his spouse (other than a spouse who is legally separated from the individual under a decree of divorce or separate maintenance), and

(ii) his children. grandchildren, and parents.

(B) EFFECT OF ADOPTION.—For purposes of subparagraph (A) (ii), a legally adopted child of an individual shall be treated as a child of such individual by blood.

(2) ATTRIBUTION FROM PARTNERSHIPS, ESTATES, TRUSTS, AND CORPORATIONS.—

(A) FROM PARTNERSHIPS AND ESTATES.—Stock owned, directly or indirectly, by or for a partnership or estate shall be considered as owned proportionately by its partners or beneficiaries.

(B) FROM TRUSTS.—

(i) Stock owned, directly or indirectly, by or for a trust (other than an employees trust described in section 401(a) which is exempt from tax under section 501(a)) shall be considered as owned by its beneficiaries in proportion to the actuarial interest of such beneficiaries in such trust.

(ii) Stock owned, directly or indirectly, by or for any portion of a trust of which a person is considered the owner under subpart E of part I of subchapter J (relating to grantors and others treated as substantial owners) shall be considered as owned by such person.

(C) FROM CORPORATIONS.—If 50 percent or more in value of the stock in a corporation is owned, directly or indirectly, by or for any person, such person shall be considered as owning the stock owned, directly or indirectly, by or for such corporation, in that proportion which the value of the stock which such person so owns bears to the value of all the stock in such corporation.

Section 318

Subsection (a)

Paragraph (2)

Subparagraph (B)

Clause (ii)

substantial owners) shall be considered as owned by the trust."
Understanding the IRC's organization is important to a tax adviser
for various reasons. First, an understanding of the organization
helps the tax adviser organize, recognize, and remember broad
areas of the tax law. For example, if an experienced tax adviser is
investigating an S corporation tax issue, he or she knows that the
applicable IRC section dealing with the question probably falls
between sections 1361 and 1379 (subchapter S of chapter 1). Second,
as previously mentioned, certain subdivisions of the IRC are frequently used in the tax adviser's vocabulary. Examples include
subchapter K (income tax issues dealing with partnerships) and
subchapter C (income tax issues dealing with corporate distributions and adjustments). Finally, because the IRC refers to itself in
these terms, a proper reading and interpretation of the IRC requires
an understanding of this organization. This internal referencing is
generally done through phrases such as, "for purposes of." For
example, section 317(a) gives a definition of the word *property*
by stating, "(a) PROPERTY.—For purposes of this part, the term
'property' means money, securities, and any other property . . . ."
The language *for purposes of this part* puts the tax adviser on notice
that this particular definition of *property* applies only to part I of
subchapter C of chapter 1. Thus, use of this definition of *property*
for any other area of the IRC would be inappropriate unless that
other provision specifically refers to section 317(a) for its definition.

Learning how to read the IRC takes a great deal of practice
and close attention to detail. Simple words such as *and, or,* and
over must be read carefully in the context of the language, using
the word to properly interpret the meaning of the statute.

Treaties

A treaty is another type of statutory law issued by the United
States. A treaty is an agreement that two countries enter into in an
effort to eliminate or mitigate the double tax that might be imposed
on a taxpayer by both of the countries involved. For example, the
United States taxes its own citizens, residents, and corporations
on their worldwide income. If a U.S. corporation has business
operations in another country, the other country may also impose
a tax on the income of the U.S. corporation. Currently, the U.S. has

entered into multiple types of tax treaties (for example, income tax treaties, excise and customs tax treaties, estate tax treaties) with many other countries in the world. Most income tax treaties follow the same format by addressing issues contained in various articles of the treaty. Some of the more common issues addressed in a treaty include (1) withholding tax rates to be imposed on investment types of income, (2) the determination of a taxpayer's residence, (3) special treatment of certain types of taxpayers such as students and professional athletes, and (4) the establishment of channels of information sharing between the two countries. A treaty is used to establish how taxpayers of one country entering into the treaty are to be taxed by the other treaty country. For example, in order to determine the potential U.S. tax liability of a Canadian corporation that has investment and business operations in the United States a tax adviser should research the United States–Canadian tax treaty. The tax adviser would not consult the treaty to determine how the United States should tax one of its own citizens or corporations. On the other hand, the tax adviser should consult the United States–Canadian tax treaty to determine how Canada would tax a U.S. corporation or individual.

Under the U.S. Constitution, the President of the United States is authorized to enter into treaties with other countries as long as the Senate consents to and agrees with the treaty provisions. Under the Constitution, treaties are considered part of the "Supreme Law of the Land." Likewise, the IRC is part of the supreme law of the land, making the IRC and a Treaty of equal authority. The IRC itself addresses this equality of authority in section 894, which states that the IRC "shall be applied to any taxpayer with due regard to any treaty obligation of the United States which applies to such taxpayer." Likewise, section 7852(d) states that in ". . . determining the relationship between a provision of a treaty and any law of the United States affecting revenue, neither the treaty nor the law shall have preferential status by reason of its being a treaty or law." At times, there may be a conflict between a treaty and the IRC. If there is a conflict between these two authorities, a general rule of thumb that is often used is to follow the authority that is most recently adopted. However, often it may be necessary to consult judicial law to ensure that the proper procedure is being followed in order to resolve the conflict.

Administrative Law

Within the federal government's executive branch, the Treasury Department has the responsibility of implementing the tax statutes Congress passes. This function is specifically carried out by the IRS division of the Treasury Department. The IRS' duties are two-fold. First, the IRS interprets the statutes according to the intent of Congress, and second, the IRS enforces the application of the statutes.

The interpretive duties of the Treasury and IRS range from the general to the specific and are carried out through the issuance of various types of administrative law. Some of this administrative law (for example, a Treasury regulation or a revenue ruling) is issued to all taxpayers and constitutes precedence or authority for all taxpayers. In contrast, other forms of administrative law deal only with a specific transaction of a particular taxpayer. These forms of administrative law issued to a particular taxpayer generally cannot be used as precedent by other taxpayers except as a means of avoiding certain penalties. However, tax advisers often research these forms of law in an attempt to understand the thinking of the IRS.

Over the years, the IRS has used a variety of different types of administrative pronouncements or documents. Some of these forms of administrative law have been used for a period of time and then have been used less frequently or discontinued. Thus, a discussion of all of the different types of administrative law that exists is impractical. However, a discussion of the administrative law that a researcher will most frequently encounter today follows.[4]

Treasury Regulations

Section 7805(a) of the IRC gives the Secretary of the Treasury or his or her delegate a general power to prescribe necessary rules and regulations to administer the tax laws as passed by Congress. As such, regulations are the highest level of administrative

---

[4] *Tax Analysts* has published a list that includes a short description of many of the different forms of administrative law. See *Tax Analysts* Doc 2002-19084 (electronic citation: 2000 TNT 138-3).

authority. Regulations issued under the general authority of section 7805 are sometimes referred to as *general* or *interpretive* regulations. In addition to section 7805, a particular IRC section dealing with a specific area of tax law may also authorize the Secretary of the Treasury or his or her delegate to prescribe such regulations as may be necessary to carry out the purposes of that particular IRC section. For example, section 385(a) specifically authorizes the Secretary to prescribe regulations that are necessary or appropriate to determine whether an interest in a corporation is to be treated as stock or debt. Regulations issued under such specific authority are often referred to as *legislative* or *statutory* regulations.

Other examples of statutory regulations are those issued under section 1502, which deals with consolidated tax returns. Because of the complexity of the subject, Congress did not legislate in detail in this area and delegated this responsibility to the Secretary of the Treasury or his or her delegate. Taxpayers electing to file consolidated returns must execute a consent form in which they agree to be bound by the provisions of the regulations.[5] Presumably, such an agreement leaves almost no appeal from the provisions of the consolidated return regulations and, in that sense, gives them a position more nearly "statutory" than the interpretive regulations.

The purpose of interpretive regulations is to clarify the language of the IRC as passed by Congress. At times, the wording of the regulations is almost identical to the language of the IRC or the accompanying committee report and is of little assistance. In recent years, however, the Treasury has made frequent attempts to add helpful examples to the regulations. In effect, even the interpretive regulations may come to have the force of law. However, if they contradict the intent of Congress, they can be overturned or held invalid by the courts.[6] Nevertheless, the odds are very much against the taxpayer who tries to win a case against the government solely by attempting to declare a specific Treasury regulation to be in conflict with the IRC or the intent of Congress. For a more complete discussion on the status of Treasury regulations, see chapter 6.

Regulations generally are issued in proposed form before they are published in final form and actually become law. Treasury

---

[5] Treas. Reg. Sec. 1.1502-75.
[6] See, for example, *Rite Aid Corp.*, 255 F. 3d (CA-FC, 2001).

issues these proposed regulations as a Notice of Proposed Rule Making (NPRM). Interested parties, such as taxpayers, the AICPA, the American Bar Association, and other professional groups and organizations generally are given at least 30 days from the date the proposed regulations appear in the *Federal Register* to submit objections or suggestions. Depending on the controversy surrounding a proposed regulation, it will be either withdrawn and issued in final form or amended and reissued as a new proposed regulation. In general, proposed regulations are not law. However, they are considered substantial authority for purposes of the substantial understatement penalty of section 6662. Furthermore, they do indicate the Treasury's thinking with respect to specific areas of the IRC.

Sometimes Treasury will issue temporary regulations to provide prompt guidance in an area in which the tax law has changed. These regulations, even though not subject to the same review and comment procedures before becoming law, have the same force of law as final regulations. In the past, temporary regulations could remain in effect for an indefinite period. However, currently the period of time temporary regulations may remain effective is limited to three years. In addition, when Treasury issues a temporary regulation, it generally must also issue a proposed regulation.[7] In summary, the tax adviser should know that temporary regulations are in full force from the day they are issued; proposed regulations are merely issued for comment and review purposes.

Final regulations are issued after the proposed regulations have gone through the comment period. Both final and temporary regulations are initially published as official Treasury Decisions (T.D.) and appear in the *Federal Register*. They are officially cited as Title 26 of the *Code of Federal Regulations*. The T.D. includes a preamble to the regulation which provides additional information such as the regulation's effective date and a summary of how Treasury addressed any taxpayer comments.

The identifying number of a regulation can be divided into three segments: (I) a number to the left of a decimal, (II) a number to the right of a decimal and to the left of a dash, and (III) a number

---

[7] Section 7805(e).

to the right of the dash. An example of how this identification scheme works is as follows:

$$\text{Treas. Reg. Sec. } \underbrace{1}.\underbrace{1245}\text{-}\underbrace{2(a)(3)(ii)}$$
$$\text{Segment} \quad \text{I} \quad \text{II} \qquad \text{III}$$

Segment I indicates that the regulation deals either with a specific type of tax or with a procedural rule. Some of the more frequently encountered segment I numbers are as follows:

Segment I Designation	Area of Law
1	Income Tax
20	Estate Tax
25	Gift Tax
31	Employment Tax
301	Administrative and Procedural Matters
601	Statement of Procedural Rules

Segment II simply coincides with the specific IRC section with which the regulation deals. Thus, in the example, one can determine that the regulation cited (1) deals with the income tax (because of the prefix 1) and (2) refers specifically to section 1245 of the IRC. Segment III is the regulation number along with its subdivisions. Thus, segment III in the example refers to paragraph (a), subparagraph (3), subdivision (ii) of the second regulation under section 1245. Generally, there is no direct correlation between the sequence designation of the IRC and the organization of a Treasury regulation. For instance, IRC section 1245(c) discusses "Adjustment to Basis," whereas the interpretive discussion of the same topic is found in Treas. Reg. Sec. 1.1245-5. In citing a proposed or temporary regulation, the word *Prop.* or *Temp.* generally is added. In addition, a "T" is generally added to the temporary regulation number. For example, Temp. Treas. Reg. Sec. 1.863-1T is a temporary regulation that is effective for tax years ending after August 1, 2006. Thus, under the three year rule dealing with temporary regulations, this regulation will expire July 31, 2009.

Frequently, there is a considerable delay between the time a IRC section is enacted or modified and the time when the Treasury issues proposed, temporary, or permanent regulations. As mentioned previously, if this is the case, taxpayers must rely on the committee reports to obtain any guidance the reports may contain.

In addition to being published in the *Federal Register*, final Treasury regulations are published in the *Internal Revenue Bulletin*, or I.R.B., the IRS's weekly newsletter. These IRBs are then bound into the IRS's semiannual publication, the *Cumulative Bulletin*, or C.B. As would be expected, regulations are an important source of precedential authority for all taxpayers.

Revenue Rulings

The revenue ruling is another interpretive tool used by the IRS that also serves as precedence for all taxpayers. A revenue ruling is an official interpretation by the National Office of the IRS dealing with the application of the IRC and regulations to a specific fact situation.[8] Revenue rulings are frequently issued as a result of specific rulings to taxpayers, technical advice to district offices, court decisions, and so on.[9]

Initially, revenue rulings are published in the IRS's weekly *Internal Revenue Bulletin*. The same rulings later appear in the permanently bound *Cumulative Bulletin*, a semiannual publication. A typical citation for a revenue ruling appears in the following forms:

Rev. Rul. 2008-5, 2008-3 I.R.B. 271, 12 Dec. 2007
or
Rev. Rul. 2003-12, 2003-1 C.B. 283

The first citation refers to the fifth revenue ruling of the 2008 fiscal year, which can be found in the third weekly *Internal Revenue Bulletin*. The second citation refers to the 12th revenue ruling issued in the 2003 fiscal year. Its source is the first volume of the 2003 *Cumulative Bulletin*, page 283. After a ruling is included in the

---

[8] Treas. Reg. Sec. 601.201(a)(1).
[9] Rev. Proc. 89-14, 1989-1 C.B. 814.

semiannual *Cumulative Bulletin* published by the IRS, the *Cumulative Bulletin* reference becomes the permanent citation. Prior to 1953, IRS rulings appeared under various titles, such as appeals and review memoranda (ARM), internal revenue mimeographs (IR-Mim.), and tax board memoranda (TBM), to name just a few.

At times the IRS may revoke, amplify, supersede, obsolete, or otherwise modify a revenue ruling. Thus, in researching an issue, a tax adviser should always verify the current status of a revenue ruling to avoid the embarrassment of relying on a ruling that has been revoked or modified in a way that makes it no longer applicable to the issue the adviser is addressing. This process is done through various citators or other reference tools (discussed in chapter 5).

According to Revenue Procedure 89-14,[10] published revenue rulings have less force than Treasury regulations because they are intended to cover only specific fact situations. Consequently, published rulings provide valid precedent to a taxpayer only if the taxpayer's facts are substantially identical to those found in the revenue ruling.

Revenue Procedures

A revenue procedure is an official statement of procedure or information.[11] Like revenue rulings, revenue procedures have less force and effect than Treasury regulations. However, revenue procedures should be binding on the IRS and may be relied upon by taxpayers. The depreciation guidelines announced in Rev. Proc. 87-56 and the depreciation tables found in Rev. Proc. 87-57 are examples of frequently used revenue procedures.[12] Other frequently used revenue procedures include those issued at the beginning of each year to inform the public of the technical tax areas in which the IRS will and will not issue private letter rulings.

Like revenue rulings, revenue procedures are published in both the *Internal Revenue Bulletin* and the *Cumulative Bulletin*. Further-

---

[10] Rev. Proc. 89-14, 1989-1 C.B. 814, para. 7.01(4).

[11] Treas. Reg. Sec. 601.601(b); Rev. Proc. 89-14, 1989-1 C.B. 814.

[12] Rev. Proc. 87-56, 1987-2 C.B. 674; Rev. Proc. 87-57, 1987-2 C.B. 687.

more, the identification methods for revenue procedures are identical to those used for revenue rulings except that the prefix "Rev. Proc." is used instead of "Rev. Rul."

Notices and Announcements

At times, taxpayers need expeditious guidance concerning an item of the tax law. This may occur for a variety of reasons, including a change in the statute, the issuance of an important judicial decision, or simply an awareness by the IRS that information needs to be given to the general public. The IRS often issues this guidance in the form of a notice published in the *Internal Revenue Bulletin*. These notices are intended to be relied on by taxpayers to the same extent as a revenue ruling or revenue procedure and may, in fact, provide the basis for a subsequent revenue ruling or regulation. An example of the use of notices is Notice 2008-1, which alerts taxpayers to the fact that two percent shareholder-employees of an S corporation can deduct health insurance premiums paid directly by the S corporation or reimbursed to the employee upon proof of payment to the S corporation.[13]

Information of general interest can also appear in the form of an announcement. In the past, announcements have been used to summarize new tax law or to publicize procedural matters. Along with revenue rulings, revenue procedures, and notices, announcements are authoritative and may be relied upon by taxpayers. An example of an announcement is Announcement 2008-2, which contains procedures for certain taxpayers to elect an alternative funding schedule for certain defined benefit plans.[14]

Notices and announcements are both published in the *Internal Revenue Bulletin*. However, only notices are subsequently published in the *Cumulative Bulletin*. Announcements and notices are both identified by the year in which they are issued, followed by the document's number.

It is important to emphasize that all of the different types of administrative law discussed thus far in the chapter (regulations,

---

[13] Notice 2008-1, 2008-1 I.R.B. 251, 13 Dec. 2007.
[14] Announcement 2008-2, 2008-3 I.R.B. 307, 21 Dec. 2007.

revenue rulings, revenue procedures, notices, and announcements) are issued either by Treasury or the IRS as official documents to all taxpayers. As such, they all may be relied on to one degree or another as authoritative. In general, final and temporary regulations are issued by Treasury and have the highest level of administrative authority. Revenue rulings are issued by the National Office of the IRS and can be used by taxpayers as precedent if the material facts in the taxpayer's situation are the same as the facts found in the revenue ruling. Taxpayers may rely on revenue procedures, notices, and announcements as long as they are pertinent to the taxpayer's situation.

The IRS also issues other types of administrative law that, in general, apply only to a specific taxpayer. Examples of rulings issued with respect to a specific taxpayer or issue include private letter rulings (PLRs or LTRs), technical advice memoranda (TAMs), determination letters, and chief counsel advice (CCA). These documents constitute legal binding authority only for the taxpayer with respect to whom the ruling is issued. In the last few years, the government has attempted to issue more precedential guidance. As a result, the number of these nonprecedential forms of guidance issued each year has declined. Nevertheless, these documents still constitute a rich source of information for other taxpayers and tax advisers for two reasons. First, they may constitute substantial authority for purposes of the avoidance of certain penalties. Second, although not precedent, they still contain a wealth of information about the way the IRS may rule in other, similar circumstances.

Another document that the IRS will periodically issue is an action on decision (AOD).

Letter Rulings

Private letter rulings (PLRs or LTRs) are issued by the National Office of the IRS directly to taxpayers who formally request advice about the tax consequences applicable to a specific business transaction. Such ruling requests are used by taxpayers to assure themselves of a preplanned tax result before they enter into a transaction. When a ruling is given, it is understood that the ruling is limited in application to the taxpayer making the request. In addition, as mentioned previously, although IRS personnel will not rely on or use PLRs as precedent in the disposition of other cases, a PLR is substantial authority for purposes of the penalty assessed for the substantial understatement of income tax.[15]

The IRS has no legal obligation to make advanced rulings on prospective transactions. Nevertheless, its policy is to offer guidance when requested, except for certain sensitive areas of the law. Furthermore, the IRS has announced that it will not issue a letter ruling with respect to an issue for which the IRS is currently developing guidance or that is clearly and adequately addressed by statute, regulation, court decisions, or other IRS published rulings. Each year the IRS issues revenue procedures that list areas in which the IRS will not rule.[16] The IRS uses a numbering system for PLRs that includes the year and week in which the ruling was issued and the number of the ruling issued that week.

Technical Advice Memoranda, Determination Letters, and Chief Counsel Advice

A technical advice memorandum (TAM) is much like a private letter ruling in that it is issued by the National Office of the IRS in response to a request for a ruling about a specific transaction. However, a TAM differs from a PLR in that it is a special after-the-fact (rather than a before-the-fact) ruling. For example, if a disagreement arises in the course of an audit between the taxpayer and an IRS agent or appeals officer, either side may ask the district director or appeals chief to request formal technical advice on the issue(s) from the National Office. If the advice is favorable to the taxpayer, IRS personnel usually will comply with the ruling. In some instances, such technical advice also has been used as the basis for the issuance of a revenue ruling. Like a PLR, a TAM may not be relied on as precedent. However, a TAM does constitute substantial authority for purposes of the substantial understatement penalty. Furthermore, because TAMs may indicate how the IRS may treat transactions in similar factual situations, they are a

---

[15] Treas. Reg. Sec. 1.6662-4(d)(3)(iii).

[16] Rev. Proc. 2008-4, 2008-1 I.R.B., 121, 07 Jan. 2008 and Rev. Proc. 2008-7, 2008-1 I.R.B. 229, 07 Jan. 2008. See also Rev. Proc. 2008-1, 2008-1 I.R.B., 04 Jan. 2008.

good source of information for tax advisers. The IRS uses the same general numbering system for TAMs that it uses for PLRs.

Another document that is very similar to a TAM is a field service advice (FSA). An FSA is not binding on the IRS, but it does provide guidance and advice regarding the tax issue at hand. An FSA is requested by an IRS attorney, appeals officer, or agent rather than the taxpayer.

At times, instead of requesting a TAM from the National Office of the IRS, a taxpayer may ask the local IRS district office for the IRS's position on a particular transaction that has already been completed. If this occurs, the IRS's response is contained in a determination letter. A determination letter generally is issued only when a determination can be made on the basis of clearly established rules in the statute or regulations.[17]

In general, the term *chief counsel advice* or CCA is a term that includes various types of written advice that is prepared by the Office of Chief Counsel. These written advice documents are issued to IRS personnel as a means of communicating a legal interpretation or position regarding a particular provision of the law.

General Counsel Memoranda

In the past, the Office of Chief Counsel has issued general counsel memoranda (GCMs). These are legal documents prepared by the Office of Chief Counsel in connection with the review of certain proposed rulings such as revenue rulings and PLRs. GCMs contain the legal analysis of the substantive issues addressed in the ruling and can be especially helpful in understanding the reasoning the IRS used in arriving at its conclusions. Because of this analysis, GCMs can provide insight into the IRS's possible response to similar issues in the future. GCMs issued after March 12, 1981 constitute substantial authority for purposes of the avoidance of certain penalties.[18] The IRS has virtually abandoned the issuance of GCMs in recent years.

---

[17] Rev. Proc. 93-1, 1993-1 C.B. 538.
[18] Treas. Reg. Sec. 1.6662-4(d)(3)(iii).

Action on Decision

When the IRS loses a case in a court other than the Supreme Court, it may choose to issue a statement known as an *action on decision* (AOD) announcing whether it will follow the holding in the case in similar situations. AODs are not issued for all cases that the IRS loses. The purpose of an AOD is to give guidance and recommendations to IRS personnel who are working on the same or similar issues. Thus, an AOD is not intended to serve as a policy statement to taxpayers. The recommendation in an AOD may take the form of an acquiescence, an acquiescence in result only, or a nonacquiescence. An acquiescence or an acquiescence in result only means that the IRS will follow the holding of the court in subsequent circumstances that have the same material facts. However, an acquiescence does not signify either an approval or disapproval of the reasoning used in arriving at the conclusion. An acquiescence in result only indicates that, although the IRS will follow the holding of the court, it disagrees or has a concern with some or all of the reasoning used by the court. A nonacquiescence indicates that the IRS will not follow the holding of the court in subsequent cases. Prior to 1991, the IRS had a policy of publishing an acquiescence or a nonacquiescence only with respect to regular Tax Court decisions that the IRS had lost. Currently, however, it may acquiesce or nonacquiesce to all types of court decisions other than those issued by the Supreme Court. If a nonacquiescence is issued for a circuit court of appeals decision, the IRS will recognize the case as precedent within the court's own circuit and will not challenge subsequent cases within that circuit. However, it will not follow the case in other jurisdictions.

Judicial Interpretations

In situations in which statutory authority alone does not provide a clear solution for a particular problem, taxpayers or their advisers must consult judicial as well as administrative authority in forming an opinion. Judicial interpretations provide varying degrees of precedent, depending upon the nature of the conflict and the jurisdiction of the court that rendered the opinion.

Even though a vast majority of all disagreements with the IRS are settled at the administrative level, unsettled disputes may be litigated in one of three courts of original jurisdiction: the U.S. Tax Court, a U.S. district court, or the U.S. Court of Federal Claims. Appeals from these courts are heard by various courts of appeals. Twelve of these courts of appeals (eleven numbered and one for the District of Columbia) hear cases based upon the geographical residence of the taxpayer. That is, their authority or jurisdiction is limited to a specific geographic area of the United States. The Thirteenth Court of Appeals (the Court of Appeals for the Federal Circuit) hears cases that are appealed from the U.S. Court of Federal Claims. Appeals from any circuit court of appeals may be directed to the U.S. Supreme Court by requesting a writ of *certiorari*, which is a request for the U.S. Supreme Court to review the case.

After receiving a request for *certiorari* from either the government or the taxpayer, the Supreme Court decides whether it should review a case. *Certiorari* is most commonly granted in situations in which a conflict exists between two or more circuit courts of appeals. Sometimes, the Supreme Court will grant *certiorari* without a prior conflict if it thinks a case has special significance. The judicial alternatives available to a taxpayer are depicted in figure 4.1. To fully understand the weight of a court decision and the degree to which it sets precedent, an elementary understanding of the jurisdiction of each court is essential.

U.S. Tax Court

The U.S. Tax Court, established under section 7441 of the IRC, specializes only in tax issues. The court consists of 19 judges who are tax law experts, appointed by the President for 15-year terms. The chief judge of the Tax Court may also appoint special trial judges. These special trial judges are primarily used to help alleviate the Tax Court's heavy caseload. The decisions that these special judges render, however, are just as authoritative as other Tax Court decisions. Although the principal office of the Tax Court is located in Washington, D.C., it conducts hearings in most large cities in the United States. Thus, the Tax Court has jurisdiction over the entire United States. Proceedings before the Tax Court may be conducted with or without a trial; if sufficient facts are stipulated,

Figure 4.1

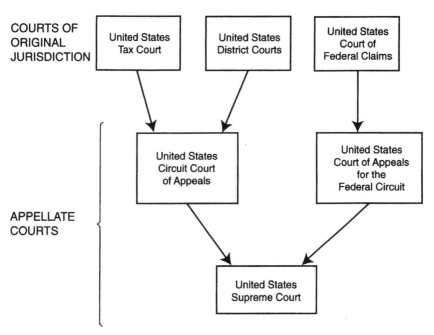

the assigned judge may render an opinion without a formal trial. Furthermore, no jury trial is available in the Tax Court.

After hearing a case, the judge submits the findings of fact and a written opinion to the chief judge. If, in the opinion of the chief judge, a case contains an unusual point of law or one on which considerable disagreement exists among the judges of the Tax Court, the chief judge may assign the case for review by other Tax Court judges or even the full Tax Court. When the full Tax Court reviews the case, it is known as an *en banc* decision. After each judge has had an opportunity to study the case, the Tax Court meets for an expression of opinions and a vote. In such instances, it is possible that one or more majority and minority opinions will be prepared, and that the trial judge—possibly the only one to have actually heard the proceedings—could write the minority opinion. The majority opinion is entered as the final decision of the Tax Court. If the chief judge decides that a review is not necessary, the original decision will stand. Tax Court decisions are issued as regular, memorandum, or small claims division decisions. A Tax Court regular decision generally involves a new or significant question regarding the tax law. Memorandum opinions, on the other hand, generally involve areas of tax law that, in the opinion of the chief judge, have been established and, thus, require only a delineation of the facts. Nevertheless, memorandum decisions do have value as precedent. In recent years, the Tax Court has handed down more memorandum opinions than regular opinions. Regular decisions are published by the Government Printing Office (GPO) in the *United States Tax Court Reports* (T.C.).[19]

Tax Court memorandum decisions are not published by the GPO. However, CCH (formerly known as Commerce Clearing House) publishes memorandum decisions in its *Tax Court Memorandum Decisions* (T.C.M.) series, and RIA (formerly known as Research Institute of America) makes them available as the *RIA TC Memorandum Decisions* (RIA TC Memo).[20]

As a general rule, the Tax Court's jurisdiction rests with the determination of deficiencies in income, excess profits, and self-employment, estate, or gift taxes. The Tax Court also has jurisdiction over declaratory judgments with respect to qualification of retirement plans[21] and over any penalty imposed for failure to pay the

---

[19] From 1943–1970, the name of the U.S. Tax Court was the Tax Court of the United States. Proceedings of the Tax Court of the United States were published as *The Tax Court of the United States Reports* (T.C.). Thus, citations for proceedings of the Tax Court under both names are the same (T.C.). For example, *Jack E. Golsen*, 54 T.C. 742 refers to the *Jack E. Golsen* case found in the 54th volume of the *United States Tax Court Reports*, page 742. Prior to 1943, the Tax Court was known as the Board of Tax Appeals. Decisions of the Board of Tax Appeals were published in the *United States Board of Tax Appeals Reports* (B.T.A.). Thus, for example, 39 B.T.A. 13 refers to the 39th volume of the *Board of Tax Appeals Reports*, page 13.

[20] In 1991, Thomson Professional Publishing acquired a line of tax products that had previously been published by the Prentice Hall Information Services Division and, since 1989, by Maxwell Macmillan. These products were then transferred by Thomson to its RIA publishing division. RIA changed the name of some publications (for example, *Federal Taxes, 2nd* became *United States Tax Reporter*). Other products (including *Citator, Citator 2nd Series, American Federal Tax Reports (AFTR)*, and *AFTR, 2nd*) kept their names. Thus, older editions of some of these products, such as the *RIA TC Memorandum Decisions*, will have either the Prentice Hall or Maxwell Macmillan name on the spine.

[21] Section 7476.

amount of tax shown on a tax return.[22] Thus, generally, to bring suit in the Tax Court, a taxpayer must have received a notice of deficiency, the so-called *90-day letter* or ticket to the Tax Court and, subsequently, have refused or failed to pay the deficiency. If the taxpayer first pays the tax before going to court, a claim for refund generally must be tried in either a federal district court or the U.S. Court of Federal Claims.

Some Tax Court transcripts state that a "decision has been entered under Rule 155" (prior to 1974, known as *Rule 50*). This notation signifies that the Tax Court has reached a conclusion regarding the facts and issues of the case but leaves the computational aspects of the decision to the opposing parties. Both parties will subsequently submit to the Tax Court their versions of the refund or deficiency computation. If both parties agree on the computation, no further argument is necessary. In the event of disagreement, the Tax Court will reach its decision on the basis of the data presented by each party. Unfortunately, data submitted or arguments heard under Rule 155 are usually not a part of the trial transcript.

Under section 7463, special trial procedures in the Tax Court's Small Tax Case Division are available for disputes involving $50,000 or less.[23] Legal counsel is not required, and taxpayers may represent themselves. Trial procedures are conducted on an informal basis, with the filing of briefs permitted but not required. Only an informal record of the trial proceedings is prepared, and every decision is final, making an appeal from a decision of the Small Tax Case Division of the Tax Court impossible. Although in the past decisions of the Small Tax Case Division have not been published, recently various publishers have started making them available electronically through their Web based research services. However, these decisions may not be cited as precedent in other cases.

U.S. District Courts

The federal judicial system is divided into 13 judicial circuits, as illustrated in figure 4.2. The 11 numbered circuits and the U.S.

---

[22] Section 6214(a).

[23] The $50,000 limitation includes the initial tax contested, potential additional amounts, and penalties. Section 7463(e).

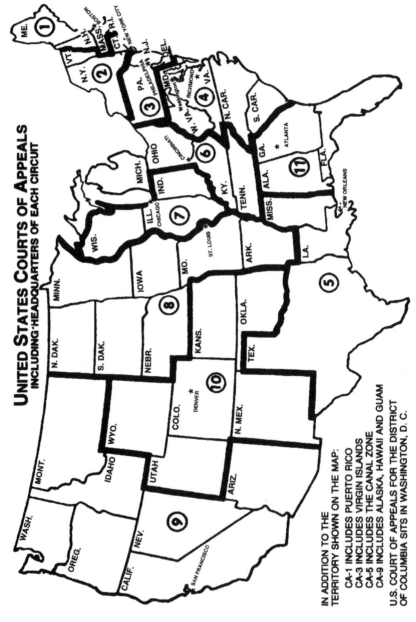

Figure 4.2

UNITED STATES COURTS OF APPEALS
INCLUDING HEADQUARTERS OF EACH CIRCUIT

IN ADDITION TO THE
TERRITORY SHOWN ON THE MAP:

CA-1 INCLUDES PUERTO RICO
CA-3 INCLUDES VIRGIN ISLANDS
CA-5 INCLUDES THE CANAL ZONE
CA-9 INCLUDES ALASKA, HAWAII AND GUAM

U.S. COURT OF APPEALS FOR THE DISTRICT
OF COLUMBIA SITS IN WASHINGTON, D. C.

Court of Appeals for the District of Columbia, which sits in Washington, D.C., have jurisdiction only over issues arising within their own geographical area. The 13th is the Court of Appeals for the Federal Circuit, which is the Court of Appeals for the U.S. Court of Federal Claims. Each of the first 12 circuits is further divided into districts. Each U.S. (or federal) district court has jurisdiction only within its own geographical area and hears, in addition to tax cases, cases involving various other types of civil and criminal issues. Thus, federal district court judges generally are not tax experts. At least one district judge is assigned to each federal district. Depending upon need, however, two or more federal district judges may hear cases in any district. Taxpayers may bring suit in a federal district court only after they have paid a tax, either with the return or as a deficiency assessment, and have processed a request for refund. A U.S. district court is the only court in which a taxpayer can request a jury trial in a tax dispute. Published proceedings of the federal district courts can be found in a primary source published by West Publishing Company, entitled the Federal Supplement (Fed. Supp.) reporter series. District court cases involving tax issues may also be found in a secondary source, such as CCH's *United States Tax Cases* (USTC) or RIA's *American Federal Tax Reports* (AFTR and AFTR 2d) series. Sample citations of district court cases found in these sources are presented in exhibit 4.2.

U.S. Court of Federal Claims

The U.S. Court of Federal Claims handles claims against the U.S. government. Although this court is headquartered in Washington, D.C., it may also hold court in other locations. To file an action in the U.S. Court of Federal Claims, the taxpayer must have paid a tax and subsequently filed a request for refund.

The proceedings of the U.S. Court of Federal Claims and its predecessor courts can be found in various primary and secondary sources.[24] For example, a primary source for proceedings of the U.S. Court of Federal Claims is the *U.S. Court of Federal Claims*

---

[24] Prior to October 29, 1992, the U.S. Court of Federal Claims was known as the *U.S. Claims Court*, which was created in 1982. The predecessor to the U.S. Claims Court was known as the *Court of Claims*.

Exhibit 4.2
Summary of Primary and Secondary Citations

	Primary		Secondary	
	Publisher	Standard Citation	Publisher	Standard Citation
Supreme Court	U.S. Government Printing Office	*Harris v. Comm.,* 340 U.S. 106 (1950)	The Lawyers' Co-Operative Publishing Company	*Harris v. Comm.,* 95 L.Ed. 111
	West Publishing Company	*Harris v. Comm.,* 71 S. Ct. 181 (1950)	RIA	*Harris v. Comm.,* 39 AFTR 1002
			CCH	*Harris v. Comm.,* 1950-2 USTC §10,786
Circuit Courts of Appeal	West Publishing Company	*Salome Jr. v. U.S.,* 395 F.2d 990 (5th Cir. 1968)	RIA	*Salome Jr. v. U.S.,* 22 AFTR, 2d 5039
			CCH	*Salome Jr. v. U.S.,* 1968-2 USTC ¶9440
District Courts	West Publishing Company	*Whittington v. Jones,* 96 F. Supp. 967 (W.D. Okla. 1951)	RIA	*Whittington v. Jones,* 40 AFTR 553
			CCH	*Whittington v. Jones,* 1951-1 USTC ¶9302
Court of Claims	West Publishing Company	*Scott v. U.S.,* 354 F. 2d 292 (Ct. Cl. 1965)	RIA	*Scott v. U.S.,* 16 AFTR, 2d 6087
	U.S. Government Printing Office	*Scott v. U.S.,* 173 Ct. Cl. 650 (1965)	CCH	*Scott v. U.S.,* 1966-1 USTC ¶9169
Claims Court	West Publishing Company	*Raphan v. U.S.,* 3 Cl. Ct. 457 (1983)	RIA	*Raphan v. U.S.,* 52 AFTR 2d 83-5987 (Cl. Ct., 1983)
			CCH	*Raphan v. U.S.,* 83-2 USTC: ¶9613 (Cl. Ct., 1983)

(Fed. Cl.) reporter, published by West Publishing Company. The proceedings of the Claims Court (the name of the U.S. Court of Federal Claims prior to October 29, 1992) can be found in the *United States Claims Court Reporter* (Cl. Ct.) series also published by West Publishing Company. The proceedings of the Court of Claims (the predecessor to the U.S. Claims Court) can be found in the *Court of Claims Reporter* (Ct. Cl.) series, published by the U.S. GPO. In addition, West's *Federal Reporter 2d and 3d* (F.2d and F.3d) series include all Court of Claims cases between 1929 and 1932 and after 1959. From 1932–1960, the Court of Claims cases were published in West's *Federal Supplement* (Fed. Supp.) series. They are also published in CCH's *U.S. Tax Cases* (USTC) and RIA's *American Federal Tax Reports* (AFTR and AFTR 2d).

U.S. Circuit Courts of Appeals

If either the taxpayer or the IRS is dissatisfied with the holding in one of the courts of original jurisdiction, an appeal may be made to one of the circuit courts of appeal. These courts hear appeals of cases dealing with tax, as well as other civil and criminal issues. In addition to the U.S. Court of Appeals for the Federal Circuit (the court to which cases from the U.S. Court of Federal Claims are appealed) and the Court of Appeals for the District of Columbia, the states and U.S. territories are geographically partitioned into judicial circuits numbered from 1–11 (see figure 4.2).[25] Decisions of the Tax Court and a district court may be appealed by either the taxpayer or the government to the circuit court in which the taxpayer resides.

Each circuit court of appeals has jurisdiction within its own geographic area, which can be exercised independently from the other circuits. Thus, with regard to a particular issue, one circuit (for example, the Tenth Circuit, which has jurisdiction over Utah) may have ruled in favor of the taxpayer, while another circuit dealing with the same question involving another taxpayer (for example, the Ninth Circuit, which has jurisdiction over California)

---

[25] The U.S. Court of Appeals for the Federal Circuit was created by P.L. 97-164, effective October 1, 1982.

may have ruled in favor of the government. Because the Tax Court has national jurisdiction, this clear distinction of jurisdiction between circuits can create a dilemma. If a third taxpayer petitions the Tax Court to rule on the same issue, under a doctrine known as the *Golsen rule*, the Tax Court will rule in favor of the taxpayer if the third taxpayer resides in the Tenth Circuit, but will rule in favor of the government if the taxpayer resides in the Ninth Circuit, even though the results are inconsistent between taxpayers. If the third taxpayer resides in another circuit which has not ruled on the issue (for example, the taxpayer lives in Houston, which is covered by the Fifth Circuit), the Tax Court, while taking both the Ninth and the Tenth Circuit decisions into consideration, will rule as it deems appropriate.

The proceedings of the circuit courts are published by West Publishing Company in the *Federal Reporter* (F2d., F3d.) series, by CCH in its USTC reporter, and by RIA in the AFTR and AFTR 2d reporters. Sample citations are found in exhibit 4.2.

U.S. Supreme Court

Final appeals from a circuit court of appeals rest with the U.S. Supreme Court. As previously explained, appeal requires a *writ of certiorari,* which the Supreme Court may or may not grant. Supreme Court decisions are of special importance because they constitute the final judicial authority in tax matters. The Supreme Court decisions can be found in any of the following publications: *United States Supreme Court Reports* (US), published by the GPO; *Supreme Court Reports* (S.Ct.), published by West Publishing Company; *United States Tax Cases* (USTC), published by CCH; and *American Federal Tax Reports* (AFTR and AFTR 2d), published by RIA. They are also published in the *Cumulative Bulletin.* Sample citations are found in exhibit 4.2.

Special Tax Reporter Series

As mentioned previously, all tax decisions rendered by the Supreme Court, the circuit courts of appeals, the Claims Court, and federal district courts are separately published by CCH in the

United States Tax Cases (USTC) series and by RIA in the *American Federal Tax Reports* (AFTR and AFTR 2d) series. Regular Tax Court decisions, which are published by the GPO in the *United States Tax Court Reports* (T.C.), are not included in either the CCH's USTC series or RIA's AFTR series.

Editorial Information

Another substantial body of tax information with which a tax adviser must be familiar is the extensive collection of editorial discussion and comment about the tax law. This body of information is not law and cannot be used as precedent. However, these sources of information often are invaluable to a tax adviser in researching a tax issue, understanding the tax law, and keeping current as the law changes.

In general, four broad categories of editorial information are available to a tax practitioner: tax research services, treatises, journals, and newsletters. Most of these sources are available both in print and electronically. A discussion of every source available in each category is impractical here. Thus, the discussion in this chapter focuses on the characteristics of only some of the more popular and frequently used sources. Chapter 5 contains a discussion and examples of how these sources are accessed and used.

Tax Research Services

In general, tax research services are designed to help the tax adviser locate statutory, administrative, and judicial authority quickly and efficiently and to give helpful editorial interpretations of the tax law. Whether published in printed or electronic form, these services are frequently and regularly updated. Tax research services may be categorized into one of two general types, based upon the way they are organized: those organized by IRC section number (an "annotated" service) and those organized by topic.[26]

---

[26] Additional tools, resources, and information for tax professionals are available on the IRS Web site at www.irs.gov/taxpros/index.html.

Annotated Services. The *Standard Federal Tax Reporter*, published by CCH, and the *United States Tax Reporter*, published by RIA, are two of the most popular annotated services that deal with federal income taxation. As mentioned previously, the materials in these services are organized or grouped by IRC section. These materials include the following:

- The text of the IRC section
- A selected legislative history of changes to the IRC section
- The text of the income tax regulations associated with the IRC section
- A brief explanation of the law contained in the IRC section
- A table of topics covered by the brief summaries (called *annotations*) of administrative law and judicial law dealing with the law covered by the applicable IRC section
- Annotations of relevant items of administrative law and judicial cases dealing with the law covered by the applicable IRC section

These annotated tax services are generally accompanied by separate IRC volumes. Thus, if a researcher is interested in reading only the appropriate IRC section, he or she may find the text of the IRC in two different locations.

The legislative history contained in these annotated tax services includes references to the public laws that have amended the IRC, along with the effective date of the change. The history may also include the language of the IRC as it existed before its amendment. Selected excerpts of the different committee reports that the editors of the service believe are particularly important or necessary may also be included. Generally this occurs when little or no interpretative authority, such as regulations, exists.

As mentioned previously in the discussion about regulations, at times there may be a significant time lag between when an IRC section is amended and when the regulations dealing with that particular IRC section are updated to reflect the change. When this occurs, the publishers of these annotated services include editorial notes or cautions along with the text of the regulations, indicating that the regulation has not been updated for amendments to the IRC. In some cases, the amendment to the IRC may have changed one issue of law contained in the IRC but not other issues dealt with in the same IRC section. Thus, the amendment to the IRC may or may not have changed the interpretation or application of the particular issue of law that the researcher is examining in the regulations. In such cases, the researcher must be able to determine which parts of the regulation are still a correct interpretation of the IRC and which parts are no longer appropriate because of the changes to the IRC. This is done by carefully examining and comparing the amendment with the IRC and its effective date with the issuance date of the regulation.

The explanations associated with each IRC section contain a relatively brief overview and explanation of the applicable law. These explanations may also contain a brief discussion about judicial law and administrative law, such as revenue rulings and revenue procedures that deal with that particular topic. These references enable the tax researcher to identify the specific source of tax law (for example, the court case or revenue ruling) that he or she wants to read and analyze. Although not as detailed as the discussions found in a topically organized tax research service or treatise, these explanations can be helpful in giving the researcher a basic understanding of the law.

The annotations themselves are perhaps one of the real strengths of these annotated tax research services. An annotation is a short summary of the judicial and administrative law that deals with the application of the law in the particular IRC section being researched. By reading these summaries, a tax researcher can quickly identify, for example, which cases, revenue rulings, or revenue procedures may be pertinent to the issues being researched. Because these annotations are only summaries of the underlying law, however, material differences in facts between the case or ruling that is annotated and the fact pattern that the researcher is dealing with may not be apparent from a reading of the annotation alone. Thus, a researcher should always read and analyze the underlying case or ruling itself before citing or using the law as precedent. When used properly, however, these annotations can be powerful tools in helping the researcher become efficient in tax research.

Once the researcher has found a judicial case or item of administrative law such as a revenue ruling or revenue procedure that appears to be relevant to the issue being researched, he or she should always verify that the law has not been overturned, superseded, or amended by subsequent decisions or rulings. This verification is done by checking the citator that is provided by these services. A description of the citator and the process used to check the currency of a particular decision or ruling is found in chapter 5.

A tax researcher may access the information in these annotated services in a variety of ways. If the researcher knows the IRC section that is pertinent to the research being done, he or she may access the information in the service by simply moving to the appropriate location, either by clicking down through the table of contents in the electronic service or, if using the printed service, by choosing the appropriate volume which contains the desired IRC section. If the researcher does not know the IRC section number, he or she may find the information through the topical index. Of course, if the researcher is using the electronic version of the service, he or she may also find the desired information by using an electronic key word search. An example of an electronic search is found in chapter 5.

Topical Services. Several tax research services are organized by topic. One of the strengths of this type of service is that the editorial discussion contained in these services is generally very detailed and thorough. Additionally, these services often contain examples that are helpful in understanding the law. Three popular topical tax research services are the *Tax Management* portfolios published by the Bureau of National Affairs (BNA), RIA's *Federal Tax Coordinator*, and CCH's *Federal Tax Service.*

For many years, the *Tax Management* portfolios published by BNA have been a very popular tax service. This service is available both electronically and in printed form. In printed form, the service consists of dozens of spiral wire bound portfolios that range in length from less than a hundred pages to several hundred pages. Each portfolio deals with a specific tax topic, although not every IRC section has its own portfolio. The material in each portfolio is organized into three major parts. Part A contains a detailed analysis of the subject matter. This analysis is organized in outline format but is written in narrative form, with extensive footnotes to statutory, administrative, and judicial authority. The format of the discussion lends itself to research progressing from general backgrounds through specific problems within the topic. Part B provides helpful working papers, such as sample letters, appropriate tax forms, and illustrations. Part C includes a bibliography of related resource material. The information in the portfolio is preceded by an extensive table of contents in outline format. Additionally, each portfolio is updated periodically by current development sheets, which are placed just in front of the table of contents. The three main portfolio series deal with (1) federal income taxation, (2) federal estate and gift taxation, and (3) U.S. taxation of international transactions. Because each portfolio consists of an extensive in-depth analysis written by an expert in the specific field the portfolio covers, the BNA portfolios are especially helpful when a tax adviser needs an extensive in-depth analysis of the tax law.

RIA's *Federal Tax Coordinator* is another topical service that has enjoyed much popularity over the years. This service, which is available both electronically and in print, contains detailed narrative discussions about the tax law. It also contains the text of the IRC and Regulations. Because it generally discusses a topic in greater detail than an annotated service, it is a nice complementary service to RIA's annotated *United States Tax Reporter*.

In addition to its annotated services, CCH also publishes a topical tax service called the *Federal Tax Service*. Here again, because its discussions are generally more detailed than the discussions in CCH's annotated *Standard Federal Income Tax Reporter*, the two services complement each other. The *Federal Tax Service* covers topics dealing with federal income and estate and gift taxes. One of its strengths is that it contains many examples of how the law is to be interpreted and applied.

Treatises

The tax law is so complex and varied that a tax adviser simply cannot know everything about every facet of the law. Thus, to provide the services a client needs, a tax adviser may be required to do some background study. At times, the adviser may gain enough understanding by reading the explanatory material in the tax research services discussed above. At other times, the adviser may need to refer to a source that discusses the law in even greater detail. Fortunately, many, very good treatises are available. These treatises are generally written by renowned experts in the field and go into great depth about the topic, often explaining the history, theory, and logic of the law. Although there are far too many to mention here, some treatises on specific tax topics have attained significant reputations among tax practitioners. Some of these popular treatises include *Federal Income Taxation of Corporations and Shareholders,* by Bittker and Eustice (Warren, Gorham & Lamont); *Partnership Taxation,* by Willis, Pennell, and Postlewaite (Warren, Gorham & Lamont); and *Federal Income Taxation of Corporations Filing Consolidated Returns,* by Dubroff et al. (Matthew Bender). Information about treatises and other works can be obtained on the Web sites of the major publishers of tax information. Some of these publishers include Matthew Bender (www.bender.com); Warren, Gorham & Lamont (www.wgl.com); RIA (www.riahome. com); and West Group (www.westgroup.com).

Tax Journals

Various journals that deal exclusively with taxation and provide valuable assistance to the tax adviser are available both in print and electronically. Some of these journals are written for the general tax practitioner, and others are written for specialists in a particular field of taxation. For example, the *Journal of Taxation,* published by Warren, Gorham & Lamont, features regular departments dealing with such topics as corporations; estates, trusts, and gifts; exempt institutions; and partnerships. The *Tax Adviser,* published monthly by the AICPA (www.aicpa.org), and *Taxation for Accountants,* published by Warren, Gorham & Lamont, are additional examples of popular tax journals for the general practitioner. Examples of specialized tax journals include the *International Taxation Journal* and the *Journal of Corporate Taxation,* published by Warren, Gorham & Lamont. Because of the number of tax journals published, a discussion of all of them here is impractical. However, information about other tax journals can be obtained on the publishers' Web sites.

To locate articles in these journals, the tax adviser can consult the cumulative indexes provided in the issues of the journals themselves. Another way of locating journal information is through various other indexes, including CCH's *Federal Tax Articles* and Warren, Gorham & Lamont's *Index to Federal Tax Articles*. CCH's *Federal Tax Articles* includes a topical index, an IRC section index, and an author's index. Warren, Gorham & Lamont's *Index to Federal Tax Articles* has a topical and an author index. Alternatively, articles may also be discovered using a key word search using an appropriate electronic service, such as Lexis-Nexis.

Tax Newsletters

Tax newsletters are also excellent sources of tax information dealing with recent developments. Newsletters help keep the tax adviser in touch with the dynamics of the tax laws. Some are published daily, while others are published weekly, biweekly, or monthly. Most are available in both printed and electronic format. A very popular source is Tax Analysts' (www.tax.org) weekly *Tax Notes* or its daily *Tax Notes Today*. Occasionally, in scanning a newsletter, a practitioner spots an item that has relevance to a client's problem. More often, however, the newsletter simply provides the tax practitioner with ideas that may be recalled and used in later work. They are also very useful in keeping abreast of potential future changes in the tax law. Being aware of these potential changes is important to the tax adviser as he or she advises clients on contemplated transactions and business structuring. Virtually every major publisher of tax information publishes newsletters in some form or another. Here again, information about these newsletters can be obtained through the publishers' Web sites.

Summary

Each of the various research services, treatises, journals, and newsletters has its own strengths and weaknesses. There are also differences in their writing style and organization. Thus, some tax advisers prefer working with some of the resources, while others will prefer using the other resources. Because of these differences, at times it may be useful or wise to consult more than one service or other reference. How many research services, treatises, journals, and newsletters a tax adviser should subscribe to is, of course, an individual decision. In spite of their differences, these publications duplicate much of the information. Furthermore, reading or using all of these publications for research would demand too much of a tax adviser's time. The decision must, therefore, be based on the size and nature of the adviser's practice. The larger the firm, the more varied the personalities, and the greater the areas of specialization represented, the greater the variety of subscriptions required.

5

Locating Appropriate Authority

In chapter 4, we discussed primary sources of the tax law, including statutory, administrative, and judicial sources. We also discussed numerous secondary sources of the tax law, such as tax research services, that may be used by tax researchers to understand the tax law and to discover relevant primary sources.

In this chapter, we focus on locating primary and secondary tax law sources. Given recent trends in the availability and attractiveness of Web based tax research tools relative to traditional print media, Web based tax research has become the primary methodology for locating appropriate tax authority. Consequently, we discuss the process, assuming researchers have access to one of these powerful research tools.

Traditionally, the process of locating tax authority required the researcher to pore through multiple volumes of printed material located in a tax or law library. However, in recent years commercial providers have made the same materials accessible by computer, first by direct modem connection to provider databases, then by CD-ROM, and over the past few years, through the World Wide

Web. Using commercial Web based services to locate tax authority offers numerous advantages over using primary and secondary tax law sources in print. For example, Web based services allow researchers to conduct powerful keyword searches in addition to using a table of contents or an index. Also, once they locate a source document, researchers may cut and paste material into a research file or memorandum, as well as quickly access related documents by selecting hypertext links embedded within the original document. Moreover, new tax authority is incorporated into Web based commercial services almost instantaneously. Conversely, there is typically a lag from the time new authority is released until it appears in print. Finally, Web based services free researchers to search for tax authority anywhere they have access to an Internet connection— at a client's office, from a hotel room, or from home. Together, these advantages have generally made the process of locating relevant tax authority more efficient.

Web Based Services

A number of commercial firms currently offer Web based tax subscription services. (See exhibit 5.1 and appendix A for a list of some of these firms along with their Web addresses.) Typically, the services differ by content and cost; the cost is typically proportionate to the level of content provided. In this chapter, we profile

Exhibit 5.1
Commercial Subscription Services

Service	Publisher	Web Address
BNA Tax and Accounting Center	Bureau of National Affairs	www.bnatax.com
CCH Tax Research Network	CCH, a Wolters Kluwer business	tax.cchgroup.com
LexisNexis	LexisNexis, a member of Reed Elsevier Inc.	www.lexisnexis.com
RIA Checkpoint	Thomson Tax & Accounting	checkpoint.riag.com
Tax Analysts	Tax Analysts	www.tax.org
Westlaw	Thomson West	www.westlaw.com

two of the more popular services: CCH's *Tax Research Network* and Thomson's *Checkpoint*.

The major difference between Web based services lies in the content that each provides. Although they all provide the legislative, statutory, administrative, and judicial authority discussed in chapter 4, they differ in the type and amount of editorial and analytical information available. Some Web based services are *aggregators* (that is, they license content from other providers), some offer only their own proprietary content, while others offer a combination. For example, CCH's *Tax Research Network* provides its annotated service *Standard Federal Tax Reporter* and the topical service *Tax Research Consultant*. Similarly, RIA's annotated service *United States Tax Reporter* and topical service *Federal Tax Coordinator* are available on *Checkpoint*. Lexis-Nexis' *lexis.com* provides content licensed from other sources, including the Bureau of National Affairs (BNA). All three Web based services contain treatises, tax journals, and tax newsletters. The differences in content between the *Tax Research Network* and *Checkpoint* are summarized in exhibit 5.2.

Search Strategies

Conceptually, the process involved in locating appropriate tax law authority is essentially the same, no matter which of the Web based

Exhibit 5.2
Web Based Services Content Summary

Content	RIA Checkpoint	CCH Tax Research Network
Primary tax law sources	All primary sources	All primary sources
Annotated services	*United States Tax Reporter*	*Standard Federal Tax Reporter*
Topical services	*Federal Tax Coordinator*	*Tax Research Consultant*
Treatises and journals	Numerous treatises, Warren, Gorham & Lamont tax journals	Several treatises, *Taxes—The Tax Magazine*
Newsletters	*Federal Taxes Weekly Alert*, *RIA Tax Watch*, other specialized newsletters	*CCH Tax Tracker News*

services the researcher uses. However, the actual sequence of steps required may differ somewhat from one service to another. Moreover, each of these providers is constantly upgrading its services— (presumably) improving its functionality and expanding its sources and offerings-so that by the time you read this book, the actual content, as well as the search processes, may have already changed. Therefore, we do not attempt to describe in detail how to execute a search in each of the highlighted services. Instead, we demonstrate each of several generic search strategies using examples from *Checkpoint* and the *Tax Research Network* to illustrate the process.

Finding a Known Primary Authority

Any of the types of primary authority discussed in chapter 4— statutory, administrative, or judicial—as well as a particular statute's legislative history may be found if researchers know the appropriate citation. By entering the citation in the template provided within *Checkpoint* and the *Tax Research Network*, the desired document may be read, printed, or saved for later use. Exhibits 5.3–5.4 show the templates found in both services.[1] Due to the template design used in *Checkpoint* and *CCH Tax Research Network*, researchers may locate a particular primary source even when they may not know the exact citation.[2]

As an example of how to retrieve a document using this approach, suppose a researcher wants to locate a circuit court of appeals case called ACM but does not know the citation for the case. As long as the researcher knows the case name, the case can be retrieved using any of the Web based services. Exhibits 5.5–5.8 demonstrate the particular steps a researcher would follow to locate the ACM case using the *Checkpoint* service.

---

[1] The citation templates for the *Tax Research Network* are formatted onto one Web page. In *Checkpoint,* however, the researcher must select from multiple citation templates depending on the type of document to be retrieved. Exhibit 5.3 displays the *Cases* citation template for *Checkpoint.*

[2] Chapter 4 illustrates the correct citation formats for various types of statutory, administrative, and judicial tax authorities.

Exhibit 5.3
Checkpoint Citations Search Template

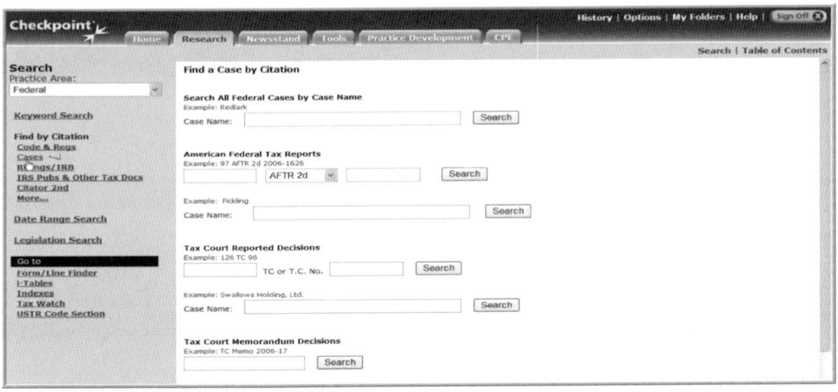

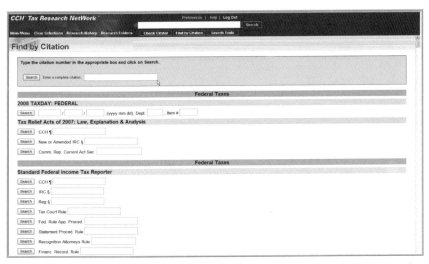

Select specific **Find by Citation** link within Research tab.

Exhibit 5.4
CCH Tax Research Network Citation Search Template

Select **Find by Citation** button from the main menu.

Exhibit 5.5
Step 1: Finding a Case by Case Name

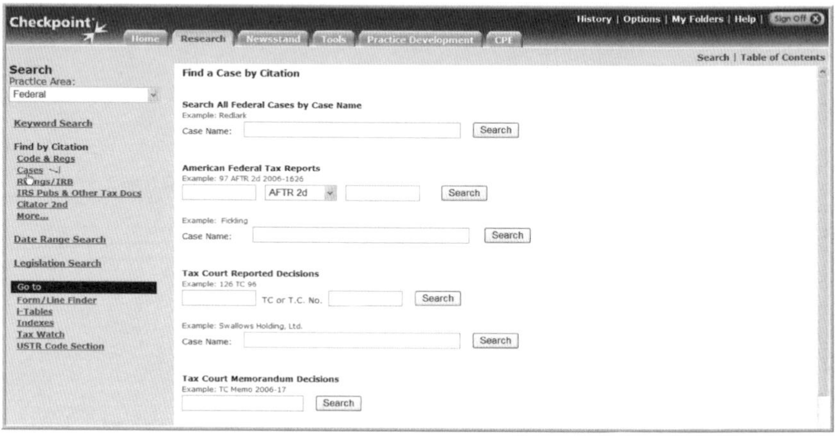

Select **Cases** link from with the Research tab.

Exhibit 5.6
Step 2: Finding a Case by Case Name

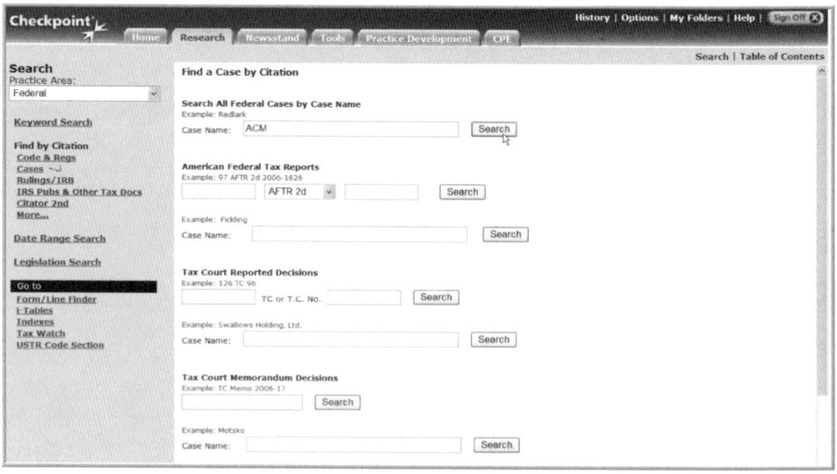

Enter **ACM** as case name before selecting **Search** button.

Exhibit 5.7
Step 3: Finding a Case by Case Name

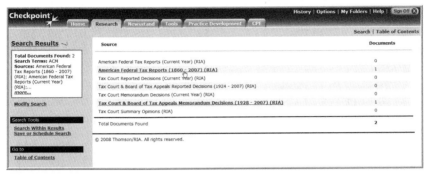

Select **American Federal Tax Reports** link.

Exhibit 5.8
Step 4: Finding a Case by Case Name

Select the appropriate case.

Using a Table of Contents to Locate Authority

If researchers are unfamiliar with what primary authority might apply to their research question, they might begin by consulting one of the annotated or topical services discussed in chapter 4. *Checkpoint* and *CCH Tax Research Network* permit researchers to search their annotated and topical services using a table of contents. To illustrate how a table of contents might be used, let us assume a researcher wants to determine when corporate distributions are treated for tax purposes as dividends. If the researcher knows only that Section 301 of the Internal Revenue Code (IRC) might apply, he or she could consult the table of contents for an annotated service, such as the *Standard Federal Tax Reporter*. Because the tables of contents for annotated services are organized by IRC section, he or she could quickly locate an explanation pertaining to Section 301 in the *Tax Research Network* using the steps illustrated in exhibits 5.9–5.15. (Note that the pointer position in each exhibit indicates which button must be selected when using the service to move to the next step in the sequence.) Once the appropriate explanation is located, the researcher may then move to related IRC sections, regulations, and annotations by selecting the buttons at the top of the explanation.

Searching by table of contents is not limited to editorial information. *Checkpoint* and the *Tax Research Network* provide tables of contents for selected sources of statutory and administrative authority. Returning to the prior example, if the researcher wanted to read Section 301 before consulting any editorial information, he or she could locate Section 301 using a table of contents. The pointer in exhibits 5.16–5.28 illustrates the steps he or she would take using the Checkpoint service. Once the IRC language is located, the researcher has the option to move to related editorial information, administrative authority, and legislative history by simply selecting one of the shaded boxes.

Exhibit 5.9
Step 1: Using a Table of Contents to Locate Editorial Information

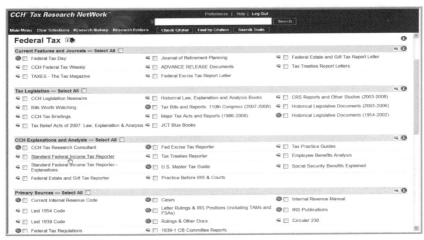

Exhibit 5.10
Step 2: Using a Table of Contents to Locate Editorial Information

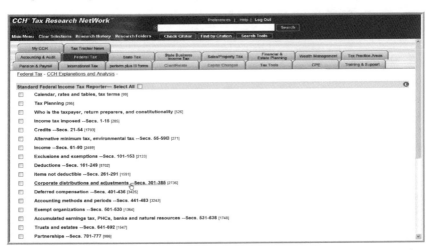

Exhibit 5.11
Step 3: Using a Table of Contents to Locate Editorial Information

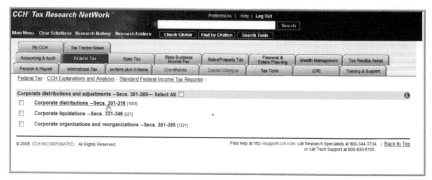

Click on **Corporate distributions—Secs. 301–318** (top screen); then click on **Distributions of property—Sec. 301** on the resulting screen (bottom screen).

Exhibit 5.12
Step 4: Using a Table of Contents to Locate Editorial Information

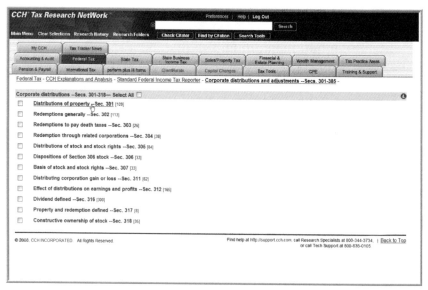

Exhibit 5.13
Step 5: Using a Table of Contents to Locate Editorial Information

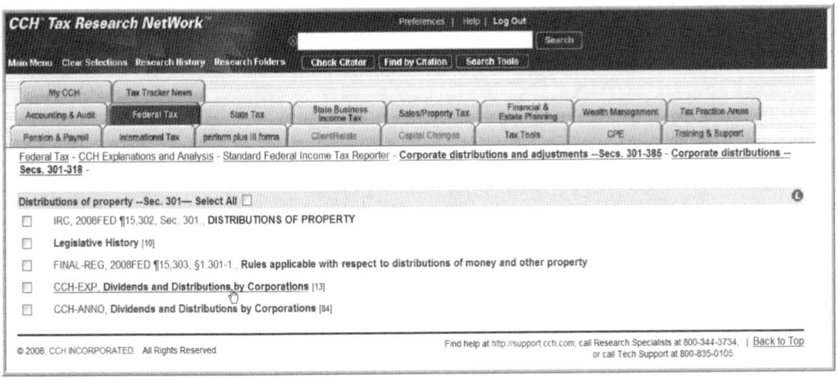

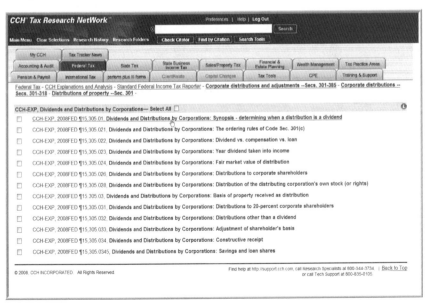

© 2008, CCH Incorporated, a Wolters Kluwer Business. All Rights Reserved. Reprinted with permission from CCH Tax Research Network.

Exhibit 5.14
Step 6: Using a Table of Contents to Locate Editorial Information

Exhibit 5.15
Step 7: Using a Table of Contents to Locate Editorial Information

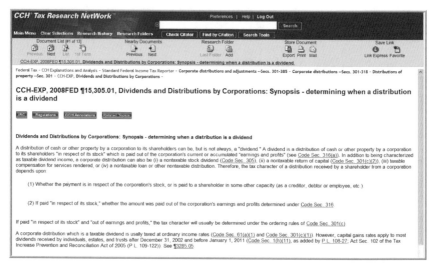

Exhibit 5.16
Step 1: Using a Table of Contents to Find Statutory Authority

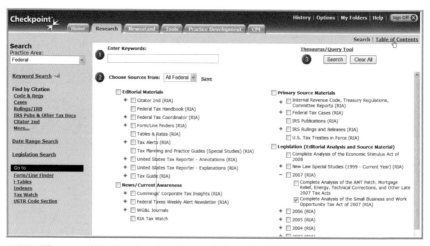

Exhibit 5.17
Step 2: Using a Table of Contents to Find Statutory Authority

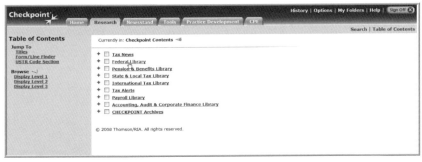

Exhibit 5.18
Step 3: Using a Table of Contents to Find Statutory Authority

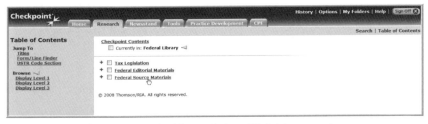

Exhibit 5.19
Step 4: Using a Table of Contents to Find Statutory Authority

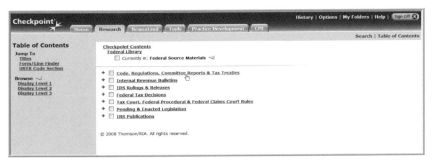

Exhibit 5.20
Step 5: Using a Table of Contents to Find Statutory Authority

Exhibit 5.21
Step 6: Using a Table of Contents to Find Statutory Authority

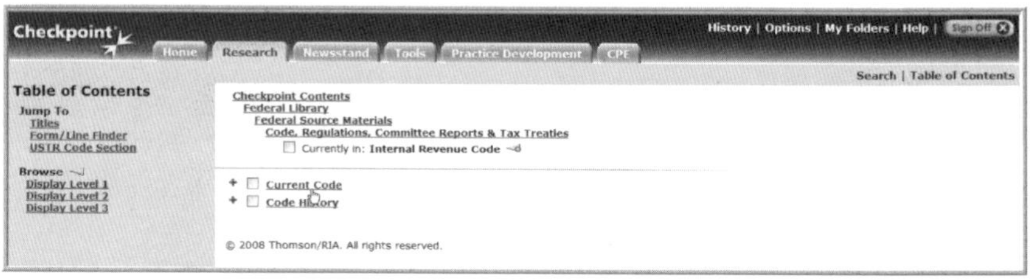

Exhibit 5.22
Step 7: Using a Table of Contents to Find Statutory Authority

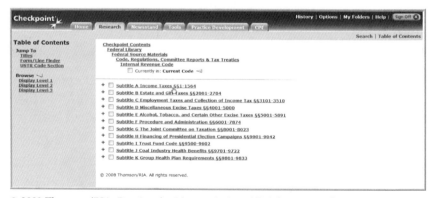

Exhibit 5.23
Step 8: Using a Table of Contents to Find Statutory Authority

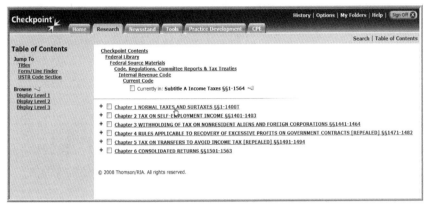

© 2008 Thomson/RIA. Reprinted with permission. All rights reserved.

Exhibit 5.24
Step 9: Using a Table of Contents to Find Statutory Authority

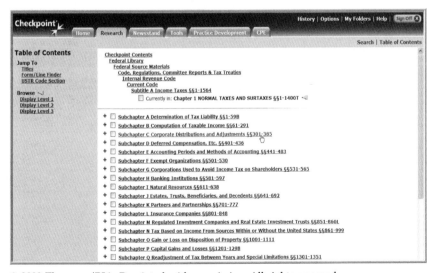

© 2008 Thomson/RIA. Reprinted with permission. All rights reserved.

Exhibit 5.25
Step 10: Using a Table of Contents to Find Statutory Authority

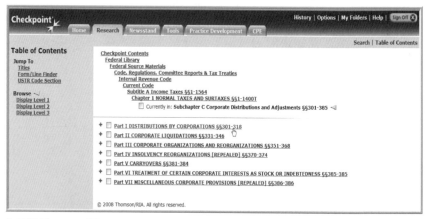

Exhibit 5.26
Step 11: Using a Table of Contents to Find Statutory Authority

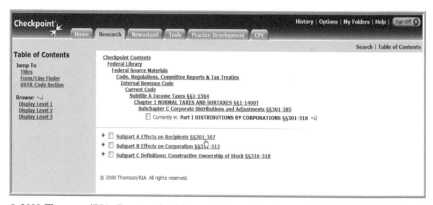

Exhibit 5.27
Step 12: Using a Table of Contents to Find Statutory Authority

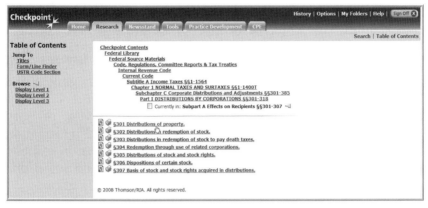

Exhibit 5.28
Step 13: Using a Table of Contents to Find Statutory Authority

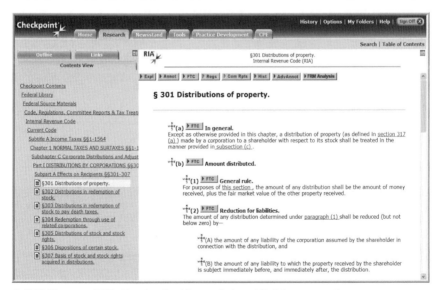

Using an Index to Locate Editorial Information

The annotated and topical services found in the *Checkpoint* and *CCH Tax Research Network* services may also be searched by using a topical index. This would be an appropriate strategy for researchers who may not know which IRC section applies to their research issue. Again, if the research question concerns the taxability of corporate distributions, the researcher might initially consult the *Tax Research Consultant* within the *Tax Research Network* to help identify the relevant issues and to locate the relevant primary authorities. The steps he or she would take to find information on corporate distributions using the index are shown in exhibits 5.29–5.32. From the final screen, the researcher would select one of the hyperlinks to access the related editorial information.

Exhibit 5.29
Step 1: Using an Index to Find Editorial Information

© 2008, CCH Incorporated, a Wolters Kluwer Business. All Rights Reserved. Reprinted with permission from CCH Tax Research Network.

Exhibit 5.30
Step 2: Using an Index to Find Editorial Information

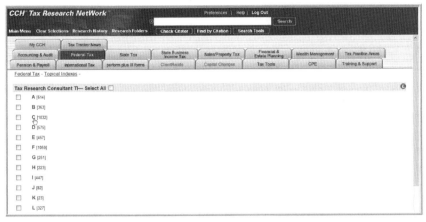

© 2008, CCH Incorporated, a Wolters Kluwer Business. All Rights Reserved. Reprinted with permission from CCH Tax Research Network.

Exhibit 5.31
Step 3: Using an Index to Find Editorial Information

CCH Tax Research NetWork	Preferences | Help | Log Out
Main Menu Clear Selections Research History Research Folders Check Citator Find by Citation Search Tools	
TOP-INDX, TAX RESEARCH CONSULTANT, CORPORATE AIRCRAFT See AIR TRANSPORTATION, EMPLOYER-PROVIDED	
TOP-INDX, TAX RESEARCH CONSULTANT, CORPORATE ATTRIBUTION RULES	
TOP-INDX, TAX RESEARCH CONSULTANT, CORPORATE BONDS	
TOP-INDX, TAX RESEARCH CONSULTANT, CORPORATE BYLAWS	
TOP-INDX, TAX RESEARCH CONSULTANT, CORPORATE CHARITABLE CONTRIBUTIONS	
TOP-INDX, TAX RESEARCH CONSULTANT, CORPORATE CHARTERS	
TOP-INDX, TAX RESEARCH CONSULTANT, CORPORATE CONSOLIDATIONS See CONSOLIDATIONS	
TOP-INDX, TAX RESEARCH CONSULTANT, CORPORATE DEBT INSTRUMENTS	
TOP-INDX, TAX RESEARCH CONSULTANT, CORPORATE DIRECTORS	
TOP-INDX, TAX RESEARCH CONSULTANT, CORPORATE DISSOLUTIONS	
TOP-INDX, TAX RESEARCH CONSULTANT, CORPORATE DISTRIBUTIONS	
TOP-INDX, TAX RESEARCH CONSULTANT, CORPORATE DIVISIONS	
TOP-INDX, TAX RESEARCH CONSULTANT, CORPORATE EARNINGS AND PROFITS See EARNINGS AND PROFITS	
TOP-INDX, TAX RESEARCH CONSULTANT, CORPORATE ENTITY, DISREGARD OF See DISREGARD OF CORPORATE ENTITY	
TOP-INDX, TAX RESEARCH CONSULTANT, CORPORATE EQUITY REDUCTION TRANSACTIONS (CERT)	
TOP-INDX, TAX RESEARCH CONSULTANT, CORPORATE EXECUTIVES See CORPORATE OFFICERS AND EXECUTIVES	
TOP-INDX, TAX RESEARCH CONSULTANT, CORPORATE FILES ON-LINE (CFOL)	
TOP-INDX, TAX RESEARCH CONSULTANT, CORPORATE FORM	
TOP-INDX, TAX RESEARCH CONSULTANT, CORPORATE INVERSIONS	
TOP-INDX, TAX RESEARCH CONSULTANT, CORPORATE MERGERS See MERGERS	
TOP-INDX, TAX RESEARCH CONSULTANT, CORPORATE MINUTES	
TOP-INDX, TAX RESEARCH CONSULTANT, CORPORATE NAME	

© 2008, CCH Incorporated, a Wolters Kluwer Business. All Rights Reserved. Reprinted with permission from CCH Tax Research Network.

Exhibit 5.32
Step 4: Using an Index to Find Editorial Information

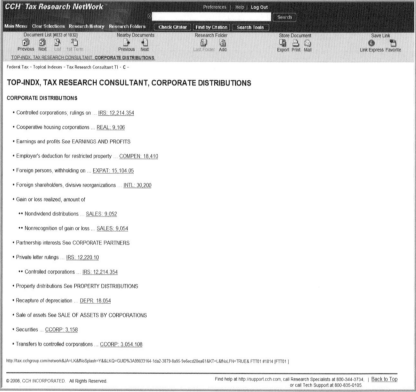

© 2008, CCH Incorporated, a Wolters Kluwer Business. All Rights Reserved. Reprinted with permission from CCH Tax Research Network.

Using a Keyword Search

The search strategies previously discussed rely heavily on tables of contents or topical indexes created by the editors of the Web based services. In that sense, the process of locating tax authority using a Web based service is similar to that using a service in print. However, the tax researcher may truly harness the power of a Web based service by creating his or her own index. The researcher creates a search request, or query formulation, to access documents in a Web based service; the search proceeds using the exact words the researcher chooses. Therefore, the researcher relies on an index he or she creates specifically for the fact situation underlying the research effort rather than on a subject index created by someone else.

All Web based services organize primary authority and editorial information into various source databases. (Exhibit 5.2 indicates the content available in *Checkpoint* and the *Tax Research Network*.)

To locate the desired information, the researcher must (1) determine which database is likely to contain the material he or she is seeking and (2) enter the appropriate search request. The search request includes any words or phrases that the user expects to find in the relevant documents. The system searches all files in the database for those particular words or phrases and displays citations for the documents that include the specific terms in the correct grammatical relationship. At this point, the researcher may view any of the documents satisfying the search criteria, save them to disk, or print them.

Formulating a Search Request

Although researchers using a Web based service are not forced to rely on a service-provided table of contents or topical index to initiate the research process, they still depend on the words and phrases used by the author of the particular document. Only documents that match the search request exactly are retrieved. Thus, perhaps the greatest challenge to the effective use of a Web based service is developing the ability to formulate a meaningful research query. A user ill-informed of efficient search techniques runs the risk of accessing many irrelevant documents or missing relevant documents.

Issues

As in any method of tax research, the success of a search using a Web based service is largely dependent on how well the user has defined the tax issues. For illustration purposes, assume the following situation:

Example 5.1. A client has approached a tax adviser with a question relating to corporate distributions of property. Specifically, the tax adviser is asked to determine how a distribution of property with a built-in loss would affect a corporation and its shareholders.

The first step in researching this case is to properly define the issues. Defining the issues is simplified when the issues are couched in question form. For example, the issues in the preceding situation could be stated as follows:

1. Is the built-in loss from the distributed property recognized by the distributing corporation?
2. What is the effect of the distribution on the distributing corporation's earnings and profits?
3. Should the distribution be treated as a dividend by the shareholders?
4. What will be the shareholder's tax basis in the property received?

When the issues have been sufficiently defined, the tax adviser can begin to choose the terms or phrases that best describe the issue.

Terms or Phrases

Knowledge of the issue and area helps to identify appropriate terms or keywords. After selecting an appropriate database, the researcher might perform an initial search with the term *distributions*. Variations in the keyword syntax required by *Checkpoint* and the *Tax Research Network* are reflected in exhibit 5.33. Using this particular search term, every document in the selected database with the keyword *distribution* or *distributions* would be returned because all the Web based services discussed here automatically search for both the singular and plural variations of keywords. If, instead, the researcher wanted to search for the keyword *distributions* and variations of the keyword, such as *distribute,* he or she could change the keyword to include a wildcard character in the

Exhibit 5.33
Keyword Syntax for Web Based Services

	RIA Checkpoint	CCH Internet Tax Research Network
Terms or Phrases:		
Find term	distributions	distributions
Find term variations	distribut*	distribut!
Find exact phrase	"corporate distributions"	corporate distributions
Logical Connectors:		
Find all terms	corporate **AND** distributions	corporate **AND** distributions
Find either term	corporate **OR** distributions	corporate **OR** distributions
Proximity Connectors:		
Term within *n* words of each other	corporate / **20** distributions	corporate **w/20** distributions
Term within the same sentence	corporate / **s** distributions	corporate **w/sen** distributions
Term within the same paragraph	corporate / **p** distributions	corporate **w/par** distributions

search term. Using this strategy, the new search term using *Checkpoint* would be *distribut** (see exhibit 5.33).

Either search strategy would likely return many irrelevant documents. To refine the search, the researcher might consider modifying the search query to include a phrase instead of a single term. For example, using the phrase *"corporate distributions"* as a query in *Checkpoint* would return only those documents in the database with the exact phrases *"corporate and distributions"* or *"corporate distributions"* (see exhibit 5.33).[3] Exhibits 5.34–5.35 illustrate how to execute this particular search using *Checkpoint* to query the Federal Tax Coordinator database. Exhibit 5.36 displays the results of the search.

---

[3] *Checkpoint* uses what is known as a Folio search process whereas *CCH Tax Research Network* uses a Boolean search process. In most instances, the differences between the two processes are minor. However, the Folio search engine would interpret the query *corporate distributions* as a request to return all documents with the words *corporate* and *distributions*. To search for an exact phrase with *Checkpoint*, the researcher must enclose the phrase in quotations (see exhibit 5.33).

Exhibit 5.34
Step 1: Using a Keyword Search to Find Editorial Information

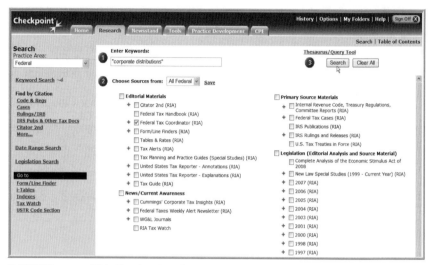

Select **Federal Tax Coordinator** database, enter keywords, and select **Search** button.

Exhibit 5.35
Step 2: Using a Keyword Search to Find Editorial Information

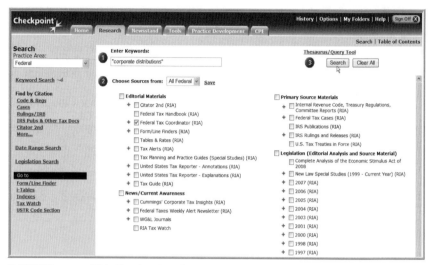

Select **Federal Tax Coordinator** link.

Exhibit 5.36
Step 3: Using a Keyword Search to Find Editorial Information

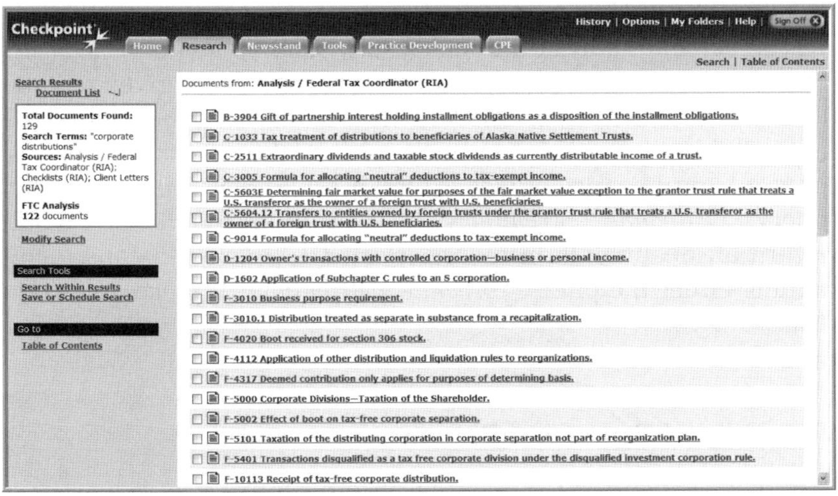

View list of documents containing search phrase.

Logical Connectors

Searching with the terms or phrases alone may return many irrelevant documents. Therefore, the researcher may need to refine the search. Researchers use connectors to properly link terms or phrases. Connectors allow the search terms to be arranged so the computer retrieves only relevant documents.

Some of the possible components of a research request have already been identified in our discussion of the tax issues. For example, in writing a tax opinion of a case dealing with property distributions to corporate shareholders, a judge might use the term *corporate*. However, a search of a tax database that is based solely on the term corporate yields far too many documents, many of which are irrelevant to our situation. *Corporate* used in isolation, therefore, is not an efficient choice of terms. The researcher, by using both *corporate* and *distributions* in the search query, may reduce the amount of irrelevant documents accessed by Web based services. In the *Tax Research Network,* the search request " *'corporate'* and *'distributions' "* would yield only the documents in the database containing both search terms (see exhibit 5.33). To further narrow the number of documents retrieved by Web based services, the researcher may add additional terms, such as *loss* or *shareholder*. However, the researcher also must be aware that if a given research query is too exclusive, relevant documents may be missed. To expand the number of documents found, the researcher may use or as a logical connector (see exhibit 5.33). For example, the search query *" 'corporate distributions'* or *'property distributions' "* would return all documents in the designated *Checkpoint* database containing either the phrase *corporate distributions* or *property distributions.*

Proximity of Terms and Phrases

Another element of formulating an efficient search request is to identify how close together the words in the search request must be for the document to be relevant. For example, a document that discusses distributions on the first page of the document and property on the 20th page of the document may not be relevant to a search. However, if the two terms are discussed within the same sentence or paragraph, it is more likely that the document is relevant.

Proximity in Web based services is specified with the use of proximity connectors. Proximity connectors are terms or words used to link together the keywords or phrases in the search request. Connectors allow the researcher to specify the distance between the terms that he or she will allow for a document to be retrieved. In our example, suppose the tax adviser decides that any document that contains the terms *property* and *distributions* within close proximity should be examined. With the appropriate proximity connector, the researcher may isolate those documents in which the two terms are, for example, within 20 words of each other, within the same sentence, or within the same paragraph. By using the proper connectors or combination of connectors displayed in exhibit 5.33, the researcher can custom-fit the search request and examine only those documents in which the occurrence of *property* and *distributions* meets the specified requirements.

Scope

Limiting the scope of search queries is another method for reducing the number of irrelevant documents retrieved from a keyword search. One way of limiting the scope of a keyword search is by narrowing the search to the specific databases that will yield the most pertinent documents. Specifically, if the researcher is interested in administrative rulings, accessing only the database containing administrative authority may reduce the number of retrieved documents. To illustrate, suppose the researcher, in attempting to resolve the research questions posed in example 5.1, wanted to only view revenue rulings containing the phrase *corporate distributions*. The steps required to select the correct database, execute the search, and review the search results in *Checkpoint* are shown in exhibits 5.37–5.41.

The *Tax Research Network* and *Checkpoint* offer additional methods for limiting the scope of search queries. For example, both services permit researchers to retrieve documents published within a specified date range using either options embedded in their search

Exhibit 5.37
Step 1: Using a Keyword Search to Find Administrative Authority

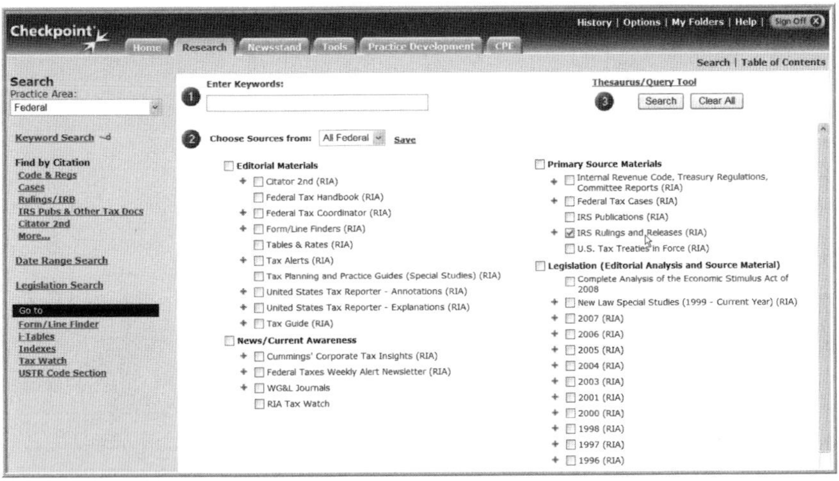

Select **Primary Source Materials: IRS Rulings and Releases**.

Exhibit 5.38
Step 2: Using a Keyword Search to Find Administrative Authority

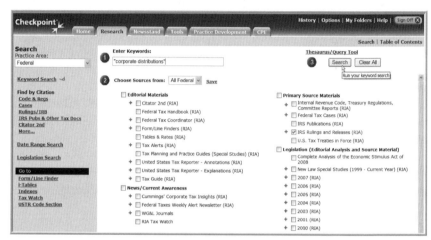

Enter keywords **"corporate distributions"**; then select **Search**.

Exhibit 5.39
Step 3: Using a Keyword Search to Find Administrative Authority

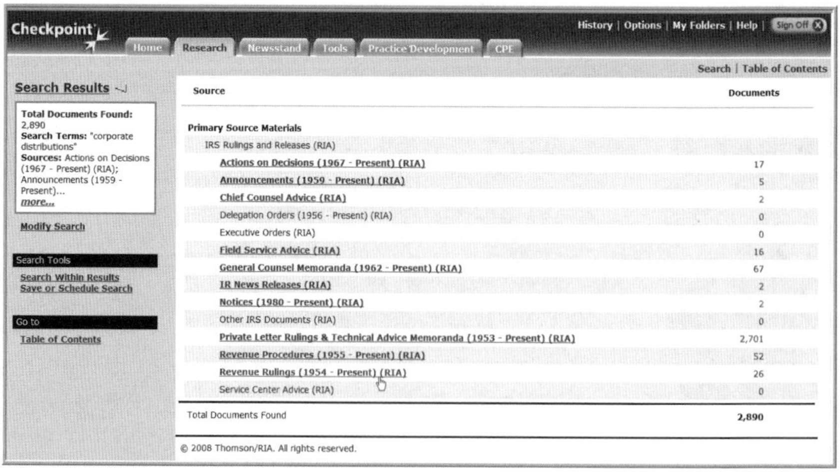

Click on **Revenue Rulings** link.

Exhibit 5.40
Step 4: Using a Keyword Search to Find Administrative Authority

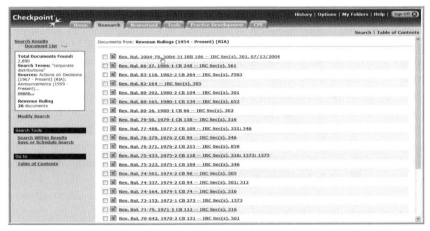

Select **Revenue Ruling 2004-79.**

Exhibit 5.41
Step 5: Using a Keyword Search to Find Administrative Authority

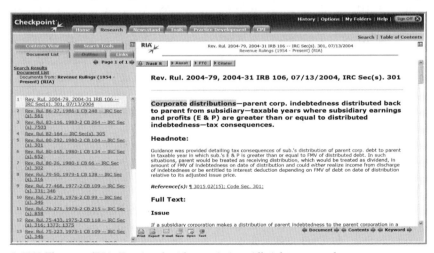

View **Revenue Ruling 2004-79.**

templates or by selectively searching a table of contents. This search strategy might be useful, for example, if the researcher wanted to view only revenue rulings with the phrase corporate distributions published after 1984.

The *Tax Research Network* search templates also give researchers the option to limit their keyword searches to certain document segments. To illustrate, if a researcher wanted to use a keyword search to locate a particular case using the case name as the search query, he or she could search more efficiently by limiting the scope of the search to the case name segment of the cases in the desired database. If he or she did not limit the scope of the search in this way, the search would not only retrieve the case she had been seeking, but also any cases citing the desired case.

Combining Search Strategies

Phrases, logical connectors, proximity connectors, and scope limitations may also be used in combination to execute sophisticated search strategies. For example, attempting to answer the research questions raised earlier, a tax researcher might apply the search query " 'corporate distributions' and 'property w/20 loss' " to the private letter rulings database in the *Tax Research Network*. This search query returns all private letter rulings with the phrase *corporate distributions* and the term *property* within 20 words of the term *loss*.

Although the major keyword search strategies described above apply equally to *Checkpoint* and the *CCH Tax Research Network*, (see exhibit 5.33 for differences in keyword syntax), they both offer additional keyword search capabilities. Web based service users should consult the documentation provided with services for information on these capabilities.

Validating Tax Law Authority

Once a researcher has located what appears to be the relevant tax authorities that deal with the tax question being examined, the authority needs to be reviewed to confirm that the cited authority is still a valid precedent. Judicial cases are often appealed and overturned. More recent court cases may be decided that disagree with the case that the researcher has identified. The steps of thorough tax research should always include updating the research results.

The tax researcher who must consider judicial authority has a very useful tool at his or her disposal: a citator, which is simply a compilation of cross-references to judicial decisions.[4] Following the initial entry of each judicial proceeding in an alphabetical sequence, a citator includes later cross-references to additional citations—that is, to other cases—that in some way contain a reference to the initial entry. To illustrate, assume that only five judicial decisions have ever been rendered (those being *Able, Baker, Charlie, Daley,* and *Evert,* in chronological order). Assume further that the court in *Baker* made some mention of the *Able* decision. In this instance, the *Able* decision would be referred to as the cited case and the *Baker* decision as the citing case. In addition, assume that the court in *Daley* made some reference to the decisions in *Able* and *Charlie,* but not to *Baker;* and that the court in *Evert* made reference only to the decision in *Baker.* Given these assumptions, a complete citator could be prepared as follows:

Able (initial citation)
...*Baker* (cross-reference to page in *Baker* that "cites" *Able*)
...*Daley* (cross-reference to page in *Daley* that "cites" *Able*)

Baker (initial citation)
...*Evert* (cross-reference to page in *Evert* that "cites" *Baker*)

Charlie (initial citation)
...*Daley* (cross-reference to page in *Daley* that "cites" *Charlie*)

Daley (initial citation)

Evert (initial citation)

Obviously, there are thousands of judicial decisions and many thousands of cross-references. If there were no citators, it would be virtually impossible to locate much of the pertinent judicial

---

[4] When relevant, citators also indicate whether the IRS has issued an acquiescence or nonacquiescence for a given case.

authority on most tax questions. With citators available, the task is at least feasible.

The use of the citator databases included in the Web based services profiled in this chapter can result in significant efficiencies relative to using the equivalent citators in print. When citating[5] older cases, researchers need not consult multiple volumes of citator services to locate all citing cases. Further, researchers using Web based services may cite a particular case while reading the case simply by selecting an available hyperlink. Finally, a researcher may read one of the citing cases listed in the citator by simply selecting the citing case. Once the citing case has been examined, the researcher may quickly return to the original case. These advantages explain why citator databases included with Web based services have all but replaced the equivalent citators in print.

Citator Databases

The *Tax Research Network* and *Checkpoint* both contain citator databases. The *Tax Research Network* provides the CCH *Citator* and *Checkpoint* provides the RIA *Citator 2d*. These citator databases differ along several important dimensions. For example, the CCH *Citator* contains only those citing cases dating 1913 forward that the editors consider important in determining a particular case's validity. In contrast, the RIA *Citator 2d* includes all citing cases from 1954 forward.

At first blush, this might suggest that the CCH *Citator* would be more useful when researchers have limited time to review the citing cases. However, the RIA *Citator 2d* provides explanations next to citing cases indicating how the citing cases treated the cited case, such as whether the citing case followed, distinguished, or reversed the cited case. Moreover, the RIA *Citator 2d* permits researchers to determine whether citing cases make reference to the cited case with regard to a particular issue discussed in the cited case. Because of the additional explanatory information provided in the RIA *Citator 2d* it is generally considered to be more useful than

---

[5] This is a term used in tax practice to refer to the process of validating a tax law source using a citator.

the CCH *Citator* in efficiently determining the validity of a cited case.

Searching Citator Databases

Regardless of which citator database a researcher may access, the process involved in verifying the validity of judicial authority is similar across the various citator databases. For example, suppose the researcher would like to cite *ACM Partnership v. Commissioner*, 157 F. 3d 231. The sequence of steps required to cite this case using *Checkpoint* and the *Tax Research Network* are displayed in exhibits 5.42–5.45, and 5.46–5.49, respectively.

To properly interpret the results of the search process, the researcher must understand how each citator organizes the results. The RIA Citator 2d lists the prior history of the case first, then citing cases are listed by treatment and within treatment by court in chronological order.[6] In contrast, the CCH Citator designates the

Exhibit 5.42
Step 1: Validating a Case Using *Checkpoint*

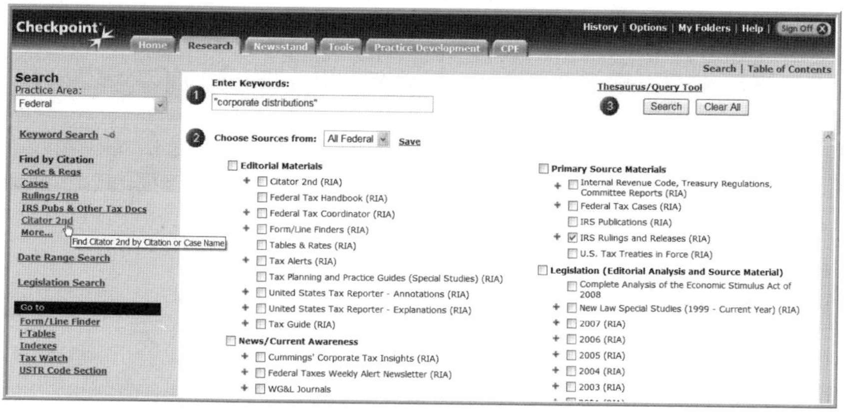

Select **Citator 2nd**.

---

[6] In addition to citing cases, RIA *Citator 2d* also lists any administrative tax law sources citing the case being examined. The same is true for the CCH *Citator*.

Exhibit 5.43
Step 2: Validating a Case Using *Checkpoint*

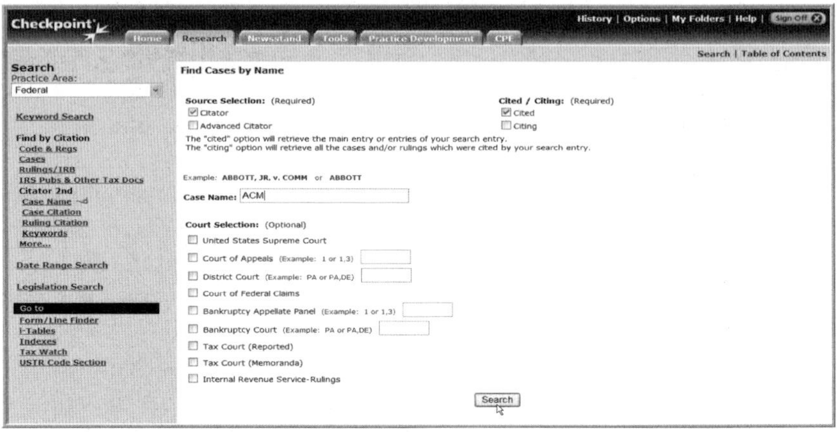

Type **ACM** in the **Case Name** box. Then click on the **Search** button.

Exhibit 5.44
Step 3: Validating a Case Using *Checkpoint*

Select the appropriate case.

Exhibit 5.45
Step 4: Validating a Case Using *Checkpoint*

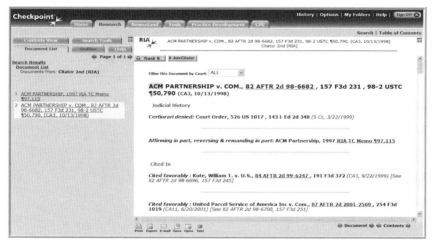

View search results.

Exhibit 5.46
Step 1: Validating a Case Using the *Tax Research Network*

Click on **Check Citator** button.

Exhibit 5.47
Step 2: Validating a Case Using the *Tax Research Network*

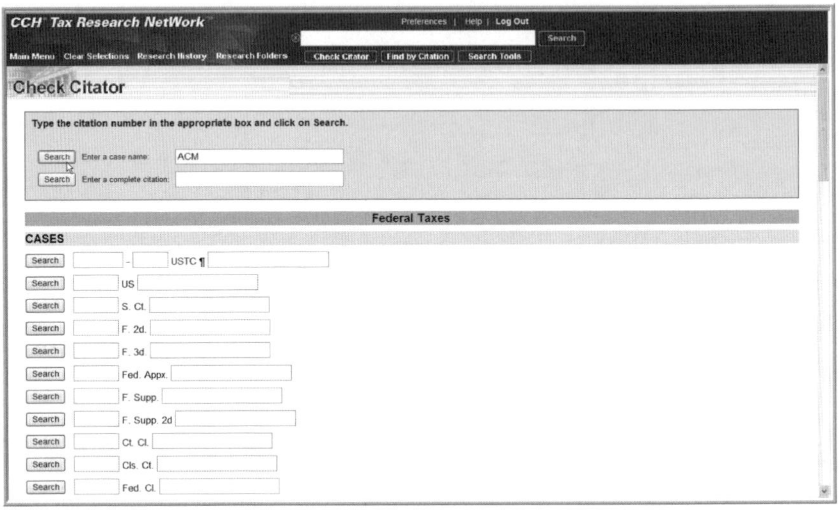

© 2008, CCH Incorporated, a Wolters Kluwer Business. All Rights Reserved. Reprinted with permission from CCH Tax Research Network.

Type **ACM** in case name box. Then click on **Search** button.

Exhibit 5.48
Step 3: Validating a Case Using the *Tax Research Network*

© 2008, CCH Incorporated, a Wolters Kluwer Business. All Rights Reserved. Reprinted with permission from CCH Tax Research Network.

Select the appropriate case.

Exhibit 5.49
Step 4: Validating a Case Using the *Tax Research Network*

CCH Tax Research NetWork · Preferences | Help | Log Out

Main Menu Clear Selections Research History Research Folders   Check Citator   Find by Citation   Search Tools

Search Results [#1 of 2]   Nearby Documents   Research Folder   Store Document   Save Link

CCH-CITATOR, 2008FED, Main Citator Table, ACM Partnership

CCH-CITATOR, 2008FED, Main Citator Table, ACM Partnership

ACM Partnership

ANNOTATED AT   2008FED ¶12,177.65, ¶25,062.26, ¶29,226.382

- SCt--Cert. denied, 3/22/99

- CA-3--(aff'g, rev'g and rem'g TC), 98-2 USTC ¶50,790; 157 F3d 231

  Coltec Industries, Inc., CA-FC, 2006-2 USTC ¶50,389, 454 F3d 1340

  Dow Chemical Co., CA-6, 2006-1 USTC ¶50,126, 435 F3d 594

  CM Holdings, Inc., CA-3, 2002-2 USTC ¶50,596, 301 F3d 96

  Neonatology Associates, P.A., CA-3, 2002-2 USTC ¶50,550, 299 F3d 221

  Strangi Est., CA-5, 2002-2 USTC ¶60,441, 293 F3d 279

  Compaq Computer Corp., CA-5, 2002-1 USTC ¶50,144, 277 F3d 778

  Saba Partnership, CA-DC, 2002-1 USTC ¶50,145, 273 F3d 1135

  United Parcel Service of America, Inc., CA-11, 2001-2 USTC ¶50,475, 254 F3d 1014

  Kute, CA-3, 99-2 USTC ¶50,853, 191 F3d 371

  Stoecker, CA-7, 2000-1 USTC ¶50,494, 179 F3d 546

View search results.

cases constituting the prior history of the case using a bold bullet point and lists them separately. In general, citing cases are listed in reverse chronological order.

Validating Administrative Authority

Administrative authority, such as revenue rulings and revenue procedures, should be validated just as court cases because revenue rulings and revenue procedures are often modified, superseded, or revoked. Fortunately, all the citator databases discussed previously allow the researcher to accomplish this task. (Recall the process for locating a revenue ruling shown in exhibits 5.37–5.41.)

The researcher may quickly check the validity of the ruling from within *Checkpoint*. The required steps are shown in exhibits 5.50–5.52. The processes required to achieve the same results using the *Tax Research Network* are very similar. The results of the search indicate that the revenue ruling is still valid since it has not been cited by subsequent revenue rulings.

Exhibit 5.50
Step 1: Validating Administrative Authority with *Checkpoint*

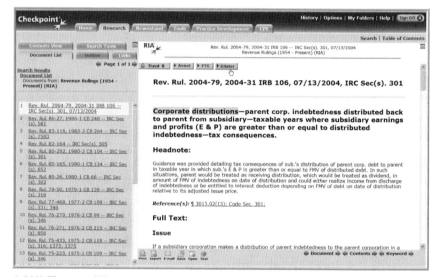

© 2008 Thomson/RIA. Reprinted with permission. All rights reserved.

From within the document, select **Citator**.

Exhibit 5.51
Step 2: Validating Administrative Authority with *Checkpoint*

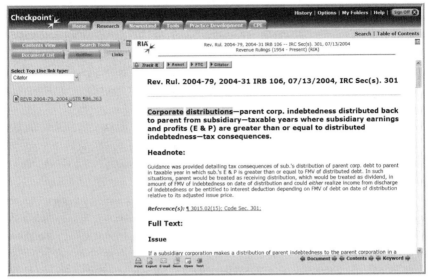

Click on the appropriate **Citator** link.

Exhibit 5.52
Step 3: Validating Administrative Authority with *Checkpoint*

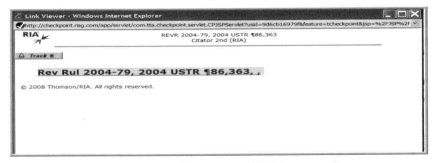

View search results.

Summary

Web based tax research services have significantly streamlined the process of locating tax law authority. However, no matter how adept tax researchers may become at using this technology, it must be used in conjunction with other skills, such as identifying appropriate authority and deciding how to weight conflicting authorities.

6

Assessing and Applying Authority

After a tax researcher has located authority that seems pertinent to a given problem, the important task of assessing that material begins. The researcher's aim is to arrive at a course of action that can be confidently communicated to the client along with identification of the risks and accompanying costs.

Locating appropriate authority for a particular tax problem is only half the battle. The technical jargon of many portions of the Internal Revenue Code (IRC) and Treasury regulations requires the tax adviser to read and comprehend unusually complex sentences to determine congressional intent. Other portions of the IRC and regulations hinge upon deceptively simple words or phrases whose definitions may be debatable. Furthermore, while available secondary authorities or such interpretive sources as Treasury regulations, revenue rulings, or court decisions may be more comprehensible than primary statutory authorities, they are less authoritative.

The researcher faces another, more serious hurdle when authorities conflict. The applicable law may be questionable due to conflicts in the language of the statute, between the language of the statute and the intent of Congress, between interpretations of the statute, between the IRS interpretations and various federal courts, and among the courts themselves at various levels of jurisdiction. Finally, a researcher may be unable to locate any authority at all on a particular problem.

In attempting to assess authority and apply it to complex practice problems, the researcher may encounter any one of three fundamentally different situations. The first involves clear, concise tax law that could be applied if the researcher were able to gather additional facts from the client. In another, the adviser may be in possession of clearly established facts but find a conflict in the applicable law. Finally, a researcher may encounter a third situation in which existing tax law is incomplete or inapplicable, requiring that issues be resolved through interpolation from related authorities and application of creative thinking.

The Law Is Clear—The Facts Are Uncertain

Frequently, a tax adviser finds it difficult to reach a conclusion and make a recommendation because of insufficient knowledge of the facts in the case rather than because of confusion in the applicable rules. In many situations, the biggest single problem is gathering sufficient evidence to support the taxpayer's contention that he or she be granted the tax treatment clearly authorized in a specific provision of the IRC.

To illustrate this kind of problem, assume that a client, Jerry Hill, includes what he describes as a *casualty loss* with the information he provides for the filing of his income tax return. A cursory line of questioning by his tax adviser reveals that the loss is claimed for a handwoven Indian wall carpet that the client claims was chewed and clawed to bits by a stray dog. Hill explains that while on vacation last summer, he left his residence in the care of his housekeeper. Apparently, one day the housekeeper neglected to close a door securely and a stray dog wandered into the house. Upon Hill's return from vacation, he was told the following story. Attracted by strange noises, the housekeeper entered the study and found a dog gnawing and tearing on the wall rug. As the housekeeper entered the room, the dog turned and ran growling from the house. Although not certain of it, the housekeeper reported noticing foam around the dog's mouth. Later, a neighbor said that a rabid dog had been seen roaming the neighborhood. The housekeeper, who cared for Hill's own dogs, stated that the dog discovered in the study was not one of Hill's. Hill checked with the city dogcatcher concerning the reported sighting of a mad dog. He was, however, unable to confirm any such report with the dogcatcher. He did not check with the police department.

Through a little research, the tax adviser is convinced that for Hill to qualify for a casualty loss deduction under Section 165(a), he must satisfy the following specific requirements:

1. The loss must have been sudden and unexpected (*Hugh M. Matheson v. Commissioner*, 54 F.2d 537 (CA-2, 1931) and Rev. Rul. 79-174, 1979-1 C.B. 99).

2. The loss generally cannot constitute a mysterious disappearance (*Paul Bakewell, Jr.*, 23 T.C. 803 (1955)). However, for a different conclusion see *Kielts v. Commissioner*, 42 T.C.M. 238 (1981).

3. The amount of the loss deduction is limited to the lesser of (*a*) the reduction in fair market value (FMV) of the asset caused by the casualty or (*b*) the adjusted basis of the asset. This amount is reduced by (1) an insurance recovery, (2) a $100 floor, and (3) 10 percent of the taxpayer's adjusted gross income (Sec. 165(h) and Treas. Reg. Sec. 1.165-7(b)).

4. The loss cannot be attributable to the taxpayer's own dog (*J.R. Dyer*, 20 T.C.M. 705 (1961)).

At this point, a tax adviser would be faced with two alternatives: accept the client's statement at face value and claim the deduction, or suggest that the client accumulate additional evidence to substantiate the loss if he desires to claim the deduction.[1] An adviser

---

[1] For example, the taxpayer should be able to show the type of casualty and when it occurred, that the loss was the direct result of the casualty, and that the taxpayer was the owner of the property with respect to which a casualty loss deduction is claimed (*White v. Commissioner*, 48 T.C. 430 (1967)).

following the former alternative is simply postponing the collection of evidence until a possible IRS audit, because the presence of a rather sizable casualty loss on a client's tax return undoubtedly would increase the risk of an audit. Furthermore, it might be self-defeating to defer the collection of evidence because two or three years from now individuals who could render statements on matters now fresh in their minds may be unavailable, or they may not recall necessary details. Furthermore, helpful police records may be destroyed. Because the taxpayer may be unaware of what is needed to substantiate the loss deduction, he or she may, in the meantime, dispose of important evidence, such as the ruined rug.

If a tax adviser pursues the second alternative, the client should be presented with a list of instructions, including the suggestion that he or she accumulate the necessary evidence to support the deduction in the event of an audit or eventual litigation. The list could include

1. sworn statements from (*a*) the housekeeper and (*b*) the individual who saw the apparently rabid dog in the neighborhood.

2. appraisal by a qualified expert or experts showing the value of the rug before and after the casualty.

3. color photographs of the rug before and after the casualty.

4. instructions to retain the damaged rug as evidence, if possible.

5. statements from, or correspondence with, insurance agents substantiating the amount of any insurance recovery.

6. purchase invoice showing proof of ownership and cost.

A client may ignore an adviser's request or he or she may be unable to obtain all of the recommended evidence. Nevertheless, the adviser will have informed the client on a timely basis of the requirements necessary to sustain the right to the claimed deduction.

In tax research work involving situations in which tax laws are clear but the facts of the situation are in question, the tax adviser should establish the facts necessary to reach a conclusion and either accumulate appropriate supporting evidence or suggest that the client do so. Then, in the event of an audit, the tax adviser would need only to persuade a revenue agent to accept the mass of overwhelming evidence and, therefore, reach the desired conclusion.

The Facts Are Clear—The Law Is Questionable

The tax researcher may encounter another kind of problem involving situations in which facts are well established but the law is uncertain. Uncertainty may arise (1) in the language of the statute itself, (2) between the language of the statute and the intent of the statute, or (3) between the interpretations of the statute.

Conflicting Statutes

Although it is rather rare, the facts of a problem can sometimes be analyzed in light of two different provisions of the statute, with each provision furnishing a different tax result. In such cases, the adviser and client should carefully evaluate which alternative to take, realizing the possibility of an IRS challenge.

An example of a possible conflict between statutes may be found in Sections 164 and 469. Section 164 states that "... *except as otherwise provided in this section*," [emphasis added] certain taxes are allowed as a deduction. Property taxes on real estate are included in this list of deductible taxes. Among other things, Section 164 continues by imposing certain limitations and special requirements for assessed taxes that tend to increase the value of the property, and the apportionment of real estate taxes between the seller and purchaser of real property. On the other hand, Section 469 disallows a deduction for losses incurred in a passive activity. Losses in a passive activity are incurred when the expenses of the activity exceed its income. Because the term *passive activity* includes any rental activity,[2] real estate taxes incurred on the passive activity's property would constitute part of the disallowed passive activity loss. Section 469(i) does provide an exception to this by allowing

---

[2] Section 469(c)(2)

a deduction of up to $25,000 per year for rental real estate activities in which the owner actively participated during the year. However, even this deduction is completely phased out for taxpayers who have adjusted gross income over $150,000. Thus, there appears to be a conflict between Section 164, which allows a deduction for the real estate taxes, and Section 469, which in many cases will disallow a deduction. Normally, in situations such as this, the statute itself resolves the conflict. For example, in Section 164 the statute could have said, "except as otherwise provided in this section, *and in section 469*, a deduction shall be allowed for the following taxes." Or in Section 469, the statute could have said, "*notwithstanding section 164*, no deduction shall be allowed for a passive activity loss." Currently, however, such explanatory phrases are not found in either Sections 164 or 469.

Conflict Between a Statute and the Intent of a Statute

A tax researcher can sometimes find conflicts between the words of a statute and the accompanying House, Senate, and conference committee reports that contain the intent of Congress. In this situation, the tax adviser must know under what circumstances he or she can rely on the committee reports. Furthermore, the adviser and the client should be prepared for a possible IRS challenge.

In *Miller v. Commissioner*, 88-1 USTC ¶9139 (CA-10, 1988), the U.S. Court of Appeals for the Tenth Circuit was faced with a conflict between the statute and the intent (legislative history) of the statute. The appellate court stated in its opinion that the Tax Court relied too heavily on the conference report, given the long-standing interpretation of the statute itself.

The appellate court did acknowledge that, in some situations, the plain meaning of a statute may be overridden if it is in apparent conflict with the purpose of the legislation. However, the court further stated that

> ... When there is a conflict between portions of legislative history and the words of a statute, the words of the statute represent the constitutionally approved method of communication, and it would require "unequivocal evidence" of legislative purpose as reflected in the legislative history to override the ordinary meaning of the statute.[3]

---

[3] *Miller v. Commissioner*, 88-1 USTC ¶9139 (CA-10, 1988)

Generally, the tax adviser should not refer to committee reports in situations where the meaning of the statute is clear. However, in situations in which the IRC is ambiguous or silent, the legislative history can be of great help.[4] The tax adviser should always remember that the purpose of using legislative history is to solve, not to create, an ambiguity.[5]

Conflicting Interpretations

A tax researcher more frequently encounters conflicting interpretations of tax statutes by various authorities. Conflicts may be found between the Treasury regulations and the courts or between two or more federal courts. In such situations, the tax adviser must consider the alternatives and weigh the risks—including the cost of lengthy administrative battles with the IRS and potential litigation—before recommending a particular conclusion or course of action. Furthermore, the taxpayer must consider the potential imposition of a penalty.[6] While it is the responsibility of the tax adviser to discover conflicting interpretations of the statutes and to advise the client of the risks and alternatives, the client should decide which course of action to pursue. Although only the client can decide whether to incur the costs of an administrative or legal confrontation with the IRS, he or she generally relies heavily on the recommendation of the tax adviser in reaching that decision. Other pertinent considerations include the general inconvenience associated with such disputes, the risk of exposure to additional audits, and the possibility of adverse publicity.

Regulations Versus Courts. If a regulation has already been challenged, one of three possible outcomes may exist. First, the IRS

---

[4] The weight of legislative history as authority may also vary according to factors such as whether the legislative history is sufficiently specific, clear, and uniform to be a reliable indicator of intent (*Miller v. Comm., supra* note 3).

[5] Sheldon I. Banoff, "Dealing with the 'Authorities': Determining Valid Legal Authority in Advising Clients, Rendering Opinions, Preparing Tax Returns and Avoiding Penalties," *Taxes—The Tax Magazine* (December 1988): 1082–1084

[6] Among others, see Section 6662, which imposes a penalty on a taxpayer for a substantial understatement of the tax liability, and Section 6694, which imposes penalties on the tax return preparer for negligent or intentional disregard of rules and regulations.

may have lost the challenge and either revised or withdrawn the contested regulation. Second, the government may have lost one or more specific tests of the regulation but is still unwilling to concede defeat. Third, the IRS has successfully defended a regulation, and, therefore, further attempts to challenge that regulation probably would not hold much promise.

An example of the first outcome previously described is the IRS's acknowledgement that part of the temporary regulations issued under Section 453 regarding wraparound installment sales were invalid. In *Professional Equities, Inc.*,[7] the Tax Court held that the 1980 Installment Sales Revision Act did not modify the taxing of gains in wraparound installment sales. Thus, Temp. Reg. Sec. 15A.453-1(b)(3)(ii) was held to be invalid. The IRS acknowledged the invalidity of the regulation by announcing its acquiescence to the Tax Court decision.[8]

What we have said concerning conflicting authority between Treasury regulations and judicial opinions is, obviously, equally applicable to conflicting authority between judicial opinions and revenue rulings, revenue procedures, and other official IRS pronouncements. While a dispute between the IRS and the courts is still in progress, taxpayers with similar questions become prime targets for litigation if they adopt a position contrary to that pursued by the IRS. The IRS is often looking for a *better fact case* (from its point of view) or for a more favorable circuit in which to litigate. Any time a tax adviser recommends a position contrary to that of the IRS, even if that contrary position is adequately supported by judicial authority, the adviser should explain to the client the potential risks and extra costs implicit in taking that position. As far as revenue agents and appellate conferees are concerned, the IRS position is the law, and they will challenge a departure from this position.

One Court's Interpretation Versus Another's. Disagreements between courts on similar issues can be characterized as *horizontal* and *vertical*. Horizontal differences mean conflicting opinions issued by courts at the same level of jurisdiction; vertical differences refer to

---

[7] 89 T.C. 165 (1987) (reviewed opinion, without dissent)
[8] 1988-2 C.B. 1

conflicts between lower and higher courts. Horizontal differences can occur between courts of original jurisdiction (Federal District Courts, the Tax Court, and the Court of Federal Claims), or between the several circuit courts. In such conflicts, the IRS is under no obligation to follow, on a nationwide basis, the precedent set by any of the courts. Thus, a district court opinion favorable to the taxpayer would technically have precedential value only for a taxpayer residing within the jurisdiction of that district court. Similarly, any circuit court opinion technically has precedential value only within the circuit where the decision originated because one circuit court is not bound to follow the precedent of another circuit court. If appealed, conflicting district court opinions from district courts within the same circuit are settled by the appropriate circuit court. The Supreme Court, if it grants *certiorari*, settles conflicts between circuits. Before the time that a circuit court or the Supreme Court disposes of such opposing views, the tax adviser and client should be fully aware of the risks involved when relying on a court decision that may subsequently be appealed and overturned.

An interesting example of a disagreement between courts involves employee expenses for transportation of the tools of one's trade. Relying on Rev. Rul. 63-100,[9] which allowed an automobile expense deduction to a musician for the transportation of his musical instrument between his personal residence and his place of employment, taxpayer Sullivan deducted his driving expenses because he transported a 32-pound bag of tools to work each day. The Tax Court denied the deduction; however, the Second Circuit reversed and remanded the case to the Tax Court. On rehearing, the Tax Court allowed more than 25 percent of the total driving expenses claimed by the taxpayer.[10] Subsequently, in *Fausner* and in *Hitt*, two airline pilots, who were required by their employers and by government regulations to carry extensive flight gear, attempted to deduct transportation expenses between their home and the airport. In *Fausner*, the Tax Court felt constrained by the *Sullivan* decision, since Fausner resided in the Second Circuit, and

---

[9] Rev. Rul. 63-100, 1963-1 C.B. 34 (now revoked by Rev. Rul. 75-380, 1975-2 C.B. 59)

[10] *Sullivan*, 368 F.2d 1007 (CA-2,1966) and T.C.M. 1968-711

it allowed the deduction for the 1965 tax year.[11] However because Hitt resided in the Fifth Circuit, the Tax Court, ruling on the same day, disregarded *Sullivan* and disallowed the deduction.[12] Fausner's returns for 1966 and 1967 were again challenged by the IRS on the same issue, and Fausner once more petitioned the Tax Court to rule on the matter. Although Fausner had resided in New York during 1966 and 1967, he had moved to Texas in 1968 and was thus petitioning from the Fifth Circuit in the latter years. In this instance, the Tax Court sustained the IRS, as it had done previously in *Hitt*.[13] Fausner appealed to the Fifth Circuit and received an adverse ruling.[14] At this point, a conflict between the Second and the Fifth Circuit courts existed, and the Supreme Court granted *certiorari* on an appeal from *Fausner*.[15] The Supreme Court finally settled the controversy by ruling against the taxpayer.[16]

The foregoing example demonstrates both horizontal and vertical differences in judicial decisions. In horizontal differences, a taxpayer cannot rely on a decision rendered by another court at the same level of jurisdiction, because courts at the same level of jurisdiction are not bound by decisions of other courts at that same level. Vertical differences are harder to explain because lower courts generally are bound by decisions of higher courts. In the case of the Tax Court, however, even vertical differences may exist because the Tax Court has national jurisdiction. The Tax Court considers itself bound by the decisions of the circuit courts of appeals only to the extent that taxpayers reside in the jurisdiction of a circuit that has rendered a decision on that issue. This maxim is frequently referred to as the Golsen Rule, since it was first expressed by the Tax Court in *J. E. Golsen*, 54 T.C. 742 (1970).

Because the Tax Court is *not* obligated to accept any circuit court opinion on a nationwide basis, it has ample opportunity to express its displeasure with a circuit court opinion by disregarding

---

[11] *Fausner*, 55 T.C. 620 (1971)

[12] *Hitt*, 55 T.C. 628 (1971)

[13] *Fausner*, P-H T.C.M. ¶71,277

[14] *Fausner*, 472 F.2d 561 (CA-5, 1973)

[15] Actually, the conflict between the circuits involved another decision, in which the court held for the taxpayer (*Tyne*, 385 F.2d 40 (CA-7, 1967)).

[16] *Fausner*, 413 U.S. 838 (1973)

it in cases involving taxpayers from other circuits. Such a result can be demonstrated with two cases, in which the Tax Court arrived at opposing conclusions, involving two "50-50" stockholders in the same S corporation where each taxpayer had sued on an identical issue. In both *Doehring* and *Puckett*, the issue to be decided was whether their loan company had lost its subchapter S status.[17] The IRS had previously disallowed the election on the grounds that more than 20 percent of the corporation's gross revenue was derived from interest (passive income).[18] The taxpayers, relying on *House v. Commissioner*, 453 F.2d 982 (CA-5, 1972), argued that the ceiling did not apply to loan companies. The Tax Court ruled against the taxpayer in *Doehring*, stating that *House* did not apply since *Doehring* would be appealed to the Eighth Circuit. In *Puckett*, however, the Tax Court upheld the taxpayer's contention, although disagreeing with it, since appeal would be to the Fifth Circuit, in which *House* was controlling. Subsequently, *Doehring* was appealed to the Eighth Circuit, where the taxpayer prevailed.[19] The sequence of events demonstrates, however, the uncertainty created, at least for a time, for taxpayers and their advisers with similar situations.

One taxpayer tested the commissioner's right to ignore established judicial precedent. In that case, the IRS sent deficiency notices to two taxpayers claiming that certain distributions received from their corporation were dividends. Both stockholders challenged the deficiency assessment in the Tax Court. While taxpayer Divine's suit was pending, the Tax Court ruled against taxpayer Luckman.[20] Upon appeal, however, the Seventh Circuit reversed the Tax Court.[21] The commissioner pressed on with the same position he had taken in *Luckman* and obtained another favorable ruling from the Tax Court in *Divine*.[22] Taxpayer Divine then appealed to the

[17] *K.W. Doehring*, T.C.M. 1974-1035; and *P.E. Puckett*, T.C.M. 1974-1038
[18] Before 1983, S corporations were limited in the amount of passive income they could earn.
[19] *K.W. Doehring*, 527 F.2d 945 (CA-8, 1975). The government also appealed *Puckett*, trying for a reversal of *House*. However, the Fifth Circuit affirmed the original Tax Court decision (*P.E. Puckett*, 522 F.2d 1385 (CA-5, 1975)).
[20] *Sid Luckman*, 50 T.C. 619 (1968)
[21] *Luckman*, 418 F.2d 381 (CA-7, 1969)
[22] *Harold S. Divine*, 59 T.C. 152 (1972)

Second Circuit Court, claiming that when the commissioner is reliti-
gating an issue that he has previously lost and the facts are distinguishable only by virtue of the identity of the taxpayer, the
commissioner should be barred from again bringing suit. Although
the Second Circuit Court held for taxpayer Divine, it struck down
his contention that the commissioner was prevented from bringing
suit.[23]

The Facts Are Clear—The Law Is Incomplete

As explained earlier, whenever a statute is silent or imprecise on
a particular tax question, tax researchers must consult other interpretive authorities, such as Treasury regulations, revenue rulings,
or court decisions. In their search for proper interpretation, tax
advisers soon discover that finding authority with facts identical
to their own will be the exception rather than the rule. In most
circumstances, therefore, the ability to distinguish cases or rulings
on the basis of facts becomes critical, for many times it is necessary
to piece together support for the researchers' positions from several
authorities.

An illustration of this third class of common tax problems follows. Assume that a client, an Austrian named Werner Hoppe,
presents the following facts. Werner visited his brother Klaus, who
had immigrated to the United States six years before and resides
in Dallas, Texas. At the time of the visit, Werner was under contract
to an Austrian soccer team and was expected to return to the team
to begin play for the fall 2008 season. Werner's brother Klaus had
fallen in love with American football and had become an enthusias-
tic fan of the Dallas Cowboys. The Cowboys had recently lost
their regular kicker to an injury, and a replacement, picked up on
waivers, proved to be less than satisfactory. Knowing of Werner's
kicking ability, Klaus was convinced that Werner could help the
Cowboys if given an opportunity. Klaus took Werner to a Cowboy
workout and introduced him to the kicking coach. As a result,
Werner was given a tryout by the Cowboys, who were desperate
for a good kicker. Werner's performance was far superior to others

---

[23] *Divine,* 500 F.2d 1041 (CA-2, 1974)

at the tryout, and the Cowboys offered him the kicking job. Werner, however, was reluctant to accept the offer because he had planned to return to Austria in a few weeks to continue his soccer career. Considerable encouragement from Klaus and the Cowboys organization seemed to be in vain until the Cowboys, at Klaus's suggestion, offered Werner a $200,000 bonus. At this point, Werner overcame his reluctance and signed a contract, which Klaus co-signed as witness and interpreter. Economically speaking, the regular salary offered by the Cowboys was considerably more attractive than was Werner's salary as a soccer player in Austria. Grateful to his brother for assisting as an interpreter and negotiator, and for encouraging him to stay, Werner instructed the Cowboys to pay $30,000 of the negotiated bonus directly to Klaus. Klaus reported the $30,000 as other income on his 2008 income tax return and paid the appropriate tax. After examining Werner's 2008 tax return, the IRS made a deficiency assessment claiming that the $30,000 paid to Klaus constituted income to Werner and should thus be included in his income under Section 61(a)(1). The IRS agent relied at least in part upon the authority of *Richard A. Allen*, 50 T.C. 466 (1968).

After determining the foregoing facts, the tax researcher decides that, according to the language of Treas. Reg. Sec. 1.61(a)(1), the total bonus payment should be included in Werner's return. The regulations specify that, in general, wages, salaries, and bonuses are income to the recipient unless excluded by law. After additional research, the tax adviser locates the decision in *Cecil Randolph Hundley, Jr.*, which appears to contain a similar situation.[24] In *Hundley*, to which the commissioner acquiesced, the taxpayer included the bonus payments in his income but was allowed a business expense deduction for that portion of the bonus paid to his father. Before relying solely on the authority of *Hundley*, the tax adviser must be certain that the facts of *Hundley* are in effect substantially similar to Werner's situation and that the expense of further negotiations with the IRS is warranted and based on a sound premise. Thus, the tax adviser will carefully compare the *Allen* and *Hundley* cases with the facts presented by Werner Hoppe. In doing this, the adviser might prepare the following list of facts.

---

[24] *Cecil Randolph Hundley, Jr.*, 48 T.C. 339, Acq. 1967-2 C.B.2

Allen	Hoppe	Hundley
1. Professional baseball player received sizable bonus.	1. Professional football player received sizable bonus.	1. Professional baseball player received sizable bonus.
2. Taxpayer was amateur before signing contract.	2. Taxpayer was professional soccer player before signing contract.	2. Taxpayer was amateur player before signing contract.
3. Parent and ball-playing minor child signed professional ball contract.	3. Ballplayer alone signed contract, but brother signed as witness and interpreter.	3. Parent and ball-playing minor child signed professional ball contract.
4. Some bonus payments were actually made to mother.	4. Some bonus payments were actually made to brother.	4. Some bonus payments were actually made to father.
5. Mother knew little about baseball.	5. Brother had average knowledge of football.	5. Father was knowledgeable in baseball and taught his son extensively.
6. Mother was passive participant in negotiations for contract and bonus.	6. Brother was an active participant in negotiations for contract and bonus.	6. Father handled most of the negotiations for contract and bonus.
7. No oral agreement existed.	7. No oral agreement existed.	7. Oral agreement existed on how to divide the bonus payments.

Because *Allen* was decided for the government and *Hundley* for the taxpayer, it may be important to distinguish the two cases on the basis of facts. Using a simple diagram technique, we begin with seven facts identified in each case (see figure 6.1).

Figure 6.1

Allen

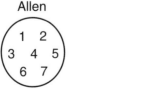

Hundley

Next, the researcher should identify those facts that are very similar in both cases and those that are more readily distinguishable (see figure 6.2).

Figure 6.2

Allen   Hundley

The second diagram shows that facts 1–4 are neutral in that they are nearly identical in both cases, and that the important facts, which perhaps swayed the outcome of the Hundley case in favor of the taxpayer, appear to be facts 5–7. Comparing *Hundley* with Hoppe produces the result as shown in figure 6.3.

Figure 6.3

Hundley   Hoppe

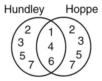

The diagram shows that Hoppe and *Hundley* agree in facts 1, 4, and 6 only. The comparison of all 3 fact situations (see figure 6.4) might provide additional insight for the tax adviser.

Figure 6.4

Allen   Hundley

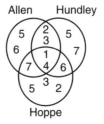

Hoppe

This analysis shows that facts 1 and 4 are neutral in all 3 cases and perhaps should not be considered to have an impact upon the final outcome. Fact 2, dealing with the professional status of Hoppe, which can be distinguished from both *Allen* and *Hundley*, might significantly bolster Hoppe's claim for an ordinary and necessary business expense under Section 162. Hoppe has already established his business as a professional athlete; fact 3, the signing of the contract by Hoppe alone (again distinguished from *Allen* and *Hundley*), seems to support the fact that Klaus was needed in the negotiations as an interpreter, the capacity in which he signed the contract. Facts 5–6, which indicate the degree of expertise exhibited by the respective relatives of the ballplayers and the roles played by the relatives in the contract negotiations, seem to be of much greater significance. In Hundley's and Hoppe's cases, both relatives took active roles in negotiating final contracts. In *Hundley*, the father was knowledgeable about baseball and contract negotiations. Hoppe's situation is certainly similar. Klaus exhibited an ability to negotiate by recommending that a bonus be offered, and he displayed his expertise as an interpreter. The final fact—fact 7—in which *Allen* and Hoppe are distinguished from *Hundley*, appears to be a liability to Hoppe's position and weakens his case considerably.

The foregoing analysis demonstrates a situation in which the statute is incomplete and a taxpayer and the adviser must rely on conflicting interpretive authority. Careful analysis indicates that previous interpretations appear to apply to some but not all the existing facts. Once a thorough examination of the facts and a review of the applicable authority have been completed, a decision must be made about the course of action. Possible risks must be evaluated and additional expenses must be estimated before the decision to contest the deficiency assessment is made. Consultation with legal counsel concerning litigation hazards will assist the taxpayer in deciding whether to carry the case beyond an administrative appeal and into the courts.

The Facts Are Clear—The Law Is Nonexistent

It is possible that a tax researcher may discover that a problem is not clearly covered by any statutory, administrative, or judicial authority. In such circumstances, the tax adviser has an opportunity to use whatever powers of creativity, logical reasoning, and persuasion he or she possesses. Because the revenue agent making an examination likewise will have little authority to substantiate any proposed adjustment, it is up to the tax adviser to present a convincing argument in support of the client's position. However, as stressed throughout this chapter, before the tax adviser proceeds with a course of action, the client should be advised of the possible risks and expenses associated with it. In these circumstances, the client may want to ask the IRS for a letter ruling before a final decision is reached.

We have suggested that in all questionable situations the cost and risk factors be considered before reaching a conclusion. Risk should be interpreted as any possible adverse consequence that might occur as a result of a specific course of action adopted by the taxpayer. One might ask whether the questionable treatment of a particular item on the return will trigger an examination, and whether such an examination is likely to subject other items on the return to scrutiny and a possible proposed adjustment.[25] Furthermore, proposed adjustments on one year's tax return may lead to similar adjustments on a prior year's return. Thus, in addition to developing a strong case against the IRS claims, potential risks must be considered in the final decision process in the treatment of all tax matters.

Standards for Recommending a Tax Return Position

Since the results of most tax planning end up on a tax return, a brief summary of the standards required to recommend a tax return position would seem appropriate. In Statement on Standards for Tax Services No. 1, *Tax Return Positions* (AICPA, *Professional Standards*, vol. 2, TS sec. 100 par. .02), the AICPA states that its members should not recommend that a tax return position be taken with

---

[25] A questionable treatment should not be confused with an illegal treatment. The former refers to items supported by adequate authority that lend themselves to honest disagreement between taxpayers and the IRS.

respect to any item unless the member has a good faith belief that the position has a "realistic possibility" of being sustained administratively or judicially on its merits if challenged. In addition, the AICPA states that its members may recommend a tax return position that the member concludes is "not frivolous" as long as the member advises the taxpayer to appropriately disclose.

The tax return preparer penalties of Section 6694 contain the standards required by the IRC. The tax return reporting standard applicable to preparers for undisclosed positions is a "reasonable belief that the position would more likely than not be sustained on its merits" (MLTN) standard. If the tax return preparer cannot achieve the MLTN threshold, the preparer can still recommend a position on a tax return if the preparer determines that a *reasonable basis* exists and the taxpayer is willing to attach a written disclosure of the position.

Section 6662 provides that a taxpayer is subject to a 20% penalty for a number of situations including a substantial understatement of tax. This penalty is avoided if *substantial authority* exists for the tax treatment of the item or a *reasonable basis* exists and the item is properly disclosed.

It is difficult to quantify each of these various standards with the exception of the MLTN and the realistic possibility standards. Since tax professionals might differ in assigning probabilities to the remaining standards, we will only attempt to list them in their relative order starting with the most rigorous first: (1) MLTN (>50%), (2) substantial authority, (3) realistic possibility (at least 33 1/3%), (4) reasonable basis, (5) not-frivolous, and (6) frivolous.

What is most peculiar about these various standards is that the tax preparer is held to a higher standard for penalty purposes than the actual taxpayer (MLTN versus substantial authority). Without question, this puts the tax professional in an awkward position when he or she tries to best represent his or her clients but at the same time conform to the IRC penalty provisions. Any recommended tax return position or course of action which results from one's tax research efforts should carefully be evaluated with respect to the myriad of applicable standards.[26]

---

[26] See additional discussion of all AICPA Statements on the AICPA Web site at http://tax.aicpa.org/Resources/Professional+Standards+and+Ethics/.

7

Communicating Tax Research

Throughout this book, we have used the terms *tax researcher* and *tax adviser* synonymously. If a distinction could be made between the two forms of practice, it would be based on the tax adviser's task of reporting the conclusion that has been so painstakingly pieced together. Although some tax conclusions can be communicated orally, much of the information gathered by tax researchers must eventually be placed in writing. The task of writing introduces two major problems for practitioners. First, the ability to write well is an acquired trait, the result of practice and more practice. Second, communicating the conclusions of tax research requires the ability to perceive how much or how little to express. This task is complicated by the fact that highly technical solutions frequently must be distilled into layman's language. Also, tax advisers often must hedge on their solutions because, as discussed in chapter 6, a definitive answer simply is not available in every case. In addition, tax advisers must, to protect their own professional integrity, foresee potential future claims against them. Like writing skills, the ability to determine precisely what needs to be said usually can be improved through practice. Inexperienced tax researchers should be given an early opportunity to present much of their initial research in written form. New researchers should also be assigned the responsibility of preparing draft copies of correspondence that will subsequently be reviewed by a supervisor for weaknesses in writing style and technical presentation. Experience and assistance can mold good researchers into good advisers with a mastery of writing style and an ability to pinpoint the finer information required in tax documents.

The form of a written tax communication is determined by the audience for which it is intended. Some documents are prepared for internal purposes, or firm use, only. Other documents, such as client letters, protest letters, and requests for rulings, are prepared for an external audience outside the firm. In the following pages, we will illustrate the appropriate formats and procedures; nevertheless, certain basic features are universal to most tax communications.

Internal Communications

Within the accounting firm, the client file is the basic tool used to communicate specific client information between the various levels of the professional staff. Pertinent information concerning each client's unique facts is contained in the file in the form of memos and working papers.

Memo to the File

A memo to the file may be written after any one of several developments. Often such memos are the result of a client's request—in person, over the telephone, or in a letter—for a solution to a tax problem. The importance of facts in tax research was explained in chapter 2; a memo to the file is commonly used to inform the researcher of the underlying facts needed to identify issues, locate authorities, and reach solutions. In most offices, the partners or managers have the initial contact with the client, whereas much of the actual research is performed by a staff person. It is critical, therefore, that accurate information be communicated between the various levels of the professional staff. A typical memorandum to the file follows:

April 1, 2008

TO: Files
FROM: Tom Partner
SUBJECT: Potential acquisition by American Rock & Sand, Inc., of
           Pahrump Ready Mix, Inc.

Today, Ron Jones, financial vice president of American Rock & Sand, Inc. (ARS), called to request information concerning the tax consequences of a proposed acquisition of Pahrump Ready Mix, Inc. (PRM). ARS is a Utah corporation (organized on October 1, 1965) licensed as a general contractor, and specializes in road and highway construction. ARS employs the accrual method of accounting and uses a calendar year end as the basis for maintaining its books. ARS's authorized capital consists of 1,000 shares of voting common stock owned principally by the Jones family.

PRM, the target corporation, is a Utah Corporation organized on June 1, 1973. PRM is engaged in the business of making and delivering concrete. PRM employs the accrual method of accounting and uses a calendar year end as the basis for maintaining its books. PRM's authorized capital consists of 5,000 shares of voting common stock owned principally by the Smith family.

ARS has approached PRM about the possibility of acquiring PRM's assets. PRM has expressed some preliminary interest if the deal can be structured so the Smith family is not taxed on the initial sale of PRM. The Smith family has stated that they would consider receiving ARS stock as long as the stock will provide them with an annual income.

Due to a shortage of cash, ARS would like to accomplish the acquisition without the use of cash. Also, the Jones family has stated that they are not interested in giving up any voting power in ARS to the Smith family. John Jones has requested that we develop, if possible, a proposal of how ARS can structure the transaction to satisfy the requests of both ARS and PRM. Mr. Jones has requested that we present at their May 1, 2008, ARS board meeting our proposal for the acquisition of PRM. If we need further information, we are to contact Mr. Jones directly.

The information contained in the memo should be sufficient for the researcher to begin work. Furthermore, the memo communicates a specific deadline and indicates that the client is willing to supplement this information with additional facts if necessary.

A less formal procedure is often followed when a long-established client calls the tax adviser for an immediate answer to a routine tax question on a well-defined, noncontroversial topic. If the tax adviser gives an oral reply, the conversation should be placed in writing, thus creating a record for the files. Such a record serves as protection against subsequent confusion or misinterpretation that may jeopardize the tax adviser's professional integrity, and it can serve as a basis for billing the client.[1]

Leaving Tracks

Once the necessary information has been recorded in a memo to the files, the researcher may begin the task of identifying questions and seeking solutions. Supporting documents for conclusions, such as excerpts from or references to specific portions of the Internal Revenue Code (IRC), Treasury regulations, revenue rulings, court decisions, tax service editorial opinions, and periodicals, should be put in the files. All questions and conclusions should be appropriately cross-indexed so the information can be retrieved quickly. Pertinent information in supporting documents should be highlighted to avoid unnecessary reading. Examples of the content and organization of a client's file are presented in chapter 8.

Because time is one of the most important commodities that any tax adviser has for sale, a well-organized client file is of the utmost importance: It can eliminate duplication of effort. Supervisory review of a staff person's research can be accomplished quickly, and additional time can be saved if and when it becomes necessary to refer to a client's file months (or even years) after the initial work was performed. Such a delayed reference to a file

---

[1] The question of whether oral advice should be confirmed in writing frequently arises. AICPA Statement on Standards for Tax Services (SSTS) No. 8, *Form and Content of Advice to Taxpayers* (AICPA, *Professional Standards*, vol. 2, TS sec. 800 par. .06), makes the following recommendation: "Although oral advice may serve a taxpayer's needs appropriately in routine matters or in well-defined areas, written communications are recommended in important, unusual, or complicated transactions. The member may use professional judgment about whether, subsequently, to document oral advice in writing."

may be required because of subsequent IRS audits, preparation of protests, or the need to solve another client's similar tax problem. Because promotions, transfers, and staff turnover are common occurrences in accounting firms, well-organized files can be of significant help in familiarizing new staff members with client problems.

Another time-saving device used by practitioners is the tax subject file. To prepare such a system, members of the practitioner's tax staff contribute tax problems together with documented conclusions. In a multioffice firm, such files are then pooled and arranged by subject matter, usually in a computer database, and made available to each office. A subject file can eliminate many hours of duplicative research.

External Communications

A tax practitioner's written communication to an audience outside the firm takes on added significance because it demonstrates expertise, renders advice, and is a reflection of the firm's reputation. Perhaps the most frequently encountered external document in a CPA's tax practice is the client letter. Communications with the IRS on behalf of a client to protest a deficiency assessment or to request a ruling for a proposed transaction are also quite common.

Client Letters

In a client letter, the tax adviser expresses a professional opinion to those who pay for his or her services. Because it is important to clearly communicate a professional opinion, writing the client letter may be the tax adviser's greatest challenge in the entire tax engagement. The format of client letters may vary from one firm to another. However, most good client letters have three things in common.

Style. Like a good speaker, a good writer must know the audience before beginning. Because tax clients and their staff vary greatly in their tax expertise, it is important to consider their technical sophistication when composing a tax opinion letter. The style of a letter may range from a highly sophisticated format, with numerous technical explanations and citations, to a simple composition that uses only layperson's terms. In many situations, of course, the best solution lies somewhere between the two extremes.

Format and Content. Regardless of the degree of technical sophistication, a well-drafted client letter follows a well-planned format. It should begin with an enumeration of the facts upon which the tax adviser's research is based. In conjunction with a statement of the facts, a statement of caution (see the following section, "Disclaimer Statements") should be included to warn the client that the research conclusions stated are valid only for the specified facts. Next, the letter should state the important tax questions implicit in the previously identified facts. Finally, the tax practitioner should list his or her conclusions and the authority for those conclusions. An example of the appropriate form and typical content of a client letter is shown in chapter 8.

A client letter may identify areas of controversy (or questions that are not authoritatively resolved) that might be disputed by the IRS. Some highly qualified tax advisers seriously question the wisdom of including any discussion of disputable points in a client letter because that letter may end up in the possession of a revenue agent at a most inopportune time. Furthermore, by authority of Section 7602, the IRS has the right to examine all relevant books, papers, and records containing information relating to the business of a taxpayer liable for federal taxes. Tax accountants are well aware that documents in their possession, relating to the computation of a client's federal tax liability, are often not considered privileged communication.

However, Section 7525 extends the attorney-client privilege to any federally authorized tax practitioner in a noncriminal tax proceeding before the IRS or the federal courts. Congress felt that the right to privileged communications should not depend on whether the adviser is licensed to practice law. However, the privilege does not apply to any communication between a CPA and his or her client if the communication would not have been privileged between an attorney and the attorney's client. For example, information disclosed to an attorney (or CPA) for the purpose of preparing a tax return is not a privileged communication.[2] The accountant in tax practice is thus faced with a dilemma. If a client letter discloses both the strengths and weaknesses of the client's tax posture, the letter could weaken the client's position (even assist the revenue agent's case) if it were to fall into the agent's hands. On the other hand, if the potential weaknesses of the position are not clearly communicated to the client, the tax adviser exposes himself or herself to potential legal liability for inappropriate advice.

Although many advisers do not agree, we believe that client letters should contain comprehensive information, including reference to those factors that the IRS could challenge. In our opinion, full disclosure and self-protection against claims by clients, which may endanger the professional reputation of all tax practitioners, is more important than the risk of an IRS challenge. Any disclosure of weaknesses must be carefully worded, and the client should be cautioned in advance to control possession of the letter.

Disclaimer Statements. Tax advisers deal with two basically different situations. In the case of after-the-fact advice, tax practitioners must assure themselves that they understand all the facts necessary to reach valid conclusions. Incomplete or inaccurate facts may lead advisers to erroneous conclusions. In planning situations, in which many of the facts are still *controllable,* tax advisers must assure themselves that they fully understand their clients' objectives and any operational constraints on achieving those objectives. Furthermore, planning situations frequently involve lengthy time periods during which changes in tax laws may occur, thus possibly changing the recommended course of action. Statement on Standards for Tax Services (SSTS) No. 8, *Form and Content of Advice to Taxpayers* (AICPA, *Professional Standards,* vol. 2, TS sec. 800), issued by the AICPA Tax Executive Committee, notes some of the problems associated with new developments in tax matters.

---

[2] *United States v. Frederick,* 182 F3d 496 (CA-7, 1999); cert. applied for Oct. 25, 1999, cert. denied, 120 SCt 1157, 2/22/2000

A member may assist a taxpayer in implementing procedures or plans associated with the advice offered. When providing such assistance, the member should review and revise such advice as warranted by new developments and factors affecting the transaction.

Sometimes a member is requested to provide tax advice but does not assist in implementing the plans adopted. Although such developments as legislative or administrative changes or further judicial interpretations may affect the advice previously provided, a member cannot be expected to communicate subsequent developments that affect such advice unless the member undertakes this obligation by specific agreement with the taxpayer.[3]

On the advisability of including a disclaimer statement in a client letter, SSTS No. 8 states:

Taxpayers should be informed that advice reflects professional judgment based on an existing situation and that subsequent developments could affect previous professional advice. Members may use precautionary language to the effect that their advice is based on facts as stated and authorities that are subject to change.[4]

In summary, SSTS No. 8 concludes that a disclaimer statement should be included. In our opinion, the client letter should include a brief restatement of the important facts, a statement to the effect that all conclusions stated in the letter are based on those specific facts, and a warning to the client of the dangers implicit in any changes or inaccuracies in those facts. In the case of tax-planning engagements, we also recommend that the tax practitioner include a warning that future changes in the law could jeopardize the planned end results. An example of such a disclaimer statement in a compliance (after-the-fact) client letter appears in chapter 8.

Protest Letters

Another external document commonly prepared by the tax practitioner is the *protest* of a client's tax deficiency as assessed by the IRS. You need to file a written protest (1) in all employee plan and

---

[3] SSTS No. 8 (AICPA, *Professional Standards*, vol. 2, TS sec. 800.08-.09).
[4] SSTS No. 8 (AICPA, *Professional Standards*, vol. 2, TS sec. 800.10).

exempt organization cases without regard to the dollar amount at issue; (2) in all partnership and S corporation cases without regard to the dollar amount at issue; and (3) in all other cases, unless you qualify for the small case request procedure. The small case request procedure may be used if the total amount of the deficiency for any tax period is not more than $25,000.[5] Some tax advisers feel, however, that a well-written formal protest enhances the chances of resolving a disagreement successfully even in cases resulting from office audits or deficiencies of $25,000 or less. The IRS suggests that a protest include

(1) the taxpayer's name and address, and a daytime phone number.

(2) a statement that the taxpayer wants to appeal the findings of the examiner to the Appeals Office.

(3) a copy of the letter showing the proposed adjustments and findings the taxpayer does not agree with (or the date and symbols from the letter).

(4) the tax periods or years involved.

(5) a list of the changes that the taxpayer does not agree with, and why the taxpayer does not agree.

(6) a statement of facts supporting the taxpayer's position on any issue with which the taxpayer does not agree.

(7) a statement outlining the law or other authority on which the taxpayer is relying.

The taxpayer must sign the written protest, stating that it is true, under the penalties of perjury as follows:

Under the penalties of perjury, I declare that I examined the facts stated in this protest, including any accompanying documents, and, to the best of my knowledge and belief, they are true, correct, and complete.

---

[5] IRS Publication 556, *Examination of Returns, Appeal Rights, and Claims for Refund,* Washington, D.C.: Government Printing Office (Rev. Aug. 2005).

If the taxpayer's representative submits the protest, he or she must substitute a declaration stating

(1) that the taxpayer's representative submitted the protest and accompanying documents, and

(2) whether the representative knows personally that the facts stated in the protest and accompanying documents are true and correct.[6]

In principle, the body of a protest follows the format of a client letter in that the protest specifies important facts, delineates contested findings, and lists the authority supporting the taxpayer's position. An example of a typical protest letter follows:

July 14, 2008

[*Full Name*]
IRS Office of Appeals
Federal Building
Salt Lake City, UT 84101

Re: Intermountain Stove, Inc.
1408 State Street
Moroni, Utah 84646

Corporate income taxes for
the year ended 12/31/2006

Dear Mr. or Ms. [*Last Name*]:

I am writing in reference to your letter of May 23, 2008 (see attached copy), which transmitted your examining officer's report dated May 8, 2008, covering his examination of Intermountain Stove's corporate income tax return for the year ended December 31, 2006. In the report, the examining officer recommended adjustments to the taxable income (loss) in the following amount:

Tax Year	Amount of Increase in Income Reported
December 31, 2006	$142,000

---

[6] IRS Publication 5, *Your Appeal Rights and How to Prepare a Protest If You Don't Agree*, Washington, D.C.: Government Printing Office (Rev. Jan. 1999)

PROTEST AGAINST ADJUSTMENT

Your letter granted the taxpayer a period of 30 days from the date thereof within which to protest the recommendations of the examining officer, which period was subsequently extended to July 22, 2008, by your letter dated June 6, 2008, a copy of which is attached. This protest to the Appeals Office is accordingly being filed within that period, as extended.

The taxpayer respectfully protests against the proposed adjustment stated below.

FINDINGS TO WHICH TAXPAYER
TAKES EXCEPTION

Exception is now taken to the following item:

Disallowance of the following expenses of
Intermountain Stove, Inc.

Description	Year	Amount
Professional Fees	December 31, 2006	$142,000

GROUNDS UPON WHICH TAXPAYER RELIES

The taxpayer submits the following information to support its contentions:

Expenses of Intermountain Stove, Inc.

Your examining officer contends that fees paid in the amount of $142,000 in connection with the employment of certain individuals who were experienced in various phases of the production and sale of cast iron stoves should be considered as the acquisition costs of assets in connection with expansion of operations and establishment of a new cast iron stove division.

Taxpayer contends, for reasons set forth below, that the examining officer's position is untenable on the facts and in law and that such costs are clearly deductible as ordinary and necessary expenses incurred in its trade or business, deductible in accordance with Section 162 of the Internal Revenue Code.

Facts concerning the operations of Intermountain Stove, Inc.

Intermountain Stove, Inc. (ISI) is a manufacturer of campers. Orders for campers in 2006 declined, and ISI decided, in addition to their camper operation, to again produce wood- and coal-burning stoves, a product ISI had manufactured until the end of World War II and for which a strong demand seemed to exist. To begin immediate operation in a new stove division, ISI contracted with a consulting firm to locate personnel with experience in the production and marketing of cast iron stoves. The fee paid for such services during 2006 amounted to $142,000.

Discussion of authorities

Section 162(a) of the Internal Revenue Code provides:

> There shall be allowed as a deduction all of the ordinary and necessary expenses paid or incurred during the taxable year in carrying on any trade or business . . . .

To contend, as the examining officer does, that assets were acquired with the employment of the newly acquired employees is not within the usual interpretation of the Internal Revenue Code.

There were no employment contracts purchased, as may sometimes be found in the hiring of professional athletes; the employees were free to sever their employment relationships at any time, and, in fact, certain of these specific individuals have done so. The examining officer's position was considered in *David J. Primuth*, 54 T.C. 374 (1970), in which the court stated:

> It might be argued that the payment of an employment fee is capital in nature and hence not currently deductible. Presumably, under this view the fee would be deductible when the related employment is terminated. However, the difficulty with this view is to conjure up a capital asset which had been purchased. Certainly, the expense was not related to the purchase or sale of a capital asset . . . .

And a concurring opinion added:

> Certainly, in the ordinary affairs of life, common understanding would clearly encompass the fee paid to the employment agency herein as "ordinary and necessary expenses in carrying on any trade or business" (sec. 162) within the "usual, ordinary and everyday meaning of the term."

Your examining officer is here attempting to disallow deductions for amounts paid to outside consultants in a situation in which the expenses would clearly be deductible if the work had been performed by the company's own staff. No such distinction should be made. The corporation employed the expertise of a knowledgeable consultant to assist in the location of personnel with specific background and experience. The payment of fees for such assistance may be compared with the direct payroll and overhead costs of operating an in-house personnel department.

The examining officer apparently believes that such costs should be capitalized primarily because they might be nonrecurring in nature. This is not the test of whether an expense is ordinary and necessary. As the Supreme Court stated in *Thomas H. Welch v. Helvering*, 290 U.S. 111, 3 USTC ¶1164 (1933), "Ordinary in this context does not mean that the payments must be habitual or normal in the sense that that same taxpayer may make them often." The fees are ordinary and necessary because it is the common experience in the business community that payments are made for assistance in the procurement of personnel. This is emphasized by the Court in *Primuth* by the following statement: " 'Fees' must be deemed ordinary and necessary from every realistic point of view in today's marketplace where corporate executives change employers with a notable degree of frequency."

These expenditures, if paid by the individual employees and reimbursed by the employer, would have been clearly deductible by both the employee and the employer, with the employee having an offsetting amount of income for the reimbursement. (See Rev. Rul. 75-120, 1975-1 C.B. 55 and Rev. Rul. 78-93, 1978-1 C.B. 38.) The expense is no less deductible when paid directly by the corporation.

It is, therefore, contended that the disallowance made by the examining officer was in error.

REQUEST FOR CONFERENCE[7]

An oral hearing is requested before the regional Appeals Office.

STATEMENT WITH RESPECT TO PREPARATION

The attached protest was prepared by the undersigned on the basis of information available to him (or her). All statements contained therein are true and correct to the best of his (or her) knowledge and belief.

_____

Signature of Tax Practitioner

---

[7] It is assumed that an appropriate power of attorney has been filed with the IRS. Otherwise, a power of attorney must be attached to the protest.

Requests for Rulings and Determination Letters

Frequently, tax practitioners find it necessary to seek a ruling from the IRS to fix the tax consequences of a client's anticipated business transaction or to settle a disagreement with a revenue agent during an examination. The general procedures with respect to advance rulings (before-the-fact) and determination letters (after-the-fact) are outlined in the first revenue procedure issued each year. (See Rev. Proc. 2008-1, 2008-1 I.R.B. 1.) The IRS has announced that a careful adherence to the specified requirements will minimize delays in processing requests for rulings and determination letters.

In addition to this annual revenue procedure, the IRS has, on occasion, issued revenue procedures that govern ruling requests for specific topics. For example, the procedures for obtaining determination letters involving Sections 401, 403(a), 409, and 4975(e)(7) are contained in Rev. Proc. 2005-6.[8] Similarly, Rev. Proc. 2003-43[9] provides guidance for corporations requesting relief for late S corporation elections and certain untimely elections required to be filed by or with respect to an S corporation.

Before 1988, the IRS responded to taxpayer inquiries without charge. However, currently fees are charged, ranging from $275 to $11,500 for ruling letters, determination letters, and opinion letters. (For a partial list of user fees, see Rev. Proc. 2008-1, appendix A.) The following is an abbreviated example of a possible ruling request:[10]

March 1, 2008

Internal Revenue Service
Associate Chief Counsel (Domestic)
Attention CC:PA:LPD:DRU
P.O. Box 7604
Ben Franklin Station
Washington, D.C. 20044

---

[8] Rev. Proc. 2006-6, 2006-1 I.R.B. 204. Employee plan determination letters; revised procedures; Sec. 401(a), 403(a), 409, 4975; Rev. Proc. 2005-6 superseded
[9] Rev. Proc. 2007-62, 2007-41 I.R.B. 786 and Rev. Proc. 2003-43, 2003-23 C.B. 998
[10] The revenue procedures dealing with a Section 355 ruling request require as many as 24 separate representations. Since the purpose of this sample ruling request is merely to illustrate the process, not all of the possible representations are included.

Re: American Rock & Sand Inc., E.I.N. 12-3456789

Dear Sir or Madam:

Rulings are respectfully requested as to the federal income tax consequences of the proposed transaction pursuant to Section 355 of the Internal Revenue Code of 1986, as amended (Code).

FACTS

The American Rock & Sand, Inc. (Distributing), E.I.N. 12-3456789, a Utah corporation, is a privately owned corporation with executive offices located at 1235 N. 1500 W., Provo, UT 84604. As of March 1, 2008, the authorized capital of Distributing consisted of 1,000 shares voting common stock. The issued and outstanding stock of Distributing is held principally by the Jones family. Distributing is engaged in the business of road and highway construction and has continually been actively engaged in such business for the past 10 years.

Distributing uses the accrual method of accounting and maintains its books of account on a fiscal year ending June 30. Distributing files a consolidated federal income tax return with its subsidiaries and is subject to examination by the District Director, Salt Lake City, UT.

Pahrump Ready Mix, Inc. (Controlled), E.I.N. 12-9876543, a Utah corporation, was formed on June 1, 1973, in order to purchase the assets of a division of an unrelated company. Since the date of that acquisition, Controlled has been actively involved in the business of making and delivering concrete.

As of March 1, 2008, the authorized capital of Controlled consisted of 1,000 shares of Class A common stock, all of which is issued and outstanding and held by Distributing. Controlled is also authorized to issue 10,000 shares of Class B nonvoting common stock, but no shares are currently issued and outstanding.

BUSINESS PURPOSE

A key employee of Controlled wishes to acquire an equity interest in Controlled, but does not wish to, nor can he afford to, purchase an equity interest as long as Controlled is a wholly owned subsidiary of Distributing. Furthermore, he does not wish to acquire an equity interest in Controlled while it has a corporate shareholder as a result of the following factors:

(1) The parent company could use the earnings and profits of Controlled to invest in other business ventures.

(2) Having a corporate parent-shareholder would give him a minority interest in Controlled with a shareholder whose interest in the future of Controlled may be different than his.

(3) Because the corporate shareholder would be entitled to a dividend received deduction, which is a benefit unavailable to him, the decisions regarding dividend distributions may differ from his.

The key employee has indicated that he would seriously consider terminating employment with Controlled if he is not offered an opportunity to purchase such a stock interest, and that when shares of Controlled stock are offered to him, he will purchase them.

PROPOSED TRANSACTION

Distributing will distribute to its shareholders, on a pro rata basis, all of the Controlled voting common stock. Controlled will then sell to the key employee 100 shares of Class B nonvoting stock within one year of receipt of an IRS ruling letter. This will represent 100 percent of the outstanding shares of this class of stock and will represent 5 percent of all of the outstanding shares of Controlled. The Class B nonvoting common stock will, in all respects, be identical to the outstanding Class A common stock, except that it is nonvoting and will contain a restriction requiring resale of Controlled at fair market value.

REPRESENTATIONS

In connection with the proposed transaction, the following representations are made:

(a) There is no plan or intention by the shareholders or security holders of Distributing to sell, exchange, transfer by gift, or otherwise dispose of any of their stock in, or securities of, either Distributing or Controlled subsequent to the proposed transaction.

(b) There is no plan or intention to liquidate either Distributing or Controlled, to merge either corporation with any other corporation, or to sell, or otherwise dispose of the assets of either corporation subsequent to the transaction, except in the ordinary course of business.

(c) Distributing, Controlled, and their respective shareholders will each pay their own expenses, if any, incurred in connection with the proposed transaction.

(d) Following the proposed transaction, Distributing and Controlled will each independently continue the active conduct of their respective businesses with their own separate employees.

(*e*) No intercorporate debt will exist between Distributing and Controlled at the time of, or subsequent to, the distribution of Controlled's stock.

(*f*) No two parties to the transaction are investment companies as defined in section 368(a)(2)(F)(iii) and (iv) of the Code.

(*g*) The five years of financial information submitted on behalf of Distributing and Controlled is representative of each corporation's present operations, and, with regard to each corporation, there have been no substantial operational changes since the date of the last financial statements submitted.

(*h*) Payments made in connection with all continuing transactions between Distributing and Controlled will be for fair market value based on terms and conditions arrived at by the parties bargaining at arm's length.

(*i*) No part of the consideration to be distributed by Distributing will be received by a shareholder as a creditor, employee, or in any capacity other than that of a shareholder of the corporation.

RULINGS REQUESTED

On the basis of the above information and representations, the following rulings are respectfully requested:

(*a*) No gain or loss will be recognized by Distributing upon the distribution of all of the Controlled stock to the shareholders of Distributing. Section 311(a).

(*b*) No gain or loss will be recognized to (and no amount will be included in the income of) the shareholders of Distributing upon the receipt of Controlled stock, as described above. Section 355(a)(1).

(*c*) Pursuant to section 358(a)(1), the basis of the stock of Controlled and Distributing in the hands of the shareholders of Distributing after the distribution will be the same as the basis of the Distributing stock held immediately before the distribution, allocated in proportion to the relative fair market value of each in accordance with section 1.358-2(a)(2) of the Regulations.

(*d*) Provided the Distributing stock was held as a capital asset on the date of the distribution of the Controlled stock, the holding period of the Controlled stock received by each shareholder of Distributing will include the holding period of the Distributing stock with respect to which the distribution was made. Section 1223(l).

(*e*) As provided in section 312(h) of the Code, proper allocation of earnings and profits between Distributing and Controlled will be made in accordance with section 1.312-10(a) of the Regulations.

MEMORANDUM OF AUTHORITIES

Section 355 provides for the tax-free spin-off of a wholly owned subsidiary. The general rules that are required for the transaction to meet the requirements of Section 355 are

(*a*) immediately before the distribution, the distributing corporation must control the corporation whose shares are being distributed. The term *control* is defined by Section 368(c) to mean stock possessing at least 80 percent of the total combined voting power and at least 80 percent of the total number of shares of all other classes of stock. Section 355(a)(1)(A).

(*b*) immediately after the distribution, both the distributing and controlled corporations must engage in the active conduct of a trade or business. Section 355(a)(1)(C) and 355(b).

(*c*) the active conduct of a trade or business is satisfied only if the trade or business was actively conducted throughout the five-year period ending on the date of the distribution with certain limitations. Section 355(b)(2).

(*d*) the distributing corporation must distribute all of its stock and securities in the controlled corporation, or distribute enough stock to constitute control and establish to the satisfaction of the Commissioner, that the retention of stock in the controlled corporation is not part of a tax avoidance plan. Section 355(a)(1)(D).

(*e*) the transaction must not be used principally as a device for the distribution of earnings and profits. Section 355(a)(1)(B).

(*f*) there must be a corporate business purpose for the transaction and continuity of interest. Regulations Section 1.355-2(b) and (c).

The test described in (*a*) above is satisfied, as Distributing owns 100 percent of Controlled.

The test in (*b*) will be satisfied given that both Distributing and Controlled will continue to actively conduct their respective businesses.

The test described in (*c*) is satisfied. The businesses of both Distributing and Controlled are active trades or businesses that have been carried on for more than five years.

The test described in (*d*) above will be satisfied because Distributing will distribute 100 percent of the stock of Controlled to its shareholders.

Distributing believes that the test described in (*e*) above is met because it has no knowledge of any plan or intention on the part of its shareholders to sell or exchange stock of either Distributing or Controlled, or to liquidate or sell the assets of Controlled. Thus, there will be no prearranged disposition of stock by the shareholders, and consummation of the transaction will effect only a readjustment of continuing interest in property under modified corporate form.

The business purpose test described in (f) is satisfied. The sole reason for effectuating the proposed transaction is to enable one of Controlled's key employees to acquire an equity interest in the corporation.

PROCEDURAL STATEMENT

To the best of the knowledge of the taxpayer and the within-named taxpayer's representatives, the identical issues involved in this request for a ruling either are not in a return of the taxpayer (or of a related taxpayer within the meaning of Section 267 of the Code, or a member of an affiliated group of which the taxpayer is also a member within the meaning of Section 1504), or if they are, then such issues (1) are not under examination by a District Director; (2) either have not been examined by a District Director, or if they have been examined, the statutory period of limitations on either assessment or for filing a claim for refund or credit of tax has expired, or a closing agreement covering the issue or liability has been entered into by a District Director; (3) are not under consideration by an Appeals Office in connection with a return of the taxpayer for an earlier period; (4) either have not been considered by an Appeals Office in connection with a return of the taxpayer for an earlier period, or if they have been considered, the statutory period of limitations on either assessment or for filing a claim for refund or credit of tax has expired, or a closing agreement covering such issues has been entered into by an Appeals Office; and (5) are not pending in litigation in a case involving the taxpayer or a related taxpayer. To the best of the knowledge of the taxpayer and the taxpayer's representatives, the identical or similar issues involved in this ruling request have not been (i) submitted to the Service, but withdrawn before a ruling was issued, or (ii) ruled on by the Service to the taxpayer or predecessor of the taxpayer.

Except as discussed above, the undersigned is not aware of any precedential published authority that is directly contrary to the rulings requested herein.

A conference is requested in the event that the issuance of an unfavorable ruling is contemplated or in the event that such conference would be of assistance to your office in the consideration of this request for a ruling.

Please address your reply and ruling letter to the undersigned, pursuant to the enclosed Power of Attorney. If any additional information is required, please telephone (Mr. or Ms.) _____ _____ at (   ) _____-_____, or the undersigned.

Respectfully submitted,
American Rock & Sand, Inc.

By _____
(Signature of Tax Practitioner)

[*Attach Section 355-Checklist Questionnaire. See Rev. Proc. 96-30, 1996-1 C.B. 696, (Apr. 22, 1996) and Rev. Proc. 2003-48, 2003-2 C.B. 86 for a more detailed discussion of the requirements for a Section 355 ruling request.*]

DECLARATION UNDER PENALTIES OF PERJURY

Under penalties of perjury, I declare that I have examined this request, including accompanying documents, and, to the best of my knowledge and belief, the request contains all the relevant facts relating to the request, and such facts are true, correct, and complete.

_____   _____
(Name of Corporate Officer)   (Date)
(Title)
(Company Name)

[*Enclose User Fee With Request.*]

STATEMENT OF PROPOSED DELETIONS UNDER SECTION 6110

With reference to the attached request for ruling dated _____, relating to _____, no information other than names, addresses, and taxpayer identifying numbers need be deleted under Section 6110(c).

_____   _____
(Name of Corporate Officer)   (Date)
(Title)
(Company Name)

[*The deletions statement must not appear in the request, but instead must be made in a separate document and placed on top of the request.*]

As mentioned in chapter 4, under the Freedom of Information Act and Section 6110(a) of the IRC, rulings and their associated background files are open for public inspection. However, the IRS is required under Section 6110(c) to delete certain information, such as, names, addresses, identification numbers, or any other information that the taxpayer feels would enable someone reading the published private letter ruling to identify the taxpayer that actually received the ruling. For that reason Rev. Proc. 2003-1 suggests that a ruling be accompanied by a statement of proposed deletions. This can be accomplished by sending the IRS a copy of the ruling request with brackets around the phrases or words the taxpayer suggests deleting.

As depicted in the sample ruling request, a request should also be signed by the taxpayer or an authorized representative. If signed by an authorized representative, the request should include an appropriate power of attorney and evidence that the representative is currently an attorney, a certified public accountant, or an enrolled agent in good standing and duly licensed to practice.

8

Tax Research in the *Closed-Fact* Case: An Example

The preparation of a well-organized working paper file cannot be overemphasized because it proves that research efforts have been thorough, are logically correct, and are adequately documented. The elements of this chapter constitute a sample client file. A client file could be maintained as either a paper file or as an electronic file. The formats of files used in practice vary substantially among firms. The new tax accountant who uses this tax study as a guide for actual research efforts should be prepared to modify this illustration to conform to the format used by his or her employer. It is hoped that the general format suggested here would be approved by most experienced tax advisers, although any employer might disagree with any of several specifics. The sample is based on a relatively simple incorporation transaction. Because the tax problems illustrated are relatively simple, the supporting file would be considered excessive by most advisers. The cost of preparing such an elaborate file would be too great to justify. In this case, the reader should concentrate more on general working paper content and arrangement than on the substantive tax issues illustrated. However, in more complex problems, this kind of detail may well be appropriate.

Throughout this chapter it is assumed that the client has contacted the accountant after all aspects of the incorporation transaction were completed. In other words, the accountant's task in this engagement is restricted to compliance-related tax research. We have combined the information for three clients into one file; that is, that of the new corporate entity and that of its president and vice president. In practice, however, three separate files would be maintained. Finally, a practice file would very likely include a substantial number of excerpts from the Internal Revenue Code, Treasury regulations, revenue rulings, judicial decisions, commercial tax services, and other reference works. These excerpts could be photocopies or, in the case of electronic databases, the excerpts might be electronically identified and organized.

Red E. Ink, Judith Dixon, and Ready, Inc.

Tax File
December 2008

Index to Working Papers

Item	Page Ref.
Client Letter (draft)	*1–3*
General Client Information	
Memo to File, R. U. Partner	*A-1–A-3*
Memo to File, Fred E. Manager	*A-4*
Red E. Ink—Personal Account	
Summary of Questions Investigated	*B-1–B-2*
Working Papers	*C-1–C-17*
Judith Dixon—Personal Account	
Summary of Questions Investigated	*D-1–D-2*
Ready, Inc.—Corporate Account	
Summary of Questions Investigated	*E-1*
Working Papers	*F-1–F-3*
Suggestions for Client's Future Consideration	*G-1*

R. U. Partner & Company
Certified Public Accountants
2010 Professional Tower
Calum City, USA 00001

December 24, 2008

Mr. Red E. Ink, President
Ms. Judith Dixon, Vice President
Ready, Incorporated
120 Publisher Lane
Calum City, USA 00002

Dear Mr. Ink and Ms. Dixon:

This letter confirms the oral agreement of December 17, 2008, in which our firm agreed to undertake the preparation of your respective federal income tax returns along with that of Ready, Inc., for next year. This letter also reports the preliminary results of our investigation into the tax consequences of the formation of Ready, Inc., last March. We are pleased to be of service to you and anticipate that our relationship will prove to be mutually beneficial. Please feel free to call upon me at any time.

Before stating the preliminary results of our investigation into the tax consequences of your incorporation transaction, I would like to restate briefly all of the important facts as we understand them. Please review this statement of facts very carefully. Our conclusions depend on a complete and accurate understanding of all the facts. If any of the following statements is either incorrect or incomplete, please call it to my attention immediately, no matter how small or insignificant the difference may appear to be.

Our conclusions are based on an understanding that on March 1, 2008, the following exchanges occurred in the process of forming a new corporation, Ready, Inc. Ms. Dixon transferred two copyrights to Ready, Inc., in exchange for 250 shares of common stock. Ms. Dixon had previously paid $1,000 for filing the copyrights. In addition, the corporation assumed a $2,500 word processing bill, which Ms. Dixon owed for these two manuscripts.

(draft)
FEM
12/24/2008

Red E. Ink
Judith Dixon
December 24, 2008
Page 2

Mr. Ink concurrently transferred all the assets and liabilities of his former sole proprietorship printing company, Red Publishings, to the new corporation in exchange for 750 shares of Ready, Inc., common stock. The assets transferred consisted of $11,700 cash, $10,000 (estimated market value) printing supplies, $50,000 (face value) trade receivables, and $58,300 (tax adjusted basis) equipment. The equipment, purchased new in 2003 for $100,000, had been depreciated for tax purposes under the modified accelerated cost recovery system (MACRS) since its acquisition. The liabilities assumed by Ready, Inc., consisted of the $65,000 mortgage remaining from the original equipment purchase in 2006 and current trade payables of $10,000. We further understand that Ready, Inc., plans to continue to occupy the building leased by Red Publishings on May 1, 2006, from Branden Properties until the expiration of that lease on April 30, 2010. Finally, we understand that Ready, Inc., has issued only 1,000 shares of common stock and that Mr. Ink retains 730 shares; that Mr. Ink's wife Neva holds 10 shares; that Mr. Tom Books, the corporate secretary-treasurer, holds 10 shares; and that Ms. Dixon holds the remaining 250 shares. The shares held by Mrs. Ink and Mr. Books were given to them by Mr. Ink, as a gift, on March 1, 2008. It is our understanding that Ready, Inc. will report its taxable income on an accrual method, calendar year basis.

Assuming that the preceding paragraphs represent a complete and accurate statement of all the facts pertinent to the incorporation transaction, we anticipate reporting that event as a wholly nontaxable transaction. In other words, neither of you, the incorporators (individually), nor your corporation will report any taxable income or loss solely because of your incorporation of the printing business. The trade receivables collected by Ready, Inc., after March 1, 2008, will be reported as the taxable income of the corporate entity; collections made between January 1, 2008, and February 28, 2008, will be considered part of Mr. Ink's personal taxable income for 2008.

There is a possibility that the Internal Revenue Service could argue (1) that Ms. Dixon is required to recognize $2,500 of taxable income or

(draft)
FEM
12/24/2008

Red E. Ink
Judith Dixon
December 24, 2008
Page 3

(2) that the corporation could not deduct the $10,000 in trade payables it assumed from the proprietorship. If either of you desire, I would be pleased to discuss these matters in greater detail. Perhaps, it would be desirable for Mr. Bent and me to meet with both of you and review these potential problems prior to our filing the corporate tax return.[1]

If Mr. Tom Books desires any help in maintaining the corporation's regular financial accounts, we shall be happy to assist him. It will be necessary for us to have access to your personal financial records no later than March 1, 2009, if the federal income tax returns are to be completed and filed on a timely basis.

Finally, may I suggest that we plan to have at least one more meeting in my office sometime prior to February 28, 2009, to discuss possible tax planning opportunities available to you and the new corporation. Among other considerations, we should jointly review the possibility that you may want to make an S election, may need to structure executive compensation arrangements carefully, and may wish to institute a pension plan. Please telephone me to arrange an appointment if you would like to do this shortly after the holidays.

Thank you again for selecting our firm for tax assistance. It is very important that some of the material in this letter be kept confidential, and we strongly recommend that you carefully control access to it at all times. If you have any questions about any of the matters discussed, feel free to request a more detailed explanation or drop by and review the complete files, which are available in my office. If I should not be available, my assistant, Fred Manager, would be happy to help you. We look forward to serving you in the future.

Sincerely yours,

Robert U. Partner

---

[1] Some advisers would delete this paragraph and handle the matter orally.

(draft)
FEM
12/24/2008

R. U. Partner & Company
Certified Public Accountants
2010 Professional Tower
Calum City, USA 00001

December 17, 2008

MEMO TO FILE

FROM: R. U. Partner

SUBJECT: Ready, Inc.—Tax Engagement

Mr. Red E. Ink (president) and Ms. Judith Dixon (vice president) this morning engaged our firm to prepare and file their personal annual federal income tax returns and the federal corporate tax return for Ready, Inc. During an interview in my office, the following information pertinent to the first year's tax returns was obtained.

On March 1, 2008, Red E. Ink and Judith Dixon incorporated the sole proprietorship publishing house that Mr. Ink has for two years previously operated as Red Publishings. There were two primary business reasons for incorporating: (1) The incorporators desired to limit their personal liability in a growing business; and (2) greater access to credit and equity markets.

Judith Dixon is a full-time practicing trial lawyer and has done a substantial amount of work in media law. Several years ago she wrote, on her own time, five articles in various professional journals. Her objective in writing the articles was to establish a reputation among her professional peers and to enjoy such resulting benefits as client referrals and seminar speaking engagements. As a matter of fact, Ms. Dixon obtained such benefits. The articles were written on a gratis basis.

For the past four years, Ms. Dixon has devoted many hours to writing two full-length books, *Trials and Tribulation* and *Media Law: Developing Frontiers*. Ms. Dixon has encountered unexpected difficulty in getting her manuscripts published. This difficulty has been very frustrating to Ms. Dixon.

A-1 (RUP 12/17/2008)

Memo to File (R. U. Partner)
December 17, 2008
Page 2

Ms. Dixon met Mr. Ink at a seminar—entitled "Media and Its Place in Our American Society"—during the fall of 2007. This was one of several seminars at which Ms. Dixon lectured annually on a fee basis. Red Publishings had never been approached by Ms. Dixon because she had wanted to be associated with a larger organization. However, at this point Ms. Dixon feared the possibility that her works would never appear in print. Thus, after a period in which Ms. Dixon sold Mr. Ink on the quality of her books and, conversely, Mr. Ink sold Ms. Dixon on the capability and growth potential of his publishing house, they convinced one another that their association would bring adequate returns to all concerned.

The following incorporation transaction was agreed upon: Judith transferred the copyrights to her two manuscripts to Ready, Inc., a newly formed corporation. Judith's tax basis in the two manuscripts was $1,000, the amount she paid another lawyer to file the copyright papers. She still owed $2,500 for the manuscript word processing. Ready, Inc., agreed to assume this liability and to issue Judith 250 shares of Ready, Inc., common stock.

Red transferred *all* the assets and liabilities of his former proprietorship to Ready, Inc., in exchange for 750 shares of Ready, Inc., common stock. Immediately after receiving the 750 shares, Red gave 10 shares to his wife, Neva, and another 10 shares to Tom Books, an unrelated and longtime employee who was named the corporate secretary-treasurer. Red stated that these two transfers were intended as gifts and not as compensation for any prior services.

Tom Books provided me with a copy of the balance sheet for Red Publishings just prior to the incorporation. It appears as follows:

Red Publishings
Balance Sheet
February 28, 2008

Assets

Cash	$ 11,700
Supplies on hand	10,000
Trade receivables	50,000
Equipment (net)	58,300
Total assets	$130,000

A-2 (RUP 12/17/2008)

Memo to File (R. U. Partner)
December 17, 2008
Page 3

Liabilities & Equity

Trade payables	$10,000	
Mortgage payable	65,000	
Total liabilities		$ 75,000
Red E. Ink, capital		55,000
Total liabilities & equity		$130,000

The balance sheet was prepared at the request of Mr. Hal Bent, who served as legal counsel to Mr. Ink and Ms. Dixon during the Ready, Inc., incorporation. Mr. Bent and Ms. Dixon are members of the same law firm. Incidentally, Mr. Bent recommended to Mr. Ink and Ms. Dixon that our firm be engaged to prepare and to file their federal tax returns.

During our interview Mr. Ink and Ms. Dixon stated that they had always reported their respective personal incomes on a calendar-year, cash basis. It is their intention to report the corporation's taxable income on an accrual basis in the future. They plan to have the corporation use the calendar year.

The $65,000 mortgage payable represents the balance payable on equipment that was purchased in 2006. This equipment has been depreciated under MACRS. The $58,300 shown on the balance sheet is tax book value. Red estimates that the fair market value of the equipment transferred was approximately $75,000 at the time of the incorporation transaction. The trade payables represent the unpaid balances for supplies, utilities, employees' wages, and so on, as of the end of February 2008. All of these accounts were paid by Ready, Inc., within 60 days following incorporation. Tom has agreed to provide us with Ready's income statement and year-end balance sheet by no later than February 1, 2009. Mr. Ink and Ms. Dixon will provide us with additional details concerning their personal tax returns in early February.

I have assigned Fred E. Manager the responsibility of investigating all tax consequences associated with the initial incorporation of Ready, Inc. He is immediately to begin preparation of our file, which will be used early next year in connection with the completion of the tax returns for these new clients. All preliminary research should be completed by Fred and reviewed by me before December 31, 2008. I have also asked Fred to prepare a draft of a client letter confirming this new engagement and stating our preliminary findings on the tax consequences of the incorporation transaction.

A-3 (RUP 12/17/2008)

R. U. Partner & Company
Certified Public Accountants
2010 Professional Tower
Calum City, USA 00001

December 19, 2008

MEMO TO FILE

FROM: Fred E. Manager

SUBJECT: Additional Information on Ready, Inc.—Tax Engagement

After reviewing Mr. Partner's file memo of December 17, 2008, and subsequently undertaking limited initial research into the tax questions pertinent to filing the Red E. Ink, Judith Dixon, and Ready, Inc., federal income tax returns, I determined that additional information should be obtained. Specifically, I observed that the February 28, 2008, balance sheet included no real property, and I believed that it was necessary for several reasons to confirm all the facts pertinent to this client's real estate arrangements. Accordingly, with R. U.'s approval, I telephoned Tom Books today and obtained the following additional information.

Tom explained that Red had signed a 48-month lease with Branden Properties, Inc., on May 1, 2006, and that Ready, Inc., had continued to occupy the same premises and had paid all monthly rentals due under this lease ($6,000 per month) since March 1, 2008. It is Tom's opinion that Red probably will construct his own building once this lease expires but that he probably will not try to get out of the present lease before its expiration on April 30, 2010. Tom said that the lease agreement calls for a two-month penalty payment (that is, a $12,000 payment) if either party should break the lease prior to its expiration. According to this agreement, whichever party breaks the lease must pay the other the stipulated sum. Tom further stated that the present lease "really is not a particularly good one." In 2006, it appeared to Red that office space in Calum City was going to be scarce, and he thought that the lease then negotiated was a wholly reasonable one. By the spring of 2008, however, the available office space exceeded the demand. Tom suggested (and, based on his square-footage estimates, I agree) that this same lease could now be negotiated for about $5,500 per month. The penalty for breaking the lease would just about equal the savings that could be obtained by renegotiating a new lease today. Under the circumstances, Red has elected to continue with the old lease for the present. This option allows him time to decide whether to build or purchase another building sometime prior to 2010.

A-4 (FEM 12/19/2008)

Red E. Ink (Personal Account)
Summary of Questions Investigated
December 2008

W.P. Ref.

1. *Was the March 1, 2008, incorporation transaction between Red E. Ink, Judith Dixon, and Ready, Inc., a tax-free transfer under Section 351?*

   Conclusion: Yes; all of the requirements of Section 351 were satisfied.   *C-1–C-2*

   a. *Collateral Question: Do Ms. Dixon's copyrights qualify as "property" for purposes of Section 351?*

      Conclusion: Yes. Substantial authority probably exists to treat Ms. Dixon's copyrights as Section 351 property.   *C-3–C-4*

   b. *Collateral Question: Do Mr. Ink and Ms. Dixon have any "control" requirement problems under Section 351(a)? Specifically, since Mr. Ink individually owns only 75% of the Ready, Inc., common stock, is the section 351(a) control requirement met?*

      Conclusion: There are no problems. The Section 351(a) control requirement is met.   *C-5–C-6*

   c. *Collateral Question: Could Ready's assumption of liabilities cause partial taxability of the incorporation transaction in regard to Mr. Ink?*

      Conclusion: No. Mr. Ink receives full nontaxable treatment pursuant to Section 357(c)(3).   *C-6–C-10*

   d. *Collateral Question: Will Ms. Dixon recognize taxable income as a result of Ready, Inc.'s assumption of her $2,500 word processing bill?*

      Conclusion: Ms. Dixon will not recognize any taxable income because of Ready, Inc.'s assumption of the $2,500 word processing bill.   *C-10–C-14*

B-1 (FEM 12/21/2008)

Red E. Ink (Personal Account)
Summary of Questions Investigated
December 2008

W.P. Ref.

2. *Is collection of the trade receivables transferred*
    by Mr. Ink to Ready, Inc. to be considered the
    taxable income of Mr. Ink, or of Ready, Inc.?

    <u>Conclusion:</u> *The trade receivables collected after*   *C-15*
    incorporation should be the taxable income of
    Ready, Inc.

3. *What is Mr. Ink's tax basis in the 730 shares of*
    Ready, Inc., common stock that he retained?

    <u>Conclusion:</u> *In our opinion, Mr. Ink's basis in the*   *C-15–C-17*
    730 shares is $4,867.

B-2 (FEM 12/21/2008)

Red E. Ink (Personal Account)
Working Papers
December 2008

W.P. Ref.

1. Was the March 1, 2008, incorporation
    transaction between Red E. Ink, Judith Dixon,
    and Ready, Inc., a tax-free transfer under
    Section 351?

<u>**Conclusion:**</u> **Yes; the incorporation of Red**   *For facts, see W.P.*
Publishings should be treated as a tax-free   *A-1–A-4.*
transaction pursuant to Section 351 which reads
as follows:

SECTION 351. TRANSFER TO CORPORATION
CONTROLLED BY TRANSFEROR.

(a) General Rule.—No gain or loss shall be recognized if   *See collateral*
property is transferred to a corporation by one or more per-   *question 1(a).*
sons solely in exchange for stock in such corporation and
immediately after the exchange such person or persons are   *See collateral*
in control (as defined in section 368(c)) of the corporation.   *question 1(b).*

(b) Receipt of Property.—If subsection (a) would apply to an
exchange but for the fact that there is received, in addition
to the stock or securities permitted to be received under subsection (a), other property or money, then—

   (1) gain (if any) to such recipient shall be recognized, but   *N/A (No boot*
   not in excess of—   *received by*
          Mr. Ink
      (A) the amount of money received, plus   *or Ms. Dixon.)*

      (B) the fair market value of such other property received;
      and

   (2) no loss to such recipient shall be recognized.

(c) Special Rule.—In determining control, for purposes of this
section, the fact that any corporate transferor distributes part   *N/A*
or all of the stock which it receives in the exchange to its
shareholders shall not be taken into account.

C-1 (FEM 12/20/2008)

Red E. Ink (Personal Account)
Working Papers
December 2008

W.P. Ref.

(d) Services, Certain Indebtedness, and Accrued Interest Not Treated as Property.—For purposes of this section, stock issued for—

(1) services,

(2) indebtedness of the transferee corporation which is not evidenced by a security, or

(3) interest on indebtedness of the transferee corporation which accrued on or after the beginning of the transferor's holding period for the debt,

shall not be considered as issued in return for property.

N/A

(e) Exceptions.—This section shall not apply to—

(1) Transfer of property to an investment company.—A transfer of property to an investment company.

(2) Title 11 or similar case.—A transfer of property of a debtor pursuant to a plan while the debtor is under the jurisdiction of a court in a title 11 or similar case (within the meaning of section 368(a)(3)(A)), to the extent that the stock or securities received in the exchange are used to satisfy the indebtedness of such debtor.

N/A

(f) Treatment of Controlled Corporation.—If—

(1) property is transferred to a corporation (hereinafter in this subsection referred to as the "controlled corporation") in an exchange with respect to which gain or loss is not recognized (in whole or in part) to the transferor under this section, and

(2) such exchange is not in pursuance of a plan of reorganization,

section 311 shall apply to any transfer in such exchange by the controlled corporation in the same manner as if such transfer were a distribution to which subpart A of part I applies.

N/A

Section 351(g) is N/A.

(h) Cross References.—

(1) For special rule where another party to the exchange assumes a liability, or acquires property subject to a liability, see section 357.

See W.P. C-6-C-14.

C-2 (FEM 12/20/2008)

Red E. Ink (Personal Account)
Working Papers
December 2008

W.P. Ref.

(2) For the basis of stock, securities, or property received in an exchange to which this section applies, see sections 353 and 362.

} *See*
W.P. C-15–C-17.

(3) For special rule in the case of an exchange described in this section but which results in a gift, see section 2501 and following.

(4) For special rule in the case of an exchange described in this section but which has the effect of the payment of compensation by the corporation or by a transferor, see section 61(a)(1).

} *N/A*

(5) For coordination of this section with section 304, see section 304(b)(3).

a. **Collateral Question: Do Ms. Dixon's copyrights qualify as "property" for purposes of Section 351?**

Conclusion: The term "property" as used in Section 351 is neither statutorily defined (the definition in Section 317(a) is applicable only to Part 1 of Subchapter C and does not apply to Section 351) nor interpreted by Treasury regulations. The problem here is determining whether Ms. Dixon has transferred intangible property or services to the corporation. In Rev. Rul. 64-56, 1964-1 C.B. 133, amplified by Rev. Rul. 71-564, 1971-2 C.B. 179, the service indicates that transfers of intangibles such as "know-how" will qualify as transfers of property under Section 351 if they meet certain requirements:

(1) Is the item transferred inherently considered property?

(2) Does the property have legal protection?

(3) Were all substantial rights to the property transferred?

C-3 (FEM 12/20/2008)

Red E. Ink (Personal Account)
Working Papers
December 2008

W.P. Ref.

(4) If the transferor agrees to perform services in connection with the transfer, are the services merely ancillary and subsidiary to the transfer?

The transfer of the copyright by Ms. Dixon appears to meet all of these requirements:

(1) In Rev. Rul. 68-194, 1968-1 C.B. 87, a taxpayer produced and copyrighted a manuscript. Later, he sold the manuscript to a publisher granting sole and exclusive rights to the manuscript. The ruling held that the transfer was a sale of the literary property. In Rev. Rul. 73-395, 1973-2 C.B. 87, the IRS held that costs incurred by an accrual basis taxpayer in writing, editing, design, and art work directly attributable to the development of textbooks and visual aids are capital expenditures under Section 263 of the Code that are depreciable under Section 167(a). Furthermore, in Rev. Rul. 64-56, it states that, "Once it is established that 'property' has been transferred, the transfer will be tax-free under Section 351 even though services were used to produce the property." This is the case unless the property transferred was specifically produced for the transferee. This is not the case with Ms. Dixon.

(2) & (3) In a telephone conversation with Ms. Dixon on Dec. 19, 2008, she indicated that the copyright had been properly filed giving exclusive U.S. protection to the property. Furthermore, she indicated that she had transferred all rights in the copyright to Ready, Inc.

(4) In the same telephone conversation with Ms. Dixon on Dec. 19, 2008, she indicated that, under the terms of the transfer, no further services were required with regard to the copyrighted manuscript.

C-4 (FEM 12/20/2008)

Red E. Ink (Personal Account)
Working Papers
December 2008

W.P. Ref.

b. Collateral Question: Do Mr. Ink and Ms.
Dixon have any "control" requirement
problems under Section 351(a)? Specifically,
since Mr. Ink individually owns only 75% of
the Ready, Inc., common stock, is the Section
351(a) control requirement met?

Conclusion: There are no problems. The
Section 351(a) control requirement is met.

In order for the general rule of Section
351(a) to apply, the shareholders involved in
the transfers must be in control of the
corporation immediately after the exchange.
Section 351 "control" is statutorily governed
by the definition of "control" contained in
Section 368(c). The requisite ownership
percentage in Section 368(c) is 80%. This
control requirement is met if, in the words of
both the statute and the regulations,
"immediately after the exchange such person
or persons are in control" [emphasis added].

In our case Mr. Ink and Ms. Dixon are
the "persons," and they own 98% of the
Ready, Inc., stock. "Control" does not have
to be maintained by a sole shareholder.
Treas. Reg. Sec. 1.351-1(a)(2) example (1)
illustrates a situation that contains an
ownership structure almost identical to our
case, that is, two shareholders, one owning
75% and one owning 25%. The example
states that no gain or loss is recognized by
either shareholder.

C-5 (FEM 12/20/2008)

Red E. Ink (Personal Account)
Working Papers
December 2008

W.P. Ref. _____

TREAS. REGS. SEC. 1.351-1. TRANSFER TO
CORPORATION CONTROLLED BY TRANSFEROR.

(a)(1) Section 351(a) provides, in general, for the nonrecognition of gain or loss upon the transfer by one or more persons of property to a corporation solely in exchange for stock or securities in such corporation, *if immediately after the exchange, such person or persons are in control* of the corporation to which the property was transferred. As used in section 351, the phrase *"one or more persons"* includes individuals, trusts, estates, partnerships, associations, companies, or corporations (see section 7701(a)(1)). To be in control of the transferee corporation, *such person or persons* must own immediately after the transfer stock possessing at least 80 percent of the total combined voting power of all classes of stock entitled to vote and at least 80 percent of the total number of shares of all other classes of stock of such corporation (see section 368(c)). . . .

(2) The application of section 351(a) is illustrated by the following examples:

Example (1). C owns a patent right worth $25,000 and D owns a manufacturing plant worth $75,000. C and D organize the R Corporation with an authorized capital stock of $100,000. C transfers his patent right to the R Corporation for $25,000 of its stock and D transfers his plant to the new corporation for $75,000 of its stock. No gain or loss to C or D is recognized.

Identical to our case

c. *Collateral Question: Could Ready's assumption of liabilities cause partial taxability of the incorporation transaction in regard to Mr. Ink?*

Conclusion: The assumption by Ready, Inc. of Red Publishing's liabilities does not cause partial taxability to Mr. Ink. Section 357 deals with the assumption of liabilities in a Section 351 transaction, and reads as follows:

C-6 (FEM 12/20/2008)

Red E. Ink (Personal Account)
Working Papers
December 2008

W.P. Ref.

SECTION 357. ASSUMPTION OF LIABILITY.

(a) General Rule.—Except as provided in subsections (b) and (c), if—

(1) the taxpayer receives property which would be permitted to be received under section 351 or 361, without the recognition of gain if it were the sole consideration, and

(2) as part of the consideration, another party to the exchange assumes a liability of the taxpayer, or acquires from the taxpayer property subject to a liability,

then such assumption or acquisition shall not be treated as money or other property, and shall not prevent the exchange from being within the provisions of section 351 or 361, as the case may be.

The rule

(b) Tax Avoidance Purpose.—

(1) In general.—If, taking into consideration the nature of the liability and the circumstances in the light of which the arrangement for the assumption or acquisition was made, it appears that the principal purpose of the taxpayer with respect to the assumption or acquisition described in subsection (a)—

(A) was a purpose to avoid Federal income tax on the exchange, or

(B) if not such purpose, was not a bona fide business purpose

then such assumption or acquisition (in the total amount of the liability assumed or acquired pursuant to such exchange) shall, for purposes of section 351 or 361 (as the case may be), be considered as money received by the taxpayer on the exchange.

N/A

(2) Burden of proof.—In any suit or proceeding where the burden is on the taxpayer to prove such assumption or acquisition is not to be treated as money received by the taxpayer, such burden shall not be considered as sustained unless the taxpayer sustains such burden by the clear preponderance of the evidence.

N/A

C-7 (FEM 12/20/2008)

Red E. Ink (Personal Account)
Working Papers
December 2008

W.P. Ref.

(c) Liabilities in Excess of Basis.—

(1) In general. In the case of an exchange—

(A) to which section 351 applies, or

(B) to which section 361 applies by reason of a plan
of reorganization within the meaning of section
368(a)(l)(D) with respect to which stock or securities of
the corporation to which the assets are transferred are
distributed in a transaction which qualifies under section
355,

if the sum of the amount of the liabilities assumed, plus
the amount of the liabilities to which the property is subject,
exceeds the total of the adjusted basis of the property transferred pursuant to such exchange, then such excess shall
be considered as a gain from the sale or exchange of a
capital asset or of property which is not a capital asset, as
the case may be.

Exception to rule
in Section 357(a)

(2) Exceptions. Paragraph (1) shall not apply to any
exchange—

(A) to which subsection (b)(l) of this section applies,

(B) which is pursuant to a plan of reorganization within
the meaning of section 368(a)(1)(G) where no former
shareholder of the transferor corporation receives any
consideration for his stock.

N/A

(3) Certain liabilities excluded.

(A) In general. If a taxpayer transfers, in an exchange to
which section 351 applies, a liability the payment of
which either—

(i) would give rise to a deduction, or

(ii) would be described in section 736(a),

then, for purposes of paragraph (1), the amount of such liability shall be excluded in determining the amount of liabilities
assumed or to which the property transferred is subject.

See collateral
question 1(d)
regarding
Ready's
assumption of
Ms. Dixon's word
processing bill of
$2,500.

(B) Exception. Subparagraph (A) shall not apply to any
liability to the extent that the incurrence of the liability
resulted in the creation of, or an increase in, the basis of
any property.

N/A

Section 357(d) is N/A.

C-8 (FEM 12/20/2008)

Red E. Ink (Personal Account)
Working Papers
December 2008

W.P. Ref. _____

Under Section 357, the transfer of liabilities in a Section 351 transaction will cause the recognition of gain only if either (1) there is a tax-avoidance purpose (Section 357(b)), or (2) the liabilities transferred exceed the basis of all the assets transferred (Section 357(c)). Section 357(b) is inapplicable here since, pursuant to the facts, there is a valid purpose for the transaction and no tax avoidance motive is present. According to Rev. Rul. 66-142, 1966-1 C.B. 66, Section 357(c) is to be applied separately to each transferor.

Per R. U. Partner's memo to file (12/17/2008), p. 2, the assets transferred to Ready, Inc., by Red E. Ink were as follows:

Asset	FMV	Basis
Cash	$11,700	$11,700
(1) Supplies	10,000	-0-
(2) Trade receivables	50,000	-0-
(3) Equipment	75,000	58,300
Total basis of assets		$70,000

FOOTNOTES:
(1) In response to my telephone inquiry of today, Tom Books confirmed that Mr. Ink has always expensed all supplies for tax purposes when paid.
(2) Mr. Ink has always reported his taxable income on a cash basis.
(3) Value estimated; adjusted basis is tax basis.

Liabilities of Red Publishings assumed by Ready, Inc., were:

Mortgage payable of Red Publishings	$65,000
Trade payables of Red Publishings	10,000
	$75,000

C-9 (FEM 12/20/2008)

Red E. Ink (Personal Account)
Working Papers
December 2008

W.P. Ref. _____

*In the incorporation transaction, Ready, Inc.
assumed all the liabilities of Red Publishings in
the amount of $75,000. However, pursuant to
Section 357(c)(3), the trade payables of
$10,000 may be excluded in applying Section
357(c) since the payment of those liabilities
would give rise to a deduction. Thus, for
purposes of Section 357(c) the total basis of the
assets transferred is $70,000 and the total
liabilities transferred are $65,000. (See Rev.
Rul. 95-74, 1995-2 CB 36.) Mr. Ink is not
taxable on the transaction because of the
transfer of the liabilities.*

d. *Collateral Question: Will Ms. Dixon recognize
taxable income as a result of Ready, Inc.'s
assumption of her $2,500 word processing bill?*

*Conclusion: No. Ms. Dixon will not recognize
any taxable income because of Ready, Inc.'s
assumption of the $2,500 word processing bill.
Here again, Section 357(b) does not apply since
there is a valid business purpose for the
transaction and no tax avoidance motive is
present. For purposes of Section 357(c), if the
$2,500 expense must be capitalized rather than
being deducted, the basis of the copyright
transferred to Ready is $1,000 (rather than
$3,500) and the liability transferred ($2,500) is
greater than the basis of the copyright
($1,000). However, pursuant to Section
357(c)(3), if the liability is deducted, it is not
counted for purposes of Section 357(c), the
liability transferred is not greater than the basis
of the asset transferred, and Ms. Dixon does not
recognize any taxable income. Pursuant to
Section 263A(h), the $2,500 word processing
expense is not required to be capitalized under
Section 263A as long as it was incurred in Ms.
Dixon's trade or business (other than as an
employee) of being a writer. The pertinent parts
of Section 263A are as follows:*

C-10 (FEM 12/20/2008)

Red E. Ink (Personal Account)
Working Papers
December 2008

W.P. Ref.

SECTION 263A. CAPITALIZATION AND
INCLUSION IN INVENTORY
COSTS OF CERTAIN EXPENSES.

(a) Nondeductibility of Certain Direct and Indirect Costs.—

(1) In general.—In the case of any property to which this
section applies, any costs described in paragraph (2)—

The general rule

(A) in the case of property which is inventory in the
hands of the taxpayer, shall be included in inventory
costs, and

(B) in the case of any other property, shall be
capitalized.

(2) Allocable costs.—The costs described in this paragraph
with respect to any property are—

(A) the direct costs of such property, and

(B) such property's proper share of those indirect costs
(including taxes) part or all of which are allocable to
such property.

Any cost which (but for this subsection) could not be taken
into account in computing taxable income for any taxable
year shall not be treated as a cost described in this paragraph.

(b) Property to Which Section Applies.—Except as otherwise
provided in this section, this section shall apply to—

(1) Property produced by taxpayer.—Real or tangible personal property produced by the taxpayer.

(2) Property acquired for resale.—

(A) In general.—Real or personal property described in
section 1221(1) which is acquired by the taxpayer for
resale.

(B) Exception for taxpayer with gross receipts of
$10,000,000 or less.—Subparagraph (A) shall not apply
to any personal property acquired during any taxable

C-11 (FEM 12/20/2008)

Red E. Ink (Personal Account)
Working Papers
December 2008

W.P. Ref.
_____

year by the taxpayer for resale if the average annual gross receipts of the taxpayer (or any predecessor) for the 3-taxable year period ending with the taxable year preceding such taxable year do not exceed $10,000,000.

(C) Aggregation rules, etc.—For purposes of subparagraph (B), rules similar to the rules of paragraphs (2) and (3) of section 448(c) shall apply.

For purposes of paragraph (1), the term "tangible personal property" shall include a film, sound recording, video tape, book, or similar property. . . .

(h) Exemption for Free-lance Authors, Photographers, and Artists.—

(1) In General.—Nothing in this section shall require the capitalization of any qualified creative expense.

Exception to general rule, see W.P. C-11.

(2) Qualified Creative Expense.—For purposes of the subsection, the term "qualified creative expense" means any expense—

(A) which is paid or incurred by an individual in the trade or business of such individual (other than as an employee) of being a writer, photographer, or artist, and

(B) which, without regard to this section, would be allowable as a deduction for the taxable year.

Such term does not include any expense related to printing, photographic plates, motion picture files, video tapes, or similar items.

(3) Definitions.—For purposes of this subsection—

(A) Writer.—The term "writer" means any individual if the personal efforts of such individual create (or may reasonably be expected to create) a literary manuscript, musical composition (including any accompanying words), or dance score.

(B) Photographer.—The term "photographer" means any individual if the personal efforts of such individual

C-12 (FEM 12/20/2008)

Red E. Ink (Personal Account)
Working Papers
December 2008

W.P. Ref.

create (or may reasonably be expected to create) a photograph or photographic negative or transparency.

(C) Artist—

(i) In general.—The term "artist" means any individual if the personal efforts of such individual create (or may reasonably be expected to create) a picture, painting, sculpture, statue, etching, drawing, cartoon, graphic design, or original print edition.

(ii) Criteria.—In determining whether any expense is paid or incurred in the trade or business of being an artist, the following criteria shall be taken into account:

(I) The originality and uniqueness of the item created (or to be created).

(II) The predominance of aesthetic value over utilitarian value of the item created (or to be created).

The deductibility of this $2,500 word processing expense depends upon whether or not Ms. Dixon was in the business of being a writer. This is a question of fact, and I believe that the facts certainly justify treating Ms. Dixon as being in the business of writing. Pursuant to the memo dated December 17, 2008, Ms. Dixon had devoted many hours to writing these two full-length books. Even though Ms. Dixon was also a practicing attorney at the time she wrote the books, it is well established that an individual may be engaged in more than one business at the same time. Furthermore, the Tax Court also ruled in Fernando Faura et al. v. Comm'r., 73 T.C. 849 (1980) that an author was engaged in a business and had the right to deduct nearly $5,000 in prepublication costs (rent, postage, telephone, transportation, and so on).

C-13 (FEM 12/20/2008)

Red E. Ink (Personal Account)
Working Papers
December 2008

W.P. Ref. _____

The service could counter that the word processing bill was a nondeductible capital expenditure or that it was a personal expenditure incurred in a transaction where profit had not been expected (that is, a hobby expenditure).

Revenue Ruling 68-194, 1968-1 C.B. 87, involved a taxpayer not engaged in a trade or business. It held that various expenses (including expenses for secretarial help, art work, supplies, and postage) incurred in producing and copyrighting a manuscript of a literary composition were directly attributable to the producing and copyrighting of the manuscript. Accordingly, the service said the expenses were not deductible for federal income tax purposes.

The service reaffirmed this position in Rev. Rul. 73-395, 1973-2 C.B. 87. The ruling also stated that the service would not follow the decision in Stern v. U.S., 27 AFTR 2d 71-1148 (D. Col. 1971).

The taxpayer in Stern, a Los Angeles resident, had spent considerable time in New York preparing a book. The necessary material for this book could be obtained only in New York. The taxpayer claimed his travel expenditures were deductible under Section 162. The service claimed that the expenditures were nondeductible capital expenditures. The court, while holding in favor of the taxpayer, summarily stated, "Nor were they expenses for securing a copyright and plates which remain the property of the person making the payments," referring to Treas. Reg. Sec. 1.263(a)-2(b).

In summary, although the treatment would not be free from attack from the service, I feel Ms. Dixon should not recognize taxable income as a result of Ready's assumption of her word processing liability. This result flows from the characterization of her word processing bill as fitting within the exception to the exception contained in Section 357(c)(3).

C-14 (FEM 12/20/2008)

Red E. Ink (Personal Account)
Working Papers
December 2008

W.P. Ref.

2. Is collection of the trade receivables transferred by Mr. Ink to Ready, Inc., to be considered the taxable income of Mr. Ink, or of Ready, Inc.?

Conclusion: For many years, relying on the "assignment-of-income" doctrine, the courts held that an individual transferor, rather than the controlled corporate transferee, was taxable on the inchoate income items transferred in a Section 351 transaction (Brown v. Comm'r., 115 F.2d 337 (CA-2, 1940), Adolph Weinberg, 44 T.C. 233 (1965), aff'd per curiam 386 F.2d 836 (CA-9, 1967), and O'Bryon v. Comm'r., 62 TCM 1347 (1991).

The Tax Court was finally persuaded, however, to allow a cash basis taxpayer to transfer accounts receivable tax-free under Section 351 (Thomas Briggs, 15 T.C.M. 440 (1956)). Since Briggs, at least two cases, Hempt Bros., Inc. v. U.S., 490 F.2d 1172 (CA-3, 1973), and Divine, Jr. v. U.S. 62-2 USTC ¶9632 (W.D. Tenn. 1962), have argued that the assignment-of-income doctrine is inapplicable in such situations. In addition, Rev. Rul. 80-198, 1980-2 C.B. 113, supports the Tax Court's decision. The ruling concludes that the transfer of accounts receivable to a controlled corporation qualifies as an exchange within the meaning of Section 351(a) and that the transferee corporation will report in its income the accounts receivable as collected. Under the circumstances of Mr. Ink's case, there seems to be good authority to argue that any receivables collected by Ready, Inc., should be treated as the taxable income of the corporation and not that of Mr. Ink individually.

3. What is Mr. Ink's tax basis in the 730 shares of Ready, Inc., common stock that he retained?

Conclusion: Section 358 determines the adjusted basis of stock and securities received in a Section 351 transaction. It reads as follows:

C-15 (FEM 12/20/2008)

Red E. Ink (Personal Account)
Working Papers
December 2008

SECTION 358. BASIS TO DISTRIBUTEES.

	W.P. Ref.

(a) General Rule.—In the case of an exchange to which section 351, 354, 355, 356, 361 applies—

(1) Nonrecognition property.—The basis of property permitted to be received under such section without the recognition of gain or loss shall be the same as that of the property exchanged—

} *Here. $70,000.* *See C-9.*

(A) decreased by—

(i) the fair market value of any other property (except money) received by the taxpayer,

} *None*

(ii) the amount of any money received by the taxpayer, and

} *$65,000. (See Section 358(d).)*

(iii) the amount of loss to the taxpayer which was recognized on such exchange, and

} *N/A*

(B) increased by—

(i) the amount which was treated as a dividend, and

(ii) the amount of gain to the taxpayer which was recognized on such exchange (not including any portion of such gain which was treated as a dividend).

} *N/A*

(2) Other property.—The basis of any other property (except money) received by the taxpayer shall be its fair market value.

} *N/A*

(b) Allocation of Basis.—

(1) In general.—Under regulations prescribed by the Secretary, the basis determined under subsection (a)(1)(I) shall be allocated among the properties permitted to be received without the recognition of gain or loss.

} *N/A*

(2) Special rule for section 355.—In the case of an exchange to which section 355 (or so much of section 356 as relates to section 355) applies, then in making the allocation under paragraph (1) of this subsection, there shall be taken into account not only the property so permitted to be received without the recognition of gain or loss, but also the stock or securities (if any) of the distributing corporation which are retained, and the allocation of basis shall be made among all such properties.

} *N/A*

C-16 (FEM 12/20/2008)

Red E. Ink (Personal Account)
Working Papers
December 2008

W.P. Ref.

(c) Section 355 Transactions Which Are Not Exchanges.—For purposes of this section, a distribution to which section 355 (or so much of section 356 as relates to section 355) applies shall be treated as an exchange, and for such purposes the stock and securities of the distributing corporation which are retained shall be treated as surrendered, and received back, in the exchange.

} *N/A*

(d) Assumption of Liability.—

(1) In general.—Where, as part of the consideration to the taxpayer, another party to the exchange assumed a liability of the taxpayer or acquired from the taxpayer property subject to a liability, such assumption or acquisition (in the amount of the liability) shall, for purposes of this section, be treated as money received by the taxpayer on the exchange.

} *For result, refer to Section 358(a)(1)(A)(ii), above.*

(2) Exception.—Paragraph (1) shall not apply to the amount of any liability excluded under section 357(c)(3).

} *Thus, N/A to any lease obligation or trade payables.*

Sections 358(e), (f), and (g) are N/A.

According to Section 358(a), therefore, Mr. Ink's basis in the 750 shares he initially received would be $5,000 (that is, $70,000 basis transferred less $65,000 liabilities assumed by Ready, Inc.).

Because Mr. Ink gave 10 shares to Mrs. Ink and 10 shares to Mr. Books, the basis in his remaining 730 shares would be $4,867 (730/ 750 x $5,000). Each donee would have a basis of $67 in the 10 shares received per Section 1015.

C-17 (FEM 12/20/2008)

Judith Dixon (Personal Account)
Summary of Questions Investigated
December 2008

W.P. Ref.

1. **Was the March 1, 2008, incorporation transaction between Red E. Ink, Ready, Inc., and Judith Dixon, a tax-free transfer under Section 351?**

   Conclusion: *Yes; all of the requirements of Section 351 were satisfied.* — *See again C-1 and C-2.*

   a. Collateral Question: *Do Ms. Dixon's copyrights qualify as "property" for purposes of section 351?*

   Conclusion: *Yes. Substantial authority probably exists to treat Ms. Dixon's copyrights as Section 351 property.* — *See again C-3 and C-4.*

   b. Collateral Question: *Do Mr. Ink and Ms. Dixon have any "control" requirement problems under Section 351(a)? Specifically, since Mr. Ink individually owns only 75% of the Ready, Inc., common stock, is the Section 351(a) control requirement met?*

   Conclusion: *There are no problems. The Section 351(a) control requirement is met.* — *See again C-5 and C-6.*

   c. Collateral Question: *Could Ready's assumption of liabilities cause partial taxability of the incorporation transaction in regard to Ms. Dixon?*

   Conclusion: *Although the issue is not totally free of doubt, there is strong authority for characterizing Ms. Dixon's incorporation as fully nontaxable.* — *See again C-6 through C-10.*

   d. Collateral Question: *Will Ms. Dixon recognize taxable income as a result of Ready, Inc.'s assumption of her $2,500 word processing bill?*

   Conclusion: *No. Ms. Dixon will not recognize any taxable income because of Ready, Inc.'s assumption of the $2,500 word processing bill.* — *See again C-10 through C-14.*

   D-1 (FEM 12/20/2008)

Judith Dixon (Personal Account)
Summary of Questions Investigated
December 2008

W.P. Ref.

2. **What is Ms. Dixon's tax basis in the 250 shares of Ready, Inc., common stock that she obtained in the incorporation transaction?**

<u>Conclusion:</u> *In our opinion, Ms. Dixon's basis in her 250 shares is $1,000. Ms. Dixon's basis in this case is determined by Section 358. According to Section 358(a), Ms. Dixon's basis in her 250 shares would be $1,000 (that is, the basis of the copyrights she transferred in exchange for the stock).*

See C-16 and C-17 for a copy of Section 358.

D-2 (FEM 12/20/2008)

Ready, Inc. (Corporate Account)
Summary of Questions Investigated
December 2008

W.P. Ref.

1. **Must Ready, Inc., report any taxable income in its first tax year because of its exchange of previously unissued stock for either the assets of Red Publishings or Ms. Dixon's copyrights?**

   Conclusion: No (Section 1032).   F-1

2. **Can Ready, Inc., claim a tax deduction under Section 162 for the $10,000 expended within 60 days following incorporation in payment of the trade payables it assumed from Red Publishings and the $2,500 expended in payment for the word processing bill assumed from Ms. Dixon?**

   Conclusion: The officers of Ready, Inc., should be   F-1 and F-2
   alerted to the remote possibility that the IRS might
   challenge the propriety of the corporation's
   deducting these expenditures. We believe, however,
   that they are properly deductible.

3. **Are the $50,000 trade receivables transferred by Mr. Ink to Ready, Inc., and collected by the corporation after the incorporation, properly deemed to be the taxable income of the corporation?**

   Conclusion: The receivables collected should be the   F-2 and F-3
   taxable income of Ready, Inc.

4. **What is Ready's adjusted tax basis in the various assets it received on March 1, 2008?**

   Conclusion: F-3
Cash	$11,700
Supplies	-0-
Receivables	-0-
Equipment	58,300
Copyrights	1,000

E-1 (FEM 12/20/2008)

Ready, Inc. (Corporate Account)
Working Papers
December 2008

W.P. Ref.
_____

1. **Must Ready, Inc., report any taxable income in its first tax year because of its exchange of previously unissued stock for either the assets of Red Publishings or Ms. Dixon's copyrights?**

    Conclusion: No; see Section 1032 below.

SECTION 1032. EXCHANGE OF STOCK FOR PROPERTY.

(a) Nonrecognition of Gain or Loss.—No gain or loss shall be recognized to a corporation on the receipt of money or other property in exchange for stock (including treasury stock) of such corporation. No gain or loss shall be recognized by a corporation with respect to any lapse or acquisition of an option to buy or sell its stock (including treasury stock).

The rule

(b) Basis.—For basis or property acquired by a corporation in certain exchanges for its stock, see section 362.

2. **Can Ready, Inc., claim a tax deduction under Section 162 for the $10,000 expended within 60 days following incorporation in payment of the trade payables it assumed from Red Publishings and the $2,500 expended in payment for the word processing bill assumed from Ms. Dixon?**

    For facts, see W.P. A-1 through A-3.

    Conclusion: *Early court decisions have denied a deduction for ordinary (Section 162) expenses incurred by the transferor but paid by the corporate transferee following a Section 351 incorporation. The Tax Court has stated:*

It is well settled that an expenditure of a preceding owner of property which has accrued but which is paid by one acquiring that property is a part of the cost of acquiring that property, irrespective of what would be the tax character of the expenditure to the prior owner. Such payment becomes part of the basis of the property acquired and may not be deducted when paid by the acquirer of that property.

[*M. Buten and Sons, Inc., 31 T.C.M. 178 (1972)*]

F-1 (FEM 12/20/2008)

Ready, Inc. (Corporate Account)
Working Papers
December 2008

   Thus, the Tax Court in <u>Buten</u> indicates that a definite uniformity of application exists in this area. Despite the cases supporting that conclusion, however, it may be significant that in <u>Peter Raich,</u> 46 T.C. 604 (1966), the parties stipulated that the accounts payable were deductible by the transferee corporation. Furthermore, in <u>Bongiovanni,</u> 470 F.2d 921 (CA-2, 1972), the Second Circuit Court in 1972 noted that ''where the acquiring corporation is on an accrual basis, such accounts are also deductible in its initial period.'' (Note: Ready, Inc., will be an accrual basis taxpayer.) Also, in <u>U.S. v. Smith,</u> 418 F.2d 589 (CA-5, 1969), the court noted, ''If this factual inquiry reveals a primary purpose other than acquisition of property, the court may properly allow a deduction to the corporation if all the requirements of Title 26 USC, section 162, are met. . . .'' Finally, in Rev. Ruls. 80-198, 1980-2 C.B. 113, 80-199, 1980-2 C.B. 122, and GCM 37528 (1978), the service has indicated that payment of the liabilities by the transferee is deductible if there was a valid business purpose for the transfer and the transferor did not defer collection of the accounts receivable or prepay the accounts payable. (See also Rev. Rul. 95-74, 1995-2 C.B. 36.)

   In Ink's incorporation it appears that the liabilities of Red Publishings were assumed by Ready, Inc., solely for business convenience reasons and not for the acquisition of property and that there has been no accumulation of the accounts payable. Ready, Inc., should be able to deduct the payment. However, the officers of Ready, Inc., should be alerted to a possibility of an IRS challenge. See <u>Magruder v. Supples,</u> 316 U.S. 394 (1942); <u>Holdcraft Transportation Co.,</u> 153 F.2d 323 (CA-8, 1946); <u>Haden Co. v. Comm'r.,</u> 165 F.2d 588 (CA-5, 1948); <u>Athol Mfg. Co.,</u> 54 F.2d 230 (CA-1, 1931); and <u>David R. Webb Company, Inc. v. Comm'r.,</u> 708 F2d 1254 (CA-7, 1983).

F-2 (FEM 12/20/2008)

Ready, Inc. (Corporate Account)
Working Papers
December 2008

W.P. Ref.

3. *Are the $50,000 trade receivables transferred by*
    Mr. Ink to Ready, Inc., and collected by the
    corporation after the incorporation, properly
    deemed to be the taxable income of the
    corporation?

    <u>*Conclusion:*</u> *Yes. The collection of the receivables*   *See again C-15.*
    should be the taxable income of Ready, Inc.

4. *What is Ready's adjusted tax basis in the various*
    assets it received on March 1, 2008?

    <u>*Conclusion:*</u> *The basis of the assets received by a*
    corporate transferee in a Section 351
    transaction is determined by Section 362(a),
    which reads as follows:

SECTION 362. BASIS TO CORPORATIONS.

(a) Property Acquired by Issuance of Stock or as Paid-In
Surplus.—If property was acquired on or after June 22, 1954,
by a corporation—

  (1) in connection with a transaction to which section 351
  (relating to transfer of property to corporation controlled
  by transferor) applies, or

  (2) as paid-in surplus or as a contribution to capital,

then the basis shall be the same as it would be in the hands
of the transferor, increased in the amount of gain recognized
to the transferor on such transfer.   *The rule*

Sections 362(b), (c), and (d) are N/A.

Accordingly, Ready's adjusted tax basis of assets   *See W.P. A-2.*
received is as follows:

Supplies	*-0-*
Receivables	*-0-*
Equipment	*$58,300*
Copyrights	*$1,000*

F-3 (FEM 12/20/2008)

Red E. Ink, Ms. Dixon, Ready, Inc.
Suggestions for Client's Future Consideration
December 2008

If Mr. Ink or Ms. Dixon desire any assistance in future tax planning we should discuss with either of them, in the near future, the following matters:

1. *"S" election*
    a. *The circumstances under which this would be desirable or undesirable*
    b. *When the decision must be made*
    c. *Need for every shareholder's approval*
    d. *Need for buyout agreements*

2. *Executive compensation possibilities*
    a. *Group term life insurance (Section 79(a))*
    b. *Health and accident insurance (Section 106)*
    c. *Death benefits (Section 101)*
    d. *Travel and entertainment (requirements and advantages)*

3. *Pension plans (costs and benefits)*

4. *Future contributions to capital*
    a. *Consider advantages of securities*
    b. *Section 1244*

9

Research Methodology for Tax Planning

This chapter examines the research methodology appropriate to tax planning. It considers (1) the general role of tax planning in the CPA firm and (2) the technical differences between research methodologies for tax planning and tax compliance.

Tax consulting[1] has become a large part of the revenues generated by tax professionals in public accounting firms. Tax consulting engagements tend to generate higher margins than tax compliance engagements. Consequently, the profitability that many public accounting firms have enjoyed has been due to an increased emphasis on building successful consulting practices. One aspect of consulting that has changed in recent years is the willingness to look to nonclients for special consulting projects. It is not unusual for

---

[1] The terms *tax planning* and *tax consulting* will be used interchangeably in this chapter. Although for some, consulting may take on a broader concept than just planning, for purposes of simplicity, no such distinction is made in this chapter.

a company to have one firm doing its audit and tax compliance work and several other firms providing special one-time consulting services.

The passage of the Sarbanes-Oxley Act of 2002 has changed the scope of providing tax services for many public accounting firms. In most cases, for their Securities and Exchange Commission (SEC) audit clients, CPA firms have to get specific preapproval from the client's audit committee for each tax engagement. In addition, certain types of tax services (appraisal and valuation, actuarial, and legal and expert services) are no longer able to be provided to an audit client.

It is not our purpose here to go into a detailed discussion of the outcomes of Sarbanes-Oxley. Such a discussion is well beyond the scope of this publication. It is clear, however, that Sarbanes-Oxley has changed the nature of how tax services are marketed to large public companies. For example, it is generally easier for management of public companies to hire another tax firm rather than attempt to get approval from the audit committee. For large tax planning engagements, especially those involving risky tax strategies, approval by the audit committee may not be forthcoming. However, there has been less impact on services related to the preparation of corporate tax returns prepared in conjunction with an audit.

CPAs who want to expand their practices and increase profitability will likely discover that tax consulting is a latent source of future growth. As we noted in chapter 2, a final tax liability depends on three variables: the facts, the law, and an administrative process. A change in any one of these variables is likely to change a client's tax liability. To devise a tax plan that is dependent on an amendment to the Internal Revenue Code (IRC) for its success is usually unrealistic. Very few taxpayers wield that much influence, and even if they did, the response of Congress in tax matters typically is unpredictable and slow. Attempts to change the administrative process would be equally ineffective for similar reasons. Good tax planning always gives adequate consideration to the administrative process, but it does not rely on changes in that process for its success. Thus, tax plans generally must be based on the existing law and administrative processes because only the facts are readily modified. The ultimate significance of those facts stems, of course, from options already in the ICC.

Tax-Planning Considerations

The fundamental problem encountered in tax planning might be compared to those inherent in, say, a decision to transport an object from New York City to Atlanta. Momentarily ignoring operational constraints, there are many ways to achieve the objective. That is, the object could be shipped by a commercial carrier (with air, rail, ship, or surface carrier possibilities); it might be personally delivered; or a friend might deliver it. However, only a few transportation methods are realistic because of various operational constraints, such as time (the object must be delivered before 9 A.M. on Monday morning), cost (the object must be shipped in the most inexpensive manner possible), or bulk (the size of the object may exclude all but a few possibilities). The transportation decision can be managed successfully only if the decision maker (1) knows which options actually exist and (2) understands the constraints. A tax problem has very similar boundaries.

Statutory Options

The IRC already contains many options from which a taxpayer must select alternative courses of action. For example, a taxpayer generally can choose to operate a business as a sole proprietorship, an S corporation, a limited liability company, or a regular corporation. By exercising any option, a taxpayer automatically causes several different portions of the IRC to apply to the business operations, any one of which may create a drastically different tax result. In addition to selecting a basic business form, a taxpayer may also have an opportunity to select a tax year, choose certain accounting methods, determine whether the entity selected should be a foreign or domestic one, choose between a taxable and a nontaxable incorporation transaction, or decide whether to capitalize certain expenditures. Selecting the most advantageous combination of statutory tax options is obviously a difficult task. The decision maker's knowledge of the very existence of those options is critical.

Client Constraints

In addition to understanding all of the options implicit in the IRC, a tax planner must also understand the objectives and constraints inherent in the client's activities. Typically, those are a combination of personal, financial, legal, and social considerations. For example, such personal objectives as a desire to increase wealth, to control the distribution of property after death, or to retire with minimal financial concerns may dictate certain actions. Personal objectives are often constrained by financial and legal obstacles. A tax planner can understand a client's objectives only if the client is willing to confide in the adviser; therefore, it is absolutely essential that mutual trust and openness exist between the client and the tax adviser before a tax-planning engagement is undertaken.

Because tax plans often involve very significant financial and legal implications, the most beneficial tax planning is achieved through a team effort rather than through individual work. For example, in an estate-planning engagement, it is not unusual to include the taxpayer's attorney, insurance agent, financial adviser, and trust officer, as well as various tax professionals, on the tax-planning team. By combining the special expertise of several individuals, the client is better served. More importantly, the team approach generally protects the client from the danger of *secondary infection*, that is, from the danger of putting into operation a plan that may succeed from a tax standpoint but that may have undesirable legal or financial consequences.

Creativity

Even if a tax adviser knows all the pertinent IRC provisions and fully understands all the client's objectives and constraints, the best tax plan may not be obvious. The best plan depends on the creative resources of the planner. Using all of his or her knowledge, the tax adviser must test tentative solutions in a methodical process that rejects some alternatives and suggests others. Without a systematic method of considering and rejecting the many alternatives, the tax planner is likely to overlook the very alternative being sought. As suggested earlier in this book, one common reason for overlooking a good alternative is simply the tax adviser's failure to think long or hard enough about the problem. There is the tendency to rush to the books or to another person for help, hoping that the best solution will automatically surface, when what is really needed is more creative thought on the subject. The authors' recommendation is not that books and consultants be avoided, but rather that the ideas obtained from these sources be given an opportunity to mature in quiet contemplation.

Tax-Planning Aids

Editorial Materials

Tax library materials can help generate successful tax-planning ideas. Most of the commercial tax services include, in some form or another, tax-planning ideas intended to assist the CPA in his or her practice. For example, the *Standard Federal Income Tax Reporter*, published by CCH, contains a tax-planning section, organized on a topical basis. The editorial comments found there are sufficiently detailed for addressing the easier tax-planning problems; they are cross-referenced to other CCH paragraphs that aid in the solution of the more difficult problems. In addition, RIA provides similar materials in its Web based service *Checkpoint*. This service has a section titled "Tax Planning & Practice Guides (Special Studies)," which provides both guidance for basic transactions and cross-references to other more detailed transactions.

The AICPA publishes *Tax Practice Guides and Checklists* (see www.cpa2biz.com), which provides extensive review checklists that are useful in dealing with the different tax entities, for example, individuals, regular corporations, S corporations, partnerships, estates, and trusts. Many other books, with varying degrees of sophistication, have been written on tax planning; it simply is not practical to mention each of them individually. Suffice it to note that readers should not be misled by all of the titles that include the phrase *tax planning*. Many of these publications are intended for specific taxpayers and their unique tax problems, for example, tax planning for professionals, for real estate transactions, for closely held corporations, or for international operations. Topics covered in one publication are often duplicated in another. Before deciding to purchase such a publication, a practitioner would be well advised to examine it in detail to make certain that it actually adds something to the material already available. Although many of these publications can be useful in tax-planning work, there is no good substitute for the ability that comes only from years of experience.

Continuing Education

The extension of formal classroom instruction beyond the college campus is partially due to the accounting profession, which requires continuing education. For tax practitioners, however, tax institutes provided continuing professional instruction long before it became mandatory in any state.

Today, continuing education programs are another major source of assistance in successful tax planning. Well developed courses are readily available from national, state, and local professional societies; universities and colleges; and private organizations. The AICPA regularly publishes catalogs in print and online (www.aicpa.org or www.cpa2biz.com) describing the continuing education programs offered by the Institute. The catalogs include descriptions of the various courses offered in taxation.

Information about other tax courses can frequently be found in tax periodicals. Some courses are designed for the beginner; others for an advanced audience. Some cover specific subjects; others are of general interest. Some are well developed and taught by highly qualified instructors; others have been hastily prepared and are poorly presented. Obviously, the caveat "let the buyer beware" is applicable in the selection of any course.

Tree Diagrams

In tax-planning work, the alternatives that an adviser must consider multiply quickly. After clearly identifying a general course of action (based on an understanding of the client's objective and knowledge of the IRC), and before reaching a conclusion, an adviser might consider structuring the possible solutions to the problem in the form of a tree diagram. Such a method ensures a thorough and systematic consideration of each alternative, because it focuses on the critical questions in sequence. The branches of the tree represent different options existing in the tax law, any one of which can achieve the client's objective. After ordering the options in this fashion, the adviser may want to quantify the tax result implicit in each alternative. This quantification will facilitate discovery of many of the risks and constraints that, in turn, eliminate some alternatives and favor others. For an example of a tree diagram, see figure 9.1.

A tree diagram cannot be prepared for a tax problem until a tax adviser fully understands the client's objectives and determines the tax rules applicable to each available method of achieving those objectives. Knowledge of the client's objectives can come only from a complete and open discussion of the transaction with the client. In tax planning, objectives and constraints are determined in the same way in which facts are established in compliance engagements. Determining the possible alternatives stems from a unique blend of prior experience and careful thinking about the problem. Ascertaining the tax outcome for each alternative is based on the same research techniques described in the earlier chapters of this study. In summary, the major differences between the tax research methods applicable to compliance work and to planning work are in the adviser's ability to identify possible alternatives and in the method for selecting the best of the several alternatives considered. In an attempt to focus on these aspects of tax planning, the following

Figure 9.1
Tree Diagram

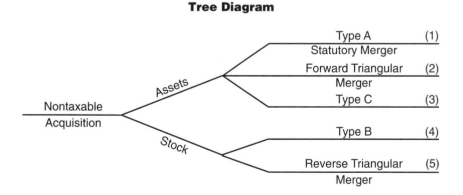

pages illustrate the process involved in a relatively simple planning engagement. We will not examine in detail the procedures by which the tax adviser determines the results implicit in each option, because they are the same as those followed in a closed-fact situation (see chapter 8).

A Tax-Planning Example

To illustrate the procedures that might be used in a tax-planning engagement, consider the following factual situation. Wonder Golf Inc. (Wonder) is a high-tech manufacturer of golf equipment. It has been experimenting with laser technology that when perfected will produce a golf club that will allow any golfer to "play golf like the pros."

Olympus Inc. (Olympus) is a large international sports equipment manufacturer. Olympus is interested in the new technology being developed by Wonder and has approached Wonder's management about possibly acquiring the company. Wonder management's initial reaction has been positive. They believe that if an agreement can be reached on certain issues, they are willing to sell Wonder.

Wonder's balance sheet currently shows assets with a fair market value of $10,000,000 and an adjusted tax basis of $1,000,000. The balance sheet also shows $2,000,000 of liabilities, leaving a fair market value of the outstanding Wonder stock of $8,000,000. Wonder is 95 percent owned by Sid Nuttal, the founder and the real genius behind the success of the company. Olympus wants desperately to retain Nuttal as the CEO of Wonder. Nuttal is very interested in the acquisition. He wants the acquisition to be tax free and, for the most part, is willing to accept Olympus stock. However, due to personal financial pressures, Nuttal needs $1,000,000 of the consideration he receives to be cash. Nuttal's basis in his Wonder stock is $600,000.

The remaining 5 percent of Wonder is owned by Dexter Childs. This stock was previously issued to retain Childs who is a critical part of the marketing function of Wonder. However, Childs is sure that if the acquisition goes through, he is out of a job. Therefore,

Childs has stated he will not sell his Wonder stock to Olympus. Childs's basis in his Wonder stock is $100,000.

Olympus is willing to acquire all Wonder's assets, with the exception of a golf course property that Wonder bought in Scottsdale, Arizona. Wonder has a $2,000,000 net operating loss (NOL) carryforward into the current year.

Wonder is currently involved in some patent infringement litigation, in which another golf manufacturer is suing for $1,000,000 for allegedly copying its golf club head design. Wonder is confident it will prevail in this case, but Olympus is not so sure. This $1,000,000 is not reflected in the balance sheet information provided earlier.

Of even greater concern is the fact that, last year, Wonder produced and sold a new laser-guided golf ball. Unfortunately, something in the golf balls' guidance system has malfunctioned and the golf balls seem to "lock on" to anything made of glass. This has caused damage to a number of residences bordering golf courses. Also, several instances have been reported of golfers being attacked by golf balls when partaking of a cool beverage from a glass container. Wonder claims it was able to recall most of the golf balls before they became widely sold. Consequently, Wonder feels that any liability is minimal. However, Olympus is concerned that it may take some time before the total damages will be known. Because of the unknown liabilities and for other business reasons, Olympus wants to operate the Wonder activities in a controlled subsidiary of Olympus.

The primary purpose of this illustration is to show the characteristics of a planning engagement and the usefulness of a tree diagram, rather than to present a detailed treatise on corporate acquisitions. A crucial element of any tax-planning engagement is to determine from the facts the possible options available to the client. As mentioned previously, if there are numerous options, a tree diagram may prove helpful in organizing the tax-planning process.

Because the acquisition is to be structured as a tax-free acquisition, five primary options will be considered. For purposes of this illustration, figure 9.1 summarizes the options and numbers them one through five for easy reference. The analysis of the five options could include a comparison of the present value of the after-tax dollars received by the sellers. Also, the buyer may develop an analysis involving the net present value of the cost to each of the alternatives. The methodologies used in modeling such acquisitions can become quite complex and are beyond the scope and purpose of this illustration. Therefore, the tax consequences of each option will be discussed in general, along with the more significant nontax issues that should be considered by both the buyers and the sellers. Through such an analysis, the benefit of a tree diagram in a tax-planning scenario can be demonstrated.

Stock Versus Asset Acquisition

Asset Acquisition. In any nontaxable corporate reorganization, the principal consideration used by Olympus must be stock. In some cases the amount of stock that must be used is fairly flexible. In other reorganizations, voting stock is the only consideration that can be used.

If a nontaxable asset structure is used, Wonder will not recognize any gain on the disposition of its appreciated assets. Instead, the basis of Wonder's assets carries over to Olympus, and Olympus inherits the $9,000,000 built-in gain. Also, no gain is recognized by Nuttal or Childs on the receipt of the Olympus stock. However, if either Nuttal or Childs receives cash, they may have a partial gain recognition. Nuttal and Childs will recognize gain to the extent of the lesser of gain realized or boot (cash) received. To the extent that Nuttal and Childs do not recognize the built-in gain in their Wonder stock, the same amount of built-in gain will be reflected in their Olympus stock. Finally, the net operating losses (NOLs) of Wonder will carry over to Olympus. However, the ability of Olympus to use the NOLs may be restricted.

Stock Acquisition. Because stock, and not assets, is being sold, a nontaxable stock acquisition refers to the tax treatment of Nuttal and Childs only. Again, no gain is recognized by Nuttal or Childs on the receipt of the Olympus stock. However, if either Nuttal or Childs receives cash, one or the other may have a partial gain recognition. Nuttal and Childs will recognize gain to the extent of the lesser of gain realized or boot (cash) received. To the extent that Nuttal and Childs do not recognize the built-in gain in their Wonder stock, the same amount of built-in gain will be reflected in their Olympus stock.

In a nontaxable stock acquisition, Wonder remains in existence for all legal purposes, and any tax and nontax attributes remain with Wonder. The NOL of Wonder remains with Wonder, but the ability to use the attribute may be limited. Wonder's asset basis is unchanged by the acquisition.

Other Considerations

Before looking at the five specific reorganizations, there are several issues that need to be addressed.

Unwanted Assets. Olympus is not interested in acquiring the Arizona golf course. For those reorganizations that have a *substantially-all* requirement, the disposition of the Arizona property could be a problem. According to Rev. Proc. 77-37, Olympus must acquire at least 70 percent of the gross assets and 90 percent of the net assets. Actual values are not provided in the facts to avoid numerous numerical calculations. What is important to realize is that the disposition of the Arizona property could present a problem for those reorganizations that have a substantially-all requirement. Let us assume that for purposes of this illustration, the disposition of the Arizona property does not violate the substantially-all requirement.

Unknown Liability. The possibility of a large potential liability from the laser-guided golf ball is a serious concern. Nothing can be done to completely eliminate this potential problem. However, in structuring the acquisition, an important factor should be choosing a reorganization that minimizes the risk of unwanted liabilities.

Dissenting Shareholder. Childs has stated that he does not want to sell his Wonder stock. However, when he realizes that as a 5 percent shareholder he has very little influence he may be convinced otherwise. In the reorganizations that involve state merger statutes, Childs will have to sell his Olympus stock if Nuttal approves the merger. Childs's only right in this type of situation is to have the courts value his shares and make the acquiring corporation cash him out. Let's assume in those situations that the courts value his 5 percent share in Wonder as being worth $400,000.

Five Corporate Reorganization Options

1. Statutory Merger: Type A Reorganization. One of the three types of nontaxable asset acquisitions is a statutory merger of Wonder into Olympus, with Wonder dissolving by operation of law. The stock consideration requirements are very flexible for a Type A reorganization. According to Treas. Reg. §1.368-1(e)(2)(v), Example 1, only 40 percent of the consideration used must be Olympus stock. Therefore, paying Nuttal $1,000,000 in cash and using $400,000 cash to buy out Childs's 5 percent dissenter interest is allowed. The disposition of the unwanted Arizona property is not an issue because a Type A reorganization does not have a substantially-all requirement. The wish to operate Wonder as a subsidiary is not a problem because a drop-down of assets is allowed in a Type A reorganization. The only real issue pertaining to a Type A reorganization is the liability concern. The use of $1,000,000 of contingent stock may alleviate the problem of the patent infringement suit. However, the unknown liability of the previously sold laser golf balls is a real problem. Olympus does not want its assets subject to that kind of liability potential. Therefore, for nontax reasons a Type A reorganization is not the best alternative.

2. Forward Triangular Merger. To qualify as a nontaxable forward triangular merger, the issue of using cash as part of the consideration is the same as discussed in the preceding Type A reorganization. The acquisition could be accomplished by having Olympus create a subsidiary, Newco. Olympus contributes $6,600,000 of Olympus stock plus the $1,400,000 in cash necessary to satisfy Nuttal and Childs. Wonder merges with and into Newco, and Wonder dissolves by operation of law. A forward triangular merger does have a substantially-all requirement, but we have already assumed that with the disposition of the Arizona property, this requirement has been satisfied. The desire to operate Wonder as a subsidiary of

Olympus is accomplished through this type of triangular merger. The advantage of a forward triangular merger is that the Olympus assets are not exposed to the known and unknown liabilities of Wonder. However, Wonder's assets, which will reside in Newco, are still subject to the potential liabilities. Thus, a forward triangular merger is a better alternative than the Type A reorganization and a reasonable way to structure the acquisition.

3. Type C Reorganization. A Type C reorganization requires that substantially all the properties of Wonder be acquired solely for the voting stock of Olympus. The substantially-all issue is the same as discussed in the previous two scenarios. If Olympus provides the Wonder shareholders with the $1,400,000 cash they have requested, the solely-for-voting stock issue is a concern. A Type C reorganization contains a 20 percent "boot relaxation" rule. As long as 80 percent of the assets of Wonder are acquired solely for voting stock, the solely-for-voting-stock requirement is satisfied. For purposes of the boot relaxation rule, any liabilities of Wonder that are assumed are treated as money. The $2,000,000 of liabilities that are agreed upon by both parties already represent 20 percent of the total assets of Wonder. Therefore, if this transaction is to qualify as a Type C reorganization, no cash can be provided by Olympus. As currently structured, the Type C reorganization is not the best option.

4. Type B Reorganization. Instead of acquiring Wonder's assets, the acquisition can be structured as a tax-free acquisition of Wonder's stock. This eliminates the substantially-all issue. Olympus is protected from the liabilities of Wonder, but Wonder's assets are not protected from Wonder's liabilities. The desire to operate Wonder as a subsidiary of Olympus is accomplished through a stock-for-stock acquisition. In fact, only in a Type B reorganization and a reverse triangular merger does Wonder corporation actually stay in existence. The real issue is that the stock of Wonder must be acquired solely for voting stock of Olympus. In a Type B reorganization, there is no boot relaxation rule. Thus, the shareholders of Wonder cannot receive any cash from Olympus if the acquisition is to qualify as a Type B reorganization. If Nuttal could be persuaded to forgo the $1,000,000 in cash, a Type B reorganization would work. The 5 percent of Wonder stock owned by Childs is not necessary as long as Olympus has control (80 percent) immediately after the acquisition. Again, as currently structured, a Type B reorganization is not the best option.

5. Reverse Triangular Merger. A reverse triangular merger can be accomplished by having Olympus create an acquisition subsidiary, Newco. Newco then merges with and into Wonder, and Wonder is the surviving corporation. The former Wonder shareholders end up with Olympus stock, and Wonder ends up a subsidiary of Olympus. This type of triangular merger satisfies the desire to operate Wonder as a subsidiary of Olympus.

The first concern is that 80 percent of the Wonder stock must be acquired in the transaction for voting stock of Olympus. Thus, the Olympus stock used in the transaction must be voting stock. Because only 80 percent of the stock of Wonder must be acquired for Olympus voting stock, Olympus can use up to $1,600,000 (20 percent of $8,000,000, the fair market value of Wonder's outstanding stock) cash in the acquisition and still qualify as a reverse triangular merger.

Wonder must hold substantially all of its assets and substantially all of Newco's assets (other than assets used as consideration for the Wonder shareholders) after the reorganization. Consistent with the discussion of the other reorganizations, the assumption is that the substantially-all requirement is satisfied. Thus, a reverse triangular merger is a reasonable way to structure the acquisition.

Summary

As the preceding analysis illustrates, both tax and nontax factors need to be considered in determining the best strategy. The Type A statutory merger is a logical choice, except for the fact that Wonder is merged directly into Olympus, which results in all of the Olympus assets being subject to the unknown liabilities of Wonder. So even though the tax results are positive, the business issue of liability assumption probably makes the Type A reorganization the least desirable option.

Both the Type C and the Type B reorganizations have solely-for-voting-stock requirements; therefore, if Nuttal and Childs want cash, neither of these options is viable. Some aspects of these two reorganizations may be appealing, but the consideration requirements are so strict that neither of these two reorganizations satisfies the taxpayers' need for cash.

The reorganizations that best satisfy the desires of the parties to the Olympus acquisition of Wonder are the two triangular mergers. Both triangular mergers have substantially-all requirements, but as discussed previously, this is not a problem because the assumption in this illustration is that the substantially-all requirement is satisfied. In the forward triangular merger, the use of $1,400,000 in cash as part of the consideration is not a problem.

The reverse triangular merger is not quite as flexible as the forward triangular merger relative to the type of consideration that can be used, but enough cash can be used to provide Nuttal with his $1,000,000 and Childs with his $400,000 in cash. However, the remaining consideration in a reverse triangular merger must be Olympus voting stock. This requirement is more stringent than for a forward triangular merger, in which any type of Olympus stock is allowed. Finally, even though it was not stated as a priority in the facts of this case, in a reverse triangular merger, Wonder actually survives the acquisition and is a wholly owned subsidiary of Olympus. In the forward triangular merger, all of Wonder's assets end up in Newco, a wholly owned subsidiary of Olympus, but Wonder itself ceases its legal existence.

All of the above alternatives need to be communicated to the respective parties. Once informed of all the possibilities and the associated benefits and risks, the client must choose which, if any, of the options to use. In the final analysis, only the client can determine which alternative is best. However, when a qualified tax adviser gives the client all the information needed to make an intelligent decision, in most instances, the client accepts the adviser's recommendation.

It is apparent from this illustration that any change in facts or stated objectives could completely change the results of the analysis. Because the acquisition is to be nontaxable, the tax consequences (gains, losses, and basis) are not significantly different for any of the options discussed. If the acquisition could be either taxable or nontaxable, a present value analysis of the related after-tax benefits of each option becomes more essential. Also, if the transaction could be taxable, the treatment of goodwill becomes much more important.

The foregoing example demonstrates a systematic approach to the research of alternative courses of action available to a taxpayer. This tax-planning process represents a rearrangement of facts over which a client can still exercise control. Such a systematic creation and evaluation of alternative strategies are the keys to profitable tax planning.

Tax-Planning Communications

Practitioners should recognize distinct differences between communicating research conclusions in a tax-compliance problem and making recommendations in a tax-planning engagement. In tax compliance work, the facts and the law pertinent to the solution are generally fixed. Therefore, once the appropriate statute and all related authorities have been identified and evaluated, the researcher generally can offer a conclusion to the client with reasonable certainty that it is correct.

Reaching an optimal conclusion in a tax-planning engagement is much less certain. The *facts* are merely preliminary proposals based on many estimates and assumptions. Furthermore, the enactment of a proposed plan is not fixed in time. It may occur the following week, the following month, or two years hence. Consequently, at the time the plan is finally executed, even the tax statutes upon which it is based may have changed, and the tax alternative originally recommended may no longer be the preferred one. Because of these uncertainties, the tax adviser should prepare for the client a written memorandum containing a statement of the assumptions and the recommended plan of action, qualified as follows:

1. A statement should be included emphasizing the fact that, unless the plan is actually implemented as originally assumed, the tax results may be substantially altered.

2. It should be stressed that the recommendations are based on current tax authority and that possible delays in implementation may change the result because of changes in the law during the interim period.

These recommendations concur with the opinion quoted in chapter 7 from AICPA Statement on Standards for Tax Services No. 8, *Form and Content of Advice to Taxpayers* (AICPA, *Professional Standards*, vol. 2, TS sec. 800). Tax advisers should seriously consider the adoption of such standard disclaimer statements in their tax-planning engagements.

APPENDIX A

Tax and Business Web Sites for Researchers, Advisers, and Students

The list of tax sites on the following pages is by no means exhaustive, but includes many tax, business, and government favorites that you should find useful in your practice. This information does not constitute an endorsement by the AICPA, the authors, editors, or publisher of any of the Web sites, entities, or individuals listed.

AICPA	www.aicpa.org	The American Institute of Certified Public Accountants is the national professional organization of CPAs, with more than 330,000 members in business and industry, public practice, government, and education.

The "Big Three" Commercial Research Sites

RIA	ria.thomson.com	RIA provides research, practice materials, and compliance tools for tax, accounting, and corporate finance professionals. RIA is a business unit of the Thomson Corporation (www.thomson.com) and was formed with the joining of Research Institute of America (now known as RIA), Computer Language Research (CLR), and Warren, Gorham & Lamont (WG&L).
CCH	tax.cchgroup.com	CCH INCORPORATED (www.cch.com) is a provider of tax and business law information and software. CCH is a wholly owned subsidiary of Wolters Kluwer U.S. The company's Directory of Web sites can be accessed at www.wolterskluwer.com/WK/Related+Nav/Products/Our+Websites.htm.
Lexis	www.lexisnexis.com	The LexisNexis Group provides information to legal, corporate, government, and academic markets, and publishes legal, tax, and regulatory information via online, hardcopy print, and CD-ROM formats. LexisNexis Group is the global legal publishing arm of Reed Elsevier, the Anglo-Dutch publisher and information provider.

The "Big Four" Professional Services Organizations

KPMG	www.kpmg.com
Deloitte & Touche	www.deloitte.com
Ernst & Young	www.ey.com
Pricewaterhouse-Coopers	www.pwc.com

Other Sites of Interest

ABA Section of Taxation Tax Site Index	www.abanet.org/tax	The American Bar Association provides this extensive list of links to tax sites.
Accountants World	www.accountantsworld.com	Links, tools, articles, and resources for the accounting profession.
American Bar Association	www.abanet.org	
American Payroll Association	www.americanpayroll.org	
American Taxation Association	www.aaahq.org/ata/index.htm	
Cornell Law School Legal Information Institute Web site	www.law.cornell.edu	The opinions of the U.S. Supreme Court can be found at supct.law.cornell.edu/supct, the statutes of the various states can be found at www.law.cornell.edu/states/index.html, and Title 26 U.S.C.A. (the Internal Revenue Code) can be found at www4.law.cornell.edu/uscode/26.

(continued)

CPA2Biz	www.cpa2biz.com	CPA2Biz is the premier source of products and services that CPAs use to fulfill their professional needs and the needs of their employers, small- to medium-sized business clients, and high-net-worth individuals. Through its strategic partnership with the AICPA, CPA2Biz is the exclusive online and offline distributor for AICPA products and services.
Internal Revenue Service	www.irs.gov	The Digital Daily is the IRS' user-friendly site. Here you can get the latest tax news and download IRS forms and publications, access IRS Regulations, Service Bulletins, Private Letter Rulings, IRS Online Fill-In Forms, and the searchable text of various IRS Publications. The Fill-In Forms may be filled in online or saved in PDF and filled in with Acrobat Reader.
Multistate Tax Commission	www.mtc.gov	Multistate Tax Commission is a joint agency of state governments.
Practicing Law Institute	www.pli.edu	
Taxsites.com Tax and accounting sites directory	www.taxsites.com	Includes listing of state-specific tax information.
Tax Analysts	www.tax.org	Tax Analysts is a leading electronic publisher of tax information. Its principal online databases are available on the Web on Lexis. Comprehensive databases are also available from Tax Analysts on CD-ROM. Tax Analysts also publishes a variety of scholarly books on tax issues as well as directories listing documents and government

Tax Executives Institute	www.tei.org	
Taxlinks	www.taxlinks.com	A Web site with links to published IRS Rulings and Revenue Procedures.
The Wall Street Executive Library	www.executivelibrary.com	Over 1450 content-rich business resources
WorldWideWeb Tax™	www.wwwebtax.com	IRS forms, IRS instructions, IRS publications, tax tables, rate schedules, charts, worksheets, and more.
IRS Tax FAQs	www.irs.gov/faqs/index.html	

Government and Related Sites

U.S. House of Representatives	www.house.gov	
U.S. Senate	www.senate.gov	
U.S. Government's Official Web Portal	www.usa.gov	"Government helping citizens, one click at a time." Conduct your government business online; find the geographic location of government offices and programs in your community—by state, city, or zip code; check out statistics and facts about your state and local community; obtain information on personal health, wellness, diseases, drugs, nutrition, and consumer safety; learn about federal benefits, including social security, unemployment insurance, children's health insurance, veterans benefits; and more.

(*continued*)

FedWorld	www.fedworld.gov	The FedWorld.gov Web site is a gateway to government information. This site is managed by the National Technical Information Service (NTIS) as part of its information management mandate.
Gov Engine	www.govengine.com	A portal of state and federal courts and government agencies.
Government Information Exchange (GIX)	www.info.gov	Search Engine with Links to Federal Government Information Sources. GIX specializes in direct linking and searching the Internet to locate information that has been posted by and for government agencies. A related program, the Federal Information Center (FIC), specializes in direct telephone assistance to callers who are trying to locate information in any format on federal agencies, programs, and services.
Social Security Online	www.ssa.gov	The official Web site of the Social Security Administration is the place to start to apply for social security benefits; request a replacement Medicare card; use the retirement, disability, or survivors planners and calculators; apply to replace, correct, or change your name on your social security card; request a social security statement; search more than 600 frequently asked questions; and contact a local office.

Library of Congress— Business Reference Services	www.loc.gov/rr/business	A starting point for conducting research in the areas of business and economics. Supported by a reference collection of over 20,000 volumes, a network of CD-ROM services, and the Adams Building Computer Catalog Center, reference specialists in specific subject areas of business assist the patron in formulating search strategies and gaining access to the information and materials contained in the library's rich collections.
The National Technical Information Service (NTIS)	www.ntis.gov	"One Search. One Source. One Solution." This growing collection, including millions of publications as well as audiovisual materials, computer datafiles, and software, originates from U.S. federal agencies, industry and university contractors with the federal government, and a worldwide compendium of research and development organizations. Search a database with items from 1990 until present.
Thomas Legislative Information from the Library of Congress	thomas.loc.gov	Here you can research Bill Text, *Congressional Record* Text, Bill Summary & Status, the *Congressional Record Index*, and the Constitution, along with other historical Congressional documents, and more.

(continued)

U.S. Business Advisor	www.business.gov	Access to federal government information and services. The U.S. Business Advisor was created by the Small Business Administration (SBA), the National Partnership for Reinventing Government (NPR), and the U.S. Business Advisor interagency task force. The site includes sections on business development, financial assistance, taxes, laws and regulations, workplace issues, and more.
U.S. Small Business Administration	www.sba.gov	
U.S. Tax Court decisions	www.ustaxcourt.gov	
U.S. Treasury	www.treas.gov	

Business and Investing Sites

AICPA 360 Degrees of Financial Literacy Web site	www.360financialliteracy.org
Yahoo!Finance	finance.yahoo.com
The Securities and Exchange Commission (SEC)	www.sec.gov
New York Stock Exchange (NYSE)	www.nyse.com
NASDAQ	www.nasdaq.com
American Stock Exchange (AMEX)	www.amex.com
Chicago Board of Trade	www.cbot.com

Business and Financial News Sites

ABCNews.com Business	abcnews.go.com/business
Barron's	www.barrons.com
BBC World Service Business	news.bbc.co.uk/2/hi/business/default.stm
Bloomberg Financial News	www.bloomberg.com
CNNMoney.com	money.cnn.com
Financial Times	news.ft.com/home/us
Fortune	www.fortune.com
Market Watch	www.marketwatch.com
MSN Money	moneycentral.msn.com
New York Times Business section	www.nytimes.com/yr/mo/day/business
Red Herring	www.redherring.com
Reuters.com	www.reuters.com
Wall Street Journal Online	online.wsj.com

APPENDIX B

Circular 230 Considerations

Treasury Department Circular 230 provides the regulations governing the practice of attorneys, certified public accountants (CPAs), enrolled agents, enrolled actuaries, and appraisers before the IRS. The recent revisions to Circular 230 provide, among other things, standards of practice for written advice. It is these provisions that have been the basis for much discussion and concern among tax practitioners of late.

Key Provisions of Circular 230

- Information to be furnished (section 10.20)
- Prompt disposition of pending matters (section 10.23)
- False and misleading information (section 10.51(d))
- Conflicting interests (section 10.29)
- Diligence as to accuracy (section 10.22)
- Standards for advising with respect to tax return positions and for preparing and signing returns (section 10.34)

Title 31 CFR Part 10 sets forth the regulations governing representation of taxpayers before the IRS. These regulations are republished by the IRS in Treasury Department Circular 230. The provisions of Circular 230 set forth who may represent taxpayers, the process for becoming an enrolled agent, duties and restrictions relating to practice, and the process for resolving allegations of violations of those duties and restrictions.

Circular 230 also sets forth the circumstances under which an individual preparer of tax returns may practice before the IRS.

Recent Circular 230 Changes

September 2007 Circular 230 Regulations Revision

These revisions contain final regulations revising the regulations governing practice before the Internal Revenue Service (IRS) (Circular 230). These regulations affect individuals who practice before the IRS. The amendments modify the general standards of practice before the IRS. The scope of these regulations is limited to practice before the IRS. These regulations do not alter or supplant ethical standards that are otherwise applicable to practitioners. These regulations are effective September 26, 2007.[1]

On September 26, 2007, the IRS also issued proposed revisions to Circular 230, Section 10.34, "Standards with respect to tax returns and documents, affidavits, and other papers." The proposed revisions were made to conform Circular 230 to the May 2007 changes made to section 6694 that raised the preparer tax return reporting standard for undisclosed positions to "more likely than not."

On May 25, 2007, the President signed into law the Small Business and Work Opportunity Tax Act of 2007, Public Law 110-28 (121 Stat. 190), which amended several provisions of the Code to extend the application of the income tax return preparer penalties to all tax return preparers, alter the standards of conduct that must be met to avoid imposition of the penalties for preparing a return

---

[1] For more information on Circular 230, and the AICPA's comments, see the AICPA Web site at http://tax.aicpa.org/Resources/Professional+Standards+and+Ethics/Treasury+Department+Circular+No.+230/.

that reflects an understatement of liability, and increase applicable penalties. On June 11, 2007, the IRS released Notice 2007-54, 2007-27 IRB 1 (see §601.601(d)(2)(ii)(b)), providing guidance and transitional relief for the return preparer provisions under section 6694 of the Code, as recently amended.

The IRS and the Treasury Department issued revisions[2] to the Circular 230[3] standards that were enacted in 2004, as part of the American Jobs Creation Act of 2004 (AJCA).[4]

The AJCA amended section 330 of Title 31 of the United States Code to clarify that the Secretary may impose standards for written advice relating to a matter that is identified as having a potential for tax avoidance or evasion. The Act also authorized the Treasury Department and the IRS to impose a monetary penalty against a practitioner who violates any provision of Circular 230.[5]

Standards of Practice for Written Advice

The new standards for written tax advice mandate disclosure requirements for various forms of opinions expressed by tax practitioners. This includes what information must be disclosed as well as specific requirements for how the information is to be disclosed on written communications, including e-mail. The requirements apply to written advice that is rendered after June 20, 2005.

Although originally drafted to address tax shelter advice, the regulations, as written, appear to be much broader in scope. And, while there are some listed exceptions, it is the breadth of the general rule that has many practitioners concerned.

---

[2] IR-2005-59, May 18, 2005; REG-159824-04, 31 CFR Part 10 (RIN 1545-BE13).

[3] Treasury Department Circular No. 230 (Rev. 6-2005), *Regulations Governing the Practice of Attorneys, Certified Public Accountants, Enrolled Agents, Enrolled Actuaries, and Appraisers Before the Internal Revenue Service* Department of the Treasury Internal Revenue Service Title 31 Code of Federal Regulations, Subtitle A, Part 10, revised as of June 20, 2005. The complete circular 230 can be accessed at www.irs.gov/pub/irs-pdf/pcir230.pdf (60-page PDF file).

[4] Public Law 108-357.

[5] See TD 9165, Final Regulations Revising the Regulations Governing Practice Before the Internal Revenue Service (Circular 230).

The Office of Professional Responsibility

The IRS Office of Professional Responsibility (OPR), which was established in January 2003, is the successor office to the former Director of Practice organization. OPR administers the laws for the practice of attorneys, CPAs, enrolled agents, enrolled actuaries, and appraisers before the IRS as set forth in Treasury Department Circular No. 230. In addition, OPR reviews applications from individuals who wish to become an enrolled agent or enrolled actuary.

Sample Language

Many law and accounting firms have begun adding "Circular 230 disclaimers" to their client communications. Although the area is still evolving, and the inevitable court cases have yet to flesh out the language, versions such as the following are already being used by many firms.[6]

> In accordance with IRS Circular 230, this communication (including any attachments) is not intended or written to be used, and cannot be used as, or considered, a "covered opinion" or other written tax advice and should not be relied upon for the purpose of avoiding tax-related penalties under the Internal Revenue Code; promoting, marketing, or recommending to another party any transaction or tax-related matter(s) addressed herein; or for IRS audit, tax dispute, or other purposes.

Sample Letter to Clients Explaining Addition of Circular 230 Disclaimer Language to Written Advice

Impact of IRS Circular 230 Written Advice Standards

[Note to the practitioner: The following sample client letter is based on the assumption that you have modified or added standard language for

---

[6] Please be advised that neither the authors nor the publisher recommend a particular "formula" for the Circular 230 disclaimer. Rather, we provide this sample language for reference only, as you consider developing your own language. As always, nonattorneys are advised to consult legal counsel.

client communications (including e-mail messages), or that you plan to do so in certain instances because of IRS Circular 230 requirements applicable to "written advice" rendered on or after June 20, 2005. The following is to notify clients of the change. Members are encouraged to modify it order to maximize its value to their professional practices.]

To Our Clients:

We are writing to inform you of how our correspondence with you (including e-mail messages) will be affected by new IRS regulations governing tax practitioners. The new rules require us to add certain standard language to many of our letters, memos, e-mails, and other correspondence concerning federal tax matters unless we are willing to undertake extensive analysis of the facts underlying a transaction and legal authorities that address the tax treatment of the transaction. This includes written advice concerning planning related to, or the application of, any federal tax to your business or personal affairs and would include business and personal tax planning and preparation written advice and written advice pertaining to estate planning or estate tax matters.

While the specific wording may vary depending on the circumstances, absent the thorough analysis of the facts, you can expect written advice from our firm to contain language similar to the following:

[**Editor's note:** Insert your firm's standard language. The following is for illustrative purposes only.]

IRS regulations require us to advise you that, unless otherwise specifically noted, any federal tax advice in this communication (including any attachments, enclosures, or other accompanying materials) was not intended or written to be used, and it cannot be used, by any taxpayer for the purpose of avoiding penalties; furthermore, this communication was not intended or written to support the promotion or marketing of any of the transactions or matters it addresses.

The new rules require such notices to be "prominently disclosed," that is, "readily apparent" to the reader. The notice must be in a separate section (but not in a footnote or as "fine print") of the correspondence. The typeface used must be at least the same size as the typeface used in any discussion of facts or law.

Be assured that this new policy does not reflect any decrease in the quality of our services or the amount of thought we put into our correspondence with you. We are adopting this policy as part of our effort to avoid fee increases; without the disclaimer, additional fees would often be required for us to fully ascertain and analyze factual matters underlying the advice.

In situations where we believe that the circumstances warrant the increased fee attributable to a communication that may provide you protection from the imposition of penalties, we will discuss the matter with you. In the event you desire a written communication on which you may rely for protection from the imposition of penalties, we encourage you to discuss the matter with us.

Please contact our office if you have any questions or concerns about the new rules and their impact on the manner in which we communicate tax advice to you.

Very truly yours,

/signed/

Circular 230 and the Standards to Which Tax Professionals Are Held

Circular 230 contains the rules and regulations governing attorneys, certified public accountants, enrolled agents, enrolled actuaries, and appraisers who represent taxpayers before the IRS. You can review the various sections of Circular 230 listed below for more information on the standards to which tax professionals are held.

The following table of questions and suggestions may help tax practitioners understand the various sections of Circular 230 for more information on the standards to which they are held:

	Did the Practitioner...	*For Example...*	*Your referral must include...*
1.	Fail to exercise due diligence?	Was the conduct: • More than a simple error but less than willful or reckless misconduct? • Negligence?	All of the basic information and explain why you believe the practitioner's submission was below the expected standard. See Circular 230 Section 10.22(a).

Did the Practitioner...	For Example...	Your referral must include...
2. Cause an unreasonable delay in the prompt disposition of any matter before the IRS?	Miss appointments? Not follow through on promised documentation? Hinder the service in processing the case?	All of the basic information and a chronology of all significant events in the case (OPR looks for a pattern of practitioner behavior rather than scheduling conflicts and "dropped balls" that routinely occur). See Circular 230 Section 10.23.
3. Demonstrate incompetence and disreputable conduct?	Give false or misleading information or participate in any way in the giving of false or misleading information in connection with any matter pending or likely to be pending before the IRS? Divert payments intended for IRS or a refund due the taxpayer? This should also be reported to the Treasury Inspector General for Tax Administration (TIGTA).	Information about where the legal argument put forth by the practitioner is patently false, or where there was a clear misstatement of fact made to IRS personnel. Demonstrate why the argument is false or why the statement made was egregious in nature. Provide any and all documentation to support diversion of funds such as cancelled checks and account transcripts. See Circular 230 Section 10.51(d) & (g).
4. Did the practitioner fail to file a federal tax return or evade the assessment of any federal tax?	Knowingly: Counsel or suggest to a client or prospective client an illegal plan to evade federal taxes or tax payment? Omit income from his or her own or a client's federal income tax return?	All of the basic information, including whether it was failure to file a Federal income tax return or failure to pay taxes when due. An annotated transcript of the accounts highlighting the relevant information (income omitted, penalties assessed, and ultimate outcome), if the issues pertain to omitted or underreported income. Consider notifying Criminal Investigation (contact your area Fraud Referral Specialist to assist you in evaluating and developing your case). See Circular 230 Section 10.51(f).

Did the Practitioner...	For Example...	Your referral must include...
5. Did the practitioner engage in contemptuous conduct?	Use abusive language or any other inappropriate conduct? Make false accusations and statements knowing them to be false? Circulate or publish malicious or libelous matter?	All of the basic information and a complete narrative account of the conduct. Actual language used, copies of any correspondence employed to falsely accuse an employee of misconduct, and a thorough recitation of the facts leading up to the situation. (It is important that the practitioner's exact language be reported.) See Circular 230 Section 10.51(k).
6. Directly or indirectly attempt to influence the official action of any officer or employee of the IRS?	Use threats, false accusations, duress, or coercion? Offer you a gift, favor, or thing of value to influence the outcome of a case?	First, report these cases to TIGTA. Once the investigation is completed, TIGTA should make a referral to OPR. You can assist both offices by ensuring your referral includes: All of the basic information and a complete narrative account of the conduct. A report of the practitioner's exact language. See Circular 230 Section 10.51(h).

[For more information, refer to the Internal Revenue Manual (IRM): www.irs.gov/irm/index.html.]

For Additional Information

A detailed discussion of Circular 230 is beyond the scope of this publication. Moreover, this area will likely evolve over the course of the coming months (or years, as case law emerges). So that readers can follow these developments, we provide the following links and resources for further research.

- September 19, 2007 Circular 230 Regulations Revision www.irs.gov/taxpros/article/0,,id=174474,00.html.
- Treasury Department Circular No. 230 (Rev. 6-2005)— www.irs.gov/pub/irs-pdf/pcir230.pdf.

- TD 9165—www.irs.gov/pub/irs-utl/td9165.pdf.
- REG-111835-99—www.irs.gov/pub/irs-regs/11183599.pdf.
- OPR Who We Are and What We Do—www.irs.gov/pub/ irs-utl/office_of_professional_responsibility_-_who_we_ are_and_what_we_do.pdf.
- Regulations Governing Practice Before the Internal Revenue Service—www.irs.gov/irb/2005-04_IRB/ar10.html.
- Internal Revenue Manual—4.11.55 Issues Involving a Tax-payer's Representative (Cont. 1)—www.irs.gov/irm/part4/ ch11s11.html.
- Announcement 2004-29—www.irs.gov/irb/2004-15_IRB/ ar17.html. IRS News release announcing amendments to Cir-cular 230—www.irs.gov/irs/article/0,,id=132445,00.html.
- IRS, Treasury Clarify Circular 230 Written Opinion Stan-dards (May 18, 2005)—www.irs.gov/newsroom/article/ 0,,id=138998,00.html.
- Regulations Governing Practice Before the Internal Revenue Service—www.irs.gov/pub/irs-regs/td9201.pdf.
- The New York State Bar Association Tax Section Report on Circular 230—www.nysba.org/Content/ContentGroups/ Section_Information1/Tax_Section_Reports/1081rpt.pdf.
- Final Rules on Written Tax Opinion Standards—www.irs. gov/pub/irs-utl/final_rule_covered_ opinion_standards.pdf.
- Proposed Standards for Certain Opinions Related to Tax Exempt Bonds—www.irs.gov/pub/irs-utl/proposed_rule_ on_bonds_opinions.pdf.
- National Society of Tax Professionals report: Ethics: "Our Joint Responsibility"—www.irs.gov/pub/irs-utl/ethics_ and_professional_resp_-_part_i.pdf.
- Circular 230 FAQs for e-Services Access—www.irs.gov/ taxpros/article/0,,id=174857,00.html.
- Circular 230 Regulations Revision—www.irs.gov/taxpros/ article/0,,id=174474,00.html.
- IRS, Treasury Clarify Circular 230 Written Opinion Standards —www.irs.gov/newsroom/article/0,,id=138998,00.html.

- Circular 230 Practitioner e-Services Access—www.irs.gov/taxpros/article/0,,id=174880,00.html.
- Form 8554 (Rev. October 2007) Application for Renewal of Enrollment to Practice Before the Internal Revenue Service—www.irs.gov/pub/irs-pdf/f8554.pdf. (213.7KB PDF)
- Internal Revenue Manual—1.25.1 Rules Governing Practice Before the IRS—www.irs.gov/irm/part1/ch18s01.html.
- Internal Revenue Manual—4.11.55 Issues Involving a Taxpayer's Representative (Cont. 1)—www.irs.gov/irm/part4/ch11s11.html.
- Internal Revenue Manual—5.1.1 Miscellaneous Guidelines—www.irs.gov/irm/part5/ch01s01.html.
- Internal Revenue Manual—39.4.1 Matters Relating To Practice Before the IRS—www.irs.gov/irm/part39/ch04s01.html.
- Standards of Practice for Tax Professionals—www.irs.gov/taxpros/content/0,,id=175435,00.html.

You may also e-mail inquiries directly to OPR at opr@irs.gov. (Please do not send OPR any confidential information via e-mail.) Inquiries containing sensitive information should be faxed to OPR at (202) 622-2207.

Note: Circular 230 is currently unavailable

As we went to press, Circular 230, *Regulations Governing the Practice of Attorneys, Certified Public Accountants, Enrolled Agents, Enrolled Actuaries, and Appraisers before the Internal Revenue Service,* required technical corrections and had been temporarily removed from the IRS Web site. The IRS notes that a revised version will be available soon. In the meantime, we encourage you to review the Federal Register or access the Code of Federal Regulations main page (www.gpoaccess.gov/cfr/index.html). When restored, the circular should be available here: www.irs.gov/taxpros/actuaries/article/0,,id=177851,00.html.

Index

A

Acquiescence, definition of, 105
Action on decision (AOD) as tax authority, 105
Administrative authority as tax authority, 87–88
  locating, 152–154
  validating, 159–161
Administrative interpretations action on decision, 105
  general counsel memoranda (GCM), 104
  letter rulings, 103
  notices and announcements, 101–103
  revenue procedures, 100–101
  revenue rulings, 99–100
  technical advice memorandum (TAM), 103
  Treasury regulations, 95–99
Advance rulings, 194
After-the-fact ruling. *See* Determination letters
AICPA
  publications by, 243–244
  role in shaping tax policy, 9
  Treasury regulations and, 97

Allen, Richard A. (case study) analysis of judicial decision about, 55–57, 175–176
  findings of facts, 44–50
  opinion, 50–54
American Federal Tax Reports (AFTR), 108, 111–115
Announcements and notices as tax authority, 101–103
Appeals and review memoranda (ARM), 100
Attorney-client privilege, 186
Authority
  assessing, chapter 6
    clear facts and incomplete laws, 174–178
    clear facts and nonexistent laws, 178–179
    clear facts and questionable laws, 167–174
    clear laws and uncertain facts, 164–167
  locating, chapter 5
    finding primary authority through, 126–129
    index, 140–142
    keywords, 142–152
    search strategies for, 125–126
    table of contents, 130–139
    Web-based services for, 124–125